Reporting on Risks

Reporting on Risks

THE PRACTICE AND ETHICS OF HEALTH AND SAFETY COMMUNICATION

Jim Willis

with Albert Adelowo Okunade

Westport, Connecticut
London

Library of Congress Cataloging-in-Publication Data

Willis, William James, 1946–
    Reporting on risks : the practice and ethics of health and safety
communication / Jim Willis with Albert Adelowo Okunade.
      p. cm.
    Includes bibliographical references and index.
    ISBN 0–275–95296–7 (alk. paper).—ISBN 0–275–95298–3 (pbk. :
alk. paper)
    1. Health risk communication. 2. Health in mass media.
I. Okunade, Albert Adelowo. II. Title.
RA423.2.W55 1997
614.4'4—dc21   96–37692

British Library Cataloguing in Publication Data is available.

Library of Congress Catalog Card Number: 96–37692
ISBN: 0–275–95296–7 (hc)
      0–275–95298–3 (pb)

First published in 1997

Praeger Publishers, 88 Post Road West, Westport, CT 06881
An imprint of Greenwood Publishing Group, Inc.

Printed in the United States of America

The paper used in this book complies with the
Permanent Paper Standard issued by the National
Information Standards Organization (Z39.48–1984).

10 9 8 7 6 5 4 3 2 1

Copyright Acknowledgments

The author and publisher are grateful for permission to reproduce portions of
the following copyrighted material:

From Philip Patterson and Lee Wilkins, *Media Ethics: Issues and Cases*, 2d
ed. Copyright © 1994 The McGraw-Hill Book Companies, Inc. Reprinted by
permission. All Rights Reserved.

From Jacqui Banaszynski, "AIDS in the Heartland," *St. Paul Pioneer Press
Dispatch*, June 21, 1987; and "AIDS in the Heartland: The Final Chapter,"
St. Paul Pioneer Press Dispatch, August 9, 1987.

From Sue Goetinck and Tom Siegfried, "Mentally Ill Fight Disease and
Stereotypes," the first of several stories in the series, "Science vs. Stigma:
Understanding Mental Illness," *Dallas Morning News*, April 28–29, 1996.

From Molly Gordy, "Quacks Prey on Immigrants," the first of a three-part
series, "Medical Menace," New York *Daily News*, July 18, 1996.

To Nancy:
A dedicated scientist with a heart.

Contents

Preface

Reporting on Risks is a survey of the field of journalistic reporting that informs the public about the health risks they could be facing in their everyday lives. These risks run the gamut from personal medical problems, to environmental hazards, to public health concerns, to safety issues and dangers wrought by disasters—both natural and man-made. It also looks at the reporting of the growing health care debate in this country and studies how the media might influence public health policy.

In its mission, this is a study designed to do three things for current and future health science reporters: (1) inform them of some of the trends in risk reporting; (2) offer guidelines of how to get closer to the truth of these health dangers; and (3) discuss some of the ethical implications involved in reporting on risks that could—if inaccurately told—either panic the public needlessly or keep it uninformed of threats its should know about.

Risk communication is an important subject area for today's media, because the public is so intent on living healthier lives than ever before. And no other area of reporting so demands that the journalist get the facts straight as risk communication.

Documentation for this book comes from a wide variety of sources, both journalistic and scientific. A few of the more important sources are the following: Dr. George Lundberg, editor of *JAMA (Journal of the American Medical Association)*; Mark V. Pauly, Ph.D., health care economist from the Wharton School of Business; Stephen G. Bloom, professor of journalism at the University of Iowa and former longtime medical reporter; Victor Cohn, former medical reporter for the *Washington Post*; Michael Calhoun, director of corporate communication for Baptist Memorial Hospital System in Memphis, Tennessee; Niles Bruzelius, science editor of the *Boston Globe*;

Sherry Jacobson, a senior writer with the *Dallas Morning News*; and Dr. Karen Amstutz, an Indianapolis physician who provided the inspiration for this book.

As always, the research found in the pages of such journals as *Journalism Quarterly, Newspaper Research Journal,* and the *Journal of Broadcasting and Electronic Media* is extremely helpful, as are the professional publications of *American Journalism Review, Editor & Publisher,* and *Columbia Journalism Review.* Among the most enlightening of books studied was Nancy Signorielli's *Mass Media Images and Impact on Health, Getting the Story* by Henry Schulte and Marcel Dufresne, and *The Reporter's Handbook,* edited by John Ullmann and Steve Honeyman. In addition, symposia like the Annenberg Washington Program's "Violence, Public Health, and the Media" and the Freedom Forum's "Under the Microscope" were extremely useful. One major conference which drew together doctors, medical reporters, health care economists, and health marketers was "Understanding and Communicating the Health Care Story," in May 1996. That conference provided a basis for a portion of this book and was sponsored by the Linder Center for Urban Journalism at the University of Memphis.

The Appendix contains three important examples of in-depth health reporting that have been done in recent years. They cover three different topics, all under the heading of risk communication, and show the wide range of the issues involved. My thanks goes to the *St. Paul Pioneer Press Dispatch,* the *Dallas Morning News,* and the New York *Daily News* for allowing us to reprint portions of these important journalistic series.

Finally, I would like to thank Albert Okunade, Ph.D., a gifted health care economist at the University of Memphis, for his contributions in writing Chapter 8 and a portion of Chapter 4 of this book; my colleagues in the Department of Journalism at the University of Memphis, for their friendship; and Jabie and Helen Hardin, for their generosity, which helped make this research possible.

1

The Field of Risk Communication

When a newspaper reporter writes a story about a chemical spill or a radiation leak, he is engaging in risk communication. When a television reporter does a story on a new wonder drug like Prozac, she is also involved in risk communication. When a magazine journalist produces an article about acid rain, she is writing about risks. When a television or theatrical movie depicts a family dealing with a disease, it is communicating information about risks. And when a journalist writes a story about a disaster like the Los Angeles earthquake or an act of terrorism like the Oklahoma City bombing, he is also dealing in risk communication.

In sum, risk communication occurs whenever the news or entertainment media depict dangers—potential, imminent, or existing—that could place at least some readers or viewers in a health risk. That risk could be to the physical, emotional, or mental state of the individual digesting the reports of these events.

These dangers run the gamut of personal health problems, public health concerns (such as the spread of AIDS), environmental concerns (such as the deteriorating ozone layer), and accidents involving hazardous materials. But risk communication can also extend beyond these boundaries to stories or shows about natural disasters, acts of terrorism, or impending weather crises, or depictions about such mental, nervous, or emotional problems as schizophrenia or autism.

Risk communication also encompasses depictions of real or alleged medical breakthroughs, new pharmaceuticals, health care services advertised by hospitals, and health care programs offered by the government to extend care to those unable to afford it under the present system.

Stories involving risks to large numbers of people are big news. For example, the Pulitzer Prize jurists in 1996 awarded six of the coveted fourteen awards to stories about medical, environmental, and public health issues. In addition, several finalists were also stories on these themes. A glimpse at some of these stories shows what is being done in the field of risk communication by newspaper reporters:

- Melanie Sill, Pat Stith, and Joby Warrick of the *News & Observer* (Raleigh, North Carolina) were awarded the Pulitzer for public service for their work on the environmental and health risks of waste disposal systems used in North Carolina's growing hog industry.

- The staff of the *Orange County Register* was awarded the Pulitzer for reporting that uncovered fraudulent and unethical fertility practices, such as egg theft at the University of California–Irvine Center for Reproductive Health. The articles prompted key regulatory reforms.

- Laurie Garrett, science and medical writer for *Newsday*, won a Pulitzer for her "courageous reporting" from Zaire on the Ebola virus outbreak. The Pulitzer board found in her dispatches considerable information and data of an explanatory nature that would alert her readers to the nature and dangers of the Ebola virus.

- A finalist in the Explanatory Journalism category (won by Garrett) was the *Los Angeles Times* for reporting on problems stemming from the lack of regulation in California's booming managed health care industry and the implications for the rest of the country.

- Another finalist in that same category was the *New York Times* for its coverage of deficient safety regulation of commuter air traffic, which is yet another type of story conveying risks to the public.

- The National Reporting Pulitzer was awarded to Alix M. Freedman of the *Wall Street Journal* for her expansive coverage of the tobacco industry that exposed how ammonia additives used by the industry heighten nicotine potency.

- A finalist in the feature writing category was Richard E. Meyer of the *Los Angeles Times* for his profile of a woman's desperate attempts to communicate after being left mute and paralyzed by strokes.

The popularity of science and medical news among the general public can also be seen in the success of the 1.2 million-circulation *Discover* magazine from Disney Magazine Publishing Group. In fact, *Discover* has negotiated a licensing deal with the 62 million-subscriber Discovery Channel for a weekly one-hour television show.

The magazine focuses on a wide range of science stories, including the following which it chose as some of its top 100 stories for 1996:

- *Archaeology.* A story on the 11,000-year-old art of the Amazon, and a new look at Jamestown, the first fort in the New World.

- *The Earth.* The map of 3 billion B.C.; a faster-spinning earth core; rumblings on Gorda Ridge and in the New Guinea Trench.

- *AIDS.* A story assessing the chances of containment of the disease, and a story about the discovery of a natural resistance.

- *Genetics.* A story about the discovery of a flock of new genes associated with various diseases such as Treacher Collins Syndrome, Retinitis Pigmentosa, and Basal Cell Carcinoma.

- *Space.* A story on NASA's discovery of a life-bearing rock from below the surface of Mars which opened new speculation as to life on that planet.

- *The Brain.* A story on how easily false memories can be formed and the search for false-memory detectors for therapists and criminal justice officials.

- *The Environment.* A story about disturbing discoveries of the long-range effects of the explosion at the Chernobyl nuclear power station on April 26, 1986. Ten years after the world's worst reported nuclear accident, researchers are finding that radioactive isotopes infiltrating the food and water supply are taking a heavy toll.

- *Sex.* A story about three male birth control methods currently being tested, and another about how sperm may one day become a surprisingly renewable resource.

This book will examine the practice and ethics of risk communication, and it will look most closely at how well the news media handle their responsibilities of representing the true nature of risks. There may be no other area of journalism where the Fourth Estate has such an awesome responsibility. Journalist-philosopher Walter Lippman reminded us decades ago there is a marked difference between the world outside and the pictures in our heads. He further noted that those pictures are put there most often by the media, because that is the way we experience most of our world. In previous writings I have labeled this mediated world the *shadow world*. It is often the world we react to—by our personal behavior, voting preferences, or in our urgings to lawmakers. Obviously, the closer that shadow world comes to representing the real world, the more appropriate are our actions which occur in that real world.

In the realm of risk communication, viewers may see a television story depicting, for instance, early warning signs of a heart attack. They compare what they see with aches and pains they have had recently, then maybe talk it over with a friend or relative, and soon are making an appointment with their internist or dropping by the nearest emergency room. If that televised depiction was accurate, then the viewer's reaction in the real world was appropriate. If it was inaccurate, then the reaction was inappropriate.

The media have the power to either heighten the awareness of the public to medical and public health risks or to lull it into thinking there is no risk. Sometimes, however, people think there is no risk simply because they don't see stories about a particular issue in the media. In other words, if it's not on TV or in the newspapers, it must not be important. Sometimes that isn't true, however. For instance, some critics have chided the news media for their slowness in reacting to news about AIDS and not treating it as a major story until celebrities like Rock Hudson and Arthur Ashe succumbed to the disease and Magic Johnson tested positive for the HIV virus. They note that the Centers for Disease Control (CDC) had established a task force on Kaposi's Sarcoma and opportunistic infections in mid-1981 and its leader had submitted a request for $833,000 to begin research by the end of that year. However, it was 1983 before substantial numbers of stories about the disease appeared in the national media, and late in 1985 when the number of stories on AIDS actually tripled. It was mid-1985 when news broke about Rock Hudson's contracting AIDS.

So the media have the power to (1) portray risks accurately, (2) unnecessarily panic the public, or (3) ignore or downplay real risks and, in so doing, convey a sense of wellness when it doesn't exist. Because the public has grown so concerned about health risks in this country, the news and entertainment media provide news and depictions about these issues. *Los Angeles Times* writer David Shaw notes:

The media, after all, pay the most attention to those substances, issues and situations that most frighten their readers and viewers. Thus, almost every day, we read and see and hear about a new purported threat to our health and safety. . . . The media are supposed to serve as an early warning system for the public, and they have long fulfilled this function in alerting people to a range of risks, from high-fat diets to cars (the Ford Pinto) to medical devices (the Dalkon Shield IUD).[1]

But, Shaw adds, some critics believe the media give us more than simply essential information and legitimate warnings and instead sound unwarranted alarms for an increasingly susceptible audience, one willing to see risk in almost everything. If this is true, one reason may be the different ethical standards some types of news media operate on. Those with a more bottom-line orientation, which see their function as entertainment as much as—or more than—news, often stretch the data and go for the dramatic punch in a health-related story. Other, more socially responsible media will stick as closely to the facts as possible. Yet even those media, because of the need to engage the reader, will put an individual focus on many medical stories and profile a victim who may or may not be a representative type of the medical problem. Boston environmental reporter David Ropiek explains: "In their zeal to have an impact, journalists are seduced . . . into playing up what is dramatic. But emphasizing stories, suggesting that everything you eat will kill you . . . profoundly colors the public psyche. We start living like Chicken Littles being told the sky is falling."[2]

There are also very different conventions operating among journalists and scientists in their approach to fact-finding. Chapters 2 and 3 will highlight some of those differences.

THE SCOPE OF RISK COMMUNICATION

Risk communication is a subject that casts a very wide net, as some of the previous examples illustrate. Health, science, crime, and the environment are all incorporated into risk communication. In the area of medical reporting alone there seem to be an infinite number and type of health hazards to write about, with new ones being discovered every month. In addition to the variety of diseases and viruses, there is also the problem of how wide the focus of the stories should be. For instance, should a story be confined to a particular individual with a disease and how the health care specialists treat it, or should it go into the deeper causes of the disease which threaten society as a whole? Pediatricians, for example, tell us that a variety of childhood illnesses—some of which turn into lifelong health problems—could be prevented with proper hygiene. Yet parents who lack the education or resources necessary to provide that hygiene for their children can't provide it. Therefore, the child grows up in a risky environment and has a greater chance of contracting the ailment.

So, doesn't risk communication also concern itself with stories about the health environment that we all live in? Shouldn't it concern itself not only with the natural environment but also with man-made environments such as workplace settings?

Several years ago I traveled to India to do a retrospective story on the deadly gas leak at the Union Carbide plant in Bhopal. I learned there were a couple of ways of approaching that story. The normal way was to look at the immediate causes for the leak. What was the breakdown in the operating system and who was responsible for the leak which killed and injured so many innocent people? But, putting a wider-angle lens on the subject, it was also necessary to discuss the overall political environment which increased the chances for such a problem occurring. As is the case with many developing countries (and much of India still falls in that category), health and safety monitoring procedures are lax, and government officials allow standards to exist in plants that would not be allowed in more advanced nations. Such was the climate in Bhopal, and a comprehensive story about that disaster should have taken the larger story into account.

Time and space restrictions—always prevalent in the news media—often cause the stories about risks to be told in a narrower focus. And, in the entertainment media, dramatic values dictate that the focus be narrow and told in very human terms. Individual scapegoats are often sought and blamed, and heroes are found who save the day. Larger, more complex issues get lost in the narrative. Often the picture of health in the media— especially in movies and television—minimizes or ignores the societal, political, or economic factors of disease while it focuses on and reinforces the individual nature of disease.[3] Nancy Signorielli puts it this way:

Television characters typically do not get sick because they do not have enough food, or live in substandard or unsanitary housing. Moreover, except in very rare situations, characters do not have to worry about having health insurance or enough money to pay for a hospital stay or a doctor's care. Sickness and disease are integral to the narrative and so are presented and treated only on an individual (or family) level. The television world's view of health is medical: Illness is treated with drugs or machines, which seemingly are available to everyone with little thought as to the cost and availability. Lifestyle or societal factors in dealing with disease are typically ignored.[4]

THE MEDIA AS ALARMISTS

If the news and entertainment media are sometimes guilty of ignoring or minimizing stories of health risks, some critics fear they are also guilty of crying wolf where no predator exists. Not only does this have negative effects on individuals, but it also causes problems for society as a whole. Government policymakers often take their lead from issues presented in the news media, especially after a large enough group of constituents are moved by what they see on TV. Government decision-makers get their information from the media more than from any other source, according to Clarence Davies, director of the Center for Risk Management at Resources for the Future, a Washington think tank specializing in environmental issues.[5]

Additionally, studies show that people in general get more information about risk and hazard from the media than from their own doctors, friends, or relatives.[6]

In the spring of 1994, ABC News produced a program entitled, "Are We Scaring Ourselves to Death?" Among other things, reporters noted that public policy is set according to what the public is most alarmed about. Since our view of dangers comes mostly from the media, then what the media show us can get translated into policy actions. Policymaking in this manner can—and often does—grow out of a series of disconnected crises, episodic events which get a lot of media attention and television exposure. Often the laws that result from these depictions are flawed because the depictions were flawed or insufficient in scope.

Some critics look at coverage of issues like hazardous waste sites and find the implied solutions for government reaction to be too simplistic or too expensive to be feasible. For instance, Estelle Fishbein, vice president of Johns Hopkins University, believes that the 1980 Superfund law written to clean up hazardous waste sites, has "failed miserably." She claims only 15 percent of the 1,300 Superfund sites identified by the EPA have been completely cleaned up, although some $13.5 billion has been spent, with one-fourth of that going to lawyers.[7]

And the *Los Angeles Times* has argued that exaggerated media coverage of pesticides has produced a similar waste of federal funds in monitoring that risk. Instead, says environmental writer Daniel Puzo, the government should focus its efforts at searching for food-borne microbes such as salmonella, which are much greater dangers.[8]

The nature of news is such that reporters often search out the unique and bizarre occurrences. This is true in medical and science reporting, as well, and often the results are unrepresentative of reality. Media coverage is infinitely more interesting to most people than the dry statistics which medical researchers develop. But the statistics are often closer to reality than the personally focused stories the media provide. Critics look to the public panics over the pesticide Alar on apples and the presence of asbestos in New York City schools.

In 1989, Ed Bradley of *60 Minutes* sat in front of the show's traditional magazine-cover backdrop, this time depicting a giant apple marked with a skull and crossbones. His warning: "The most potent cancer-causing agent in our food supply is a substance sprayed on apples to keep them on the trees longer and make them look better." A nationwide panic ensued, and that was enlarged by other media which quickly produced their own stories on Alar. But, as *Los Angeles Times* writer David Shaw notes, at the time of the broadcast (seen by as many as 40 million Americans) "the industry was already moving away from Alar, and the nation's three major baby-food makers said they were using non-Alar apples."[9]

The media's overtreatment of the Alar story was prompted in part by a report released by an activist environmental group called the Natural Resources Defense Council (NRDC) that wanted the U.S. Environmental Protection Agency to ban Alar and several other pesticides. *Newsweek* got a copy of the report and gave it strong play before it was officially released. As a result of that report and public appeals from actress Meryl Streep, many Americans felt death was close at hand for apple eaters or apple juice drinkers. In short, the media coverage produced a nationwide hysteria that resulted in school boards across the country banning apples and apple products from their school menus. Apple sales took a nosedive, and many farmers had to dispose of their crops. The cost to the apple growing industry: $100 million.[10]

In critiquing the reaction to the Alar scare, the *Washington Post* editorialized: "A complicated scientific issue was allowed to be decided not by officials charged with protecting the public, on the basis of hard evidence, but by a frightened public acting on incomplete and often erroneous press reports."[11]

Many observers believe the Alar story could have been reported more responsibly if the risk had been compared to other environmental risks, if the reasons for the conflicting estimates of danger had been cited, if the media had researched the activists' NRDC report more, and—in short—if reporters had just done their homework on the issue.

THE EFFECTS OF RISK COMMUNICATION

Because the media deal with these issues of public health and safety, it is reasonable to assume that the depictions of these stories have either a direct or indirect effect on the public's behavior concerning these perceived threats. Research does confirm a wide range of such effects, so the media's responsibility to present an accurate picture of the problems is vital.

Daniel Yankelovich, chairman of DYG, Inc. and WSY Consulting Group, Inc., says the media have a definite role to play in the formation of public opinion and public judgment about risks. Sometimes public opinion on a particular issue seems mindless, thoughtless and irresponsible; sometimes, on the same issue at a later point in time, public opinion seems almost uncannily right, he suggests. What happens is that "a quite orderly process of evolution occurs on some issues, whereby the incoherent, beastly roar evolves gradually into a coherent public voice."[12] This finalized public voice is what he calls "public judgment," and it is different from raw opinion. In the move toward public judgment, people engage in a complex, difficult task of sifting through and dealing with conflicting emotions, values, and interests that envelop a particular issue or problem.

Yankelovich defines seven phrases in the excursion from raw opinion to public judgment:

1. Awareness.
2. A sense of urgency or a demand for action.
3. A search for solutions.
4. Reaction and resistance.
5. Wrestling with alternative choices.
6. Intellectual assent, or resolution at the cognitive level.
7. Full resolution—moral, emotional, and intellectual.

He elaborates on the media's role in this journey by saying:

The mass media often do an excellent job at the beginning of the process, by bringing issues to the public's attention and creating a sense of urgency about them. But then they often move on to the next issue, contributing little to the difficult process of working the problems through. Journalists traditionally present positions as adversarial—positions on issues like abortion or gun control for example—that rarely correspond to the real views of most people. This style of presentation even retards progress, contributing to the gridlock that so often sets in when we try to grapple with these issues.[13]

So many observers like Yankelovich believe journalists could do a better job of informing by (1) reporting on the complexities of the problem, (2) defining the conflicting values surrounding—and sometimes polarizing—an issue, and (3) defining a common ground that could be the basis for effective action. Such a process would go much further than simply reporting the obvious polarity on an issue—often as typified by an open conflict—or simplifying an issue to anecdotal terms. The fact that public opinion, to many, still displays inconsistency (what Yankelovich calls "mushiness") indicates the media are not fostering a higher level of public debate.

Mark Moore, a professor in the Kennedy School of Government at Harvard University, has noted it is unclear if segments of the public are even discussing the same phenomenon. Using violence as an example, Moore believes white men often equate it with crime and seek ways of preventing it or stopping criminals. Women, on the other hand, seem more likely to focus on domestic violence. Other groups worry about the cult of violence and its impact on youths. Even on a particular topic the public may take a position which is inconsistent with itself. On gun control, for example, much of the country favors some form of it but still wants the right to keep firearms in the home for personal protection.[14]

One way in which television can assist in public understanding is by way of televised roundtable discussions using journalists as moderators and call-in shows or "town meetings" such as Bill Clinton used on the issue of universal health care.

How vulnerable do people feel to various health risks as a result of media coverage of these issues? Some researchers believe that certain segments of society consider themselves relatively invulnerable to health risks, so they don't attend to information about those risks. That attitude, in turn, makes them more vulnerable to risks.[15] To most teenagers, for instance, the concepts of death and serious disease are irrelevant to their personal well-being because they feel their whole life is ahead of them. Certainly they see more depictions of death and violence in the media than previous generations ever did, yet still the idea of their own death is far removed from their thinking in most cases. On another health issue, the high rate of teenage pregnancy shows that many of the population are not internalizing the warnings of the public service ad campaigns on safe sex.

For many years research has shown that people are apt to feel others have a stronger chance of getting hurt or succumbing to risks than they do. A typical spring or summer in Oklahoma or West Texas would show this to be true when tornado warnings are sounded for communities. The number of individuals and families who take no precautions is amazing, considering the potential harm that can come from being in the path of a tornado. Yet many people realize the twisters are very localized and feel the chance of their home or street getting hit is so minimal that they don't heed the warnings unless they see the funnel coming down the street.

Research has shown that most people also believe they are better drivers than other people and thus are less vulnerable to wrecks or serious injury.[16]

People also believe they are less vulnerable to risks from heart attack (as witnessed by the massive amount of french fries sold at fast-food restaurants), cancer, venereal diseases, or suicide.[17] Research has also shown that when people pay attention to news about health hazards, they are more apt to visualize the risk to society as a whole instead of to themselves personally.[18] All of this led a trio of researchers to write in 1987, "It is not easy to get people to acknowledge their vulnerability."[19]

A 1984 study raised the question of why some people who consider themselves immune from a certain risk go ahead and adopt precautionary tactics suggested by the media. The study's findings assert that "this could be due to the assumption by respondents that the protective measures available would be sufficient to neutralize the risk."[20]

A study reported in 1995 carries that thought further and asserts that relative personal invulnerability is not always a reflection of a person's ignorance of risk warnings. Rather, it could be an indirect effect of risk communication behaviors. The study suggests that when people are threatened by a serious risk, those who are more concerned about the risk and those who consider the risk warning as quite convincing will look for more information about the risk from media and interpersonal channels. The risk communication behaviors will then create some communication effects, such as increasing the individual's perceived self-expertise about the risk and enhancing his or her perception of controlling the risk. Ultimately, these communication effects will directly lead to the perception of relative personal invulnerability.[21]

In other words, certain populations could consider themselves relatively immune from risks because they *have* attended to the messages and are taking precautions to deal with the risks and control them.

What basic concerns motivate people to attend to news about risks? One 1989 study suggests that survival and growth are two such basic drives for people to monitor their environment for information. Because the media are the key source of this monitoring, those who feel the issue or risk involves them will pay attention.[22] Research also confirms that the experience of victimization may damage a person's belief in personal immunity, cause high stress, and lead that person to read or view stories about those risks and how to minimize them.[23]

RISK COMMUNICATORS: WHO ARE THEY?

Who are the people who write the stories about health and public safety risks and convey that information to the public? Like all beat reporters, they come from a wide range of backgrounds, although most probably began as general-assignment reporters with journalism or broadcasting degrees. Most news organizations treat the health/science area as any other beat and try to find reporters who at least have an interest in the area, if not some educational background in it. The difference with health/science news lies in its technical nature and its statistical basis which often appeal more to a quantitative mind than a verbal one. However, few health/science writers have formal training in the sciences. Instead, they learn as they cover the beat, much like any other beat reporter does. Sometimes this causes problems for both them and their readers or viewers. One illustration of that can be found in the coverage of the Three Mile Island nuclear power plant accident in Harrisburg, Pennsylvania. Radiation began leaking slowly from the plant on a Wednesday afternoon and, by Friday, two more uncontrolled bursts were emitted into the atmosphere. By the next day, more than 300 out-of-town journalists ascended on the scene, and the incident became the major story of the year. By far, most of these journalists knew little—if anything—about the subject of nuclear power. It was a story that could affect thousands of people in the surrounding communities; were a meltdown to occur, an untold number of lives would be at stake. Most nearby residents would be basing their decision on whether to evacuate on the reports they received from television, newspapers, and radio. Yet most of those doing the reporting had no formal training in science or in nuclear energy.

One reporter, Jim Panyard of the now-defunct *Philadelphia Bulletin*, said he was facing a story beyond his scope.[24] Although his methodology was much the same as reporting on the legislature, his sources now were speaking words and phrases he did not understand. These words were about unknown objects such as millirems, manrems, rads, and picocuries. He was also finding that even the scientists who did understand those terms did not always agree on the causes behind—or the potential danger of—the radiation leak. Panyard said, "There is no doubt that the situation is dangerous, but how dangerous is the question. I'm concerned, and I think other reporters are, too."[25]

In short, what reporters were facing was a technical story that turned into a technical nightmare to cover. Studying the phenomenon, Peter M. Sandman and Mary Paden wrote:

At the beginning, at least, the vast majority of reporters had no idea what anybody was talking about. Anchorless on a sea of rads and rems and roentgens, of core vessels and containments and cooling systems, they built their stories about the discrepancies between sources, confident that the news, when they finally came to understand it, would center on the facts in dispute. What is surprising about the T.M.I. coverage that emerged is not that it was sometimes technically wrong, but that it was so often technically right.[26]

Some fifteen years later, critics from within the media were still decrying the poor coverage the media exhibit in dealing with nuclear power. Jim Morris, the *Houston Chronicle*'s special projects reporter, notes:

There's a lack of coverage of the nuclear power industry in general (because) it's a complicated, very dry story and it takes a lot of effort to understand the terminology. . . . Nuclear power is a subject that can be tedious and probably sounds unappealing. . . . It's a challenge to write the stories in an understandable way, and your editors may lose interest. But you'll be doing something important. You'll put a very arrogant and secretive industry on notice that someone is watching it.[27]

Despite the tremendous importance of a well-covered health/science beat, the news industry seems to be supporting it less in recent years. For instance, according to a 1992 report by the Scientists' Institute for Public Information—now named the Media Resource Service—half of all weekly science sections appearing in newspapers were victimized by the last recession. In 1989 there were 95 such sections; by 1992 there were only 47.[28] And a growing number of journalists are nevertheless covering science as hard news instead of simply focusing on the quirkiness of science or zeroing in on the world's natural wonders.[29] Writer Stuart Schear notes:

Like their colleagues on the politics and business desks, these science reporters relish the opportunity to sort through the political, economic, institutional and social agendas influencing science and science policy. If there is truly a "new science journalism," it is this last group that deserves the mantle, since they are pushing the field well beyond its traditional boundaries.[30]

A sampling of stories from the anthology the *New Science Journalists* reveals what some of the nation's best science writers are up to these days:[31]

• An essay by Natalie Angier of the *New York Times* that looks at laziness among humans in the context of behavior in the insect and animal kingdoms.
• An investigative story by John Crewdson of the *Chicago Tribune* that discloses fraud in one of the nation's foremost research studies on the treatment of breast cancer.
• A retracing of events by Robert S. Capers and Eric Lipton of the *Hartford Courant* that shows the human mistakes and political and budgetary pressures that caused a team of technicians to misshape the mirror for the Hubble telescope.

The *Boston Globe* has one of the best weekly health/science sections appearing in newspapers today. Its editor, Niles Bruzelius, has a staff of eight full-time reporters, although none of them held a degree in the sciences as of 1995. Instead, *Globe* science writers hold mainly liberal arts or humanities-based degrees and began as general-assignment reporters, some with a dream of becoming a science or medical writer. "I would love to hire writers with an academic science background," Bruzelius says, "but what I'm mainly interested in is a demonstrated ability to cover a story well and write it well."[32]

The *Globe*'s section covers health, science, and the environment, and

Bruzelius notes there is a "considerable interest" in health and the environment. A 1995 readership study for the *Globe*'s Health/Science section showed medical and environmental stories to be running neck-and-neck in popularity, with almost 90 percent of the section's readers interested in both.[33]

At the *Globe*, science is treated as an enterprise like any other such as business or politics. Bruzelius says,

I think that, where science news once was seen as features or a kind of Gee Whiz news, that feeling has gradually been superceded by the idea that it has to be covered as an enterprise like any other enterprise that is covered by the paper. We still do stories on individual, unique phenomena, but we also look at the broader scope and impact of health and science.[34]

Contrary to what Stuart Schear feels some science journalists believe, however, Bruzelius believes medical news is very much a legitimate part of science news. He says the *Globe* tries to look as much as possible at the research aspect of medical news, as well as the symptoms of the individual disease. In fact, he believes that is what separates health reporting in newspapers from health reporting on television:

Television offers, at best, one story a night on health and medicine, whereas we can offer two or three a day in the paper, in addition to the weekly Health/Science section. Also, we tend to go more into detail on the virus and research related to it, whereas television looks more at how the symptoms affect an individual.[35]

On the plus side for television, Bruzelius believes its power to visually depict diseases and medical problems sometimes gives television a competitive edge.

No matter what their background, most science writers do not work as journalists for newspapers or magazines. Only about 250 to 300 members of the National Association of Science Writers (which boasts more than 1,000 members) are staff writers; only about 10 percent of the 1,650 daily newspapers employ science writers.[36] Additionally, most newspaper science and medical writers work on the larger metropolitan and regional dailies. General assignment reporters cover whatever science news gets reported in small dailies, or it comes from wire services or public information writers employed by local medical and science centers. In the magazine world, although some science writers work for major publications such as *Time* or *Newsweek*, the majority work for specialized science or medical magazines. Wire services also hire science and medical writers, as do network radio and television operations.

At the local television level, the medical beat most often goes to general-assignment reporters or one of the news anchors. In at least one large midwestern market, for example, one of the lead news anchors is the station's medical reporter, and he doesn't even have a college degree. Typical of medical reporting at many television stations, this reporter makes abundant use of syndicated news packages and video news releases and other media information supplied by health centers, pharmaceutical companies, and other vested-interest groups. Local interviews with physicians are sometimes spliced into this otherwise canned material. Sometimes, however, a top-ten market will feature a medical doctor as the station's medical reporter. Boston is one such market which has been served by physician/reporters.

Looking at science writers as a whole, author Dorothy Nelkins asserts, "Science writers are brokers, framing social reality for their readers and shaping the public consciousness about science-related events."[37] And writer Robert Andersen notes:

From AIDS to nuclear winter, Bhopal to Chernobyl, Challenger to Star Wars, a cat's cradle of improbable, outsized and often terrifying issues has landed in the science writer's lap. Of baffling complexity and often global consequence, these issues impose severe, perhaps impossible, demands on science reporters. Writing to deadline on a breaking story is one thing; writing to deadline while interpreting alien "social reality" is quite another. Too often the harried reporter resorts to shortcuts, stock framing, facile imagery, and pumped-up controversy.[38]

In sum, the challenge for science writers is to understand the complex technical matters that affect people's everyday lives and translate that knowledge in a way that is both interesting and informative for the average reader or viewer. The temptation is always there to romanticize science and the scientist and, as Nelkin puts it, "to rhapsodize about technology." [39] The best of the science writers, however, will find a way to do what the best reporters do: convey factual and significant information in an interesting way that doesn't distort or rob the news of its meaning.

NOTES

1. David Shaw, "Headlines and High Anxiety," *Los Angeles Times*, September 11, 1994, p. A1.

2. Ibid., p. A30.

3. Nancy Signorielli, *Mass Media Images and Impact on Health* (Westport, Conn.: Greenwood Press, 1993), p. 23.

4. Ibid.

5. David Shaw, "Cry Wolf Stories Permeate Coverage of Health Hazards," *Los Angeles Times*, September 12, 1994, p. A18.

6. Ibid.

7. Ibid.

8. Ibid.

9. David Shaw, "Alar Panic Shows Power of Media to Trigger Fear," *Los Angeles Times*, September 12, 1994, p. A19.

10. Ibid.

11. Ibid.

12. Margaret Gerteis, "Violence, Public Health, and the Media," report based on the conference, "Mass Communication and Social Agenda-Setting," the Annenberg Washington Program and Harvard School of Public Health, October 20–21, 1993.

13. Ibid.

14. Ibid.

15. Yu-Wei Hu, "Reconsidering the Theoretical Linkage between Risk Communication and Relative Personal Invulnerability: A Path Analysis," paper presented at the Association of Educators in Journalism and Mass Communication annual convention, Washington D.C., August 10, 1995, pp. 3–5.

16. Ibid.

17. Ibid.

18. Ibid.

19. Ibid.

20. Ibid.

21. Ibid., pp. 20–21.

22. Ibid.

23. Ibid.

24. Peter M. Sandman and Mary Paden, "At Three Mile Island," *Columbia Journalism Review* (July/August 1979), p. 45.

25. Ibid.

26. Ibid.

27. Elliott Negin, "In the Dark," *American Journalism Review* (April 1995), p. 43.

28. Stuart Schear, "Of Mice or Men?", *Columbia Journalism Review* (August 1995), p. 59.

29. Ibid.

30. Ibid.

31. Robert Andersen, "The Credulous and the Complacent," *Columbia Journalism Review* (September/October 1987), pp. 57–58.

32. Telephone interview with Niles Bruzelius, September 20, 1995.

33. Ibid.

34. Ibid.

35. Ibid.

36. Warren Burkett, *News Reporting: Science, Medicine, and High Technology* (Ames: Iowa State University Press, 1986), p. 27.

37. Andersen, "The Credulous and the Complacent."

38. Ibid.

39. Ibid.

2

The Journalist and the Pursuit of Truth

In no other area of journalism does the relatively unsystematic nature of reporting surface as clearly as it does in the actual pursuit of truth. Journalists take pride in their independence, autonomy and creativity, and they use all of these—often in unorthodox ways—in ferreting out the truth.

In contrast to the scientist who painstakingly follows an elaborate and time-tested scientific method in pursuing the answer to a single question, the journalist pursues a number of leads at once. In so doing, she chases a number of phenomena posing as fact and must treat them all as equally valid until verification proves them truth, lie, or rumor. And the verification the reporter seeks is often something less than a scientist would accept as proof. It often translates as getting one or two other knowledgeable sources to confirm or deny what the first source has said. In such a case, something is verified if two or three independent sources agree on it.

Additionally, reporters often find it necessary to take shortcuts to obtaining facts. Some of these shortcuts are needed for expediency, as the impending deadline looms always just ahead. Some involve questions of ethics which generally must be resolved quickly in the reporter's mind and heart. Case in point: a reporter has only 20 minutes to deadline and is having difficulty, through official channels, of obtaining the medical status of a patient who was brought in after being hit by a school bus. So she picks up the phone, calls the nursing station on the appropriate hospital floor, and announces herself as the victim's sister who is out of town but desperately wants to know her brother's condition.

Thus, if one road to truth appears blocked, a journalist will move quickly to find a detour. In reporting, these detours come in various shapes and sizes and they would often be overlooked by the untrained traveler.

So journalists often act creatively in pursuing facts, verifying them, and weaving them into a larger truth. However, it is important to note reporters do follow a general set of guidelines in searching out facts. These include, but are not limited to, the following:

• Seeking credible sources.
• Getting multiple sources on key stories and/or on key points within stories.
• When possible, pursuing the so-called "paper trail" of evidence before interviewing sources who are the actual targets of the story.
• Attempting to remain objective and detached from the story as much as possible.
• Attempting to be fair and balanced in covering all sides of the story.
• Attempting to be accurate with the information provided or ferreted out.
• Trying to present the information in an appropriate story structure, answering all the questions the readers might have about the event.

Aside from these and a few other guidelines, however, each journalist's approach to securing a story may well vary from the next. And often reporters even deviate from these guidelines.

TRUTH VERSUS ACCURACY

Before going any further, we should note that truth and accuracy are not necessarily the same thing. In the best of times the two concepts are identical, as when a source makes a statement that is a genuine reflection of reality. Often, however, a source will say something which is not true. If a newspaper prints that statement as it was given, it is being accurate although the statement itself is untrue.

You might say, however, that accuracy is the fertile soil from which truth can grow. Take, for example, the story of the Oklahoma City bombing on April 19, 1995. If a reporter were describing accurately the scene and mood of the tragedy, then a truthful account of the carnage and emotional trauma would emerge.

You could, then, assert a maxim that accuracy can exist without truth, but that truth cannot exist without accuracy. It is a reporter's job to be accurate, but it is also his job to be truthful. Facts are the common ground between the two concepts of truth and accuracy. Some facts emerge quickly, but others take time to pry out. As a whole, as essayist Roger Rosenblatt notes, truth emerges slowly and reveals itself in stages like a growing fern. This slowness factor will be discussed later.

Always elements in the creation of an accurate—and hopefully truthful—account of the day's news are the journalist and the larger institution of the news media. Media sage Marshall McLuhan coined the word "media" to indicate the go-between or mediated nature of journalists and their news organizations. McLuhan and other analysts before him such as Walter Lippman constantly explained that this journalistic mediation injects a very human reporter into the process of truth-telling. Lippman warned against confusing a report of reality with reality itself, cautioning that even the best reports are often built upon stereotypical thinking by reporters who must create word pictures in a hurry. Lippman thus spoke of "the world outside" and "the pictures in our heads." The pictures are the creation of these journalistic intermediaries, and they form a kind of shadow world which parallels the world of reality—hopefully very closely—but is not the actual world of reality.

THE CREATIVE REPORTER

In the world of day-to-day street reporting, reporters often make up their methodology as they paint their word pictures of reality. And instead of apologizing for such a shoot-from-the-hip style, many reporters believe it is the only way to do the job.

The reasons are many. One is that truth-seeking is a very fluid and dynamic process. It is also a very hard process for a number of reasons to be given later. Also, many reporters insist that each story is different and may require a little different methodology than the last, although certain similarities of means often occur. Finally, as just mentioned, truth-seeking is often a very slow process—especially if someone has something to hide, which is often the case. This slowness, however, must be fit into a profession which also prides itself on speed.

THE REQUIREMENT OF SPEED

Journalism has been described as literature in a hurry. It could be described just as appropriately as history in a hurry. The daily newspaper or the evening newscast is as up-to-date as history gets, being edged out only by live television updates and on-line information. The problem is the closer journalism gets to "real-time reporting," the more specious it becomes insofar as accuracy is concerned. ABC commentator Jeff Greenfield looked back on the real-time reporting of the Gulf War and noted the following:

We watch almost hypnotically; a *Times-Mirror* survey revealed that half of us literally cannot turn the TV set off. And yet we watch with a growing sense of frustration, a hunger to hear every fragment of information linked with the knowledge that much of what we learn we will unlearn in the next half hour. And this, perhaps, is the most signficant, most troublesome aspect of television's first "real-time" war; the uneasy blend of instant, immediate, round-the-clock access to information that is inherently incomplete, fragmented, or downright wrong. Both in terms of what we are learning and what this kind of access may be doing to us, it may well prove to be immeasurably more important than any other question about television's impact on the war—and on ourselves.[1]

It's as if there is a built-in hurdle to accuracy within the process of journalism itself. That hurdle is the requirement of speedy reporting and the accompanying deadline. Nevertheless, the entire process of truth-seeking by a journalist must fit into this quandary.

This paradox of speed and accuracy exists because the news media market both to the consuming public. It is not just information that sells; speed sells as well. In fact, one could make the case that speed is *more* marketable today than accuracy. The public's appetite for the latest factoids and blips of the bizarre seems almost insatiable. Witness the O. J. Simpson story or any tidbits about Michael Jackson.

Television tabloid programs have discovered that actual information is not a prerequisite for doing a story on any given night, especially if it's a continuing story like a Jackson or a Simpson. The important thing is to find something new, even if it is just a new piece of home videotape that runs only a few seconds in length. In television, there are definite hot-button topics, and the idea is to find them and keep feeding them to the public until they cool off and another emerges.

Historian Daniel J. Boorstin noted in the early 1960s that America is yearning for the image; for something more bizarre and startling than they saw yesterday. The news media—largely television—are rushing to provide it, he concludes. In so doing, the media fall prey to a kind of pseudo-news which confuses drama with reality and shadows with substance.

If speed were not important to the consumer, then television might not be the news medium of choice for many Americans (72 percent in 1995), and there would be no need for fax or on-line newspapers. Since it is so important, however, reporters must adopt a reporting method that seeks the truth but does it in a hurry. So daily journalism has little time for fact-finding methods that utilize a long, drawn-out systematic approach. The scientific method works in daily journalism only if it can be carried out quickly. And speed is more of an enemy to the scientific method than it is to journalism.

As in all cases, exceptions arise. Where investigative reporters are given long periods of time to research, report, and write their stories, more systematic reporting methods can be used. Large newspapers like the *Philadelphia Inquirer* and the *Miami Herald*, for instance, often give an investigative team several months or longer to develop a series. Within this time frame, more sophisticated methods of fact-finding can be used and might range from filing Freedom of Information requests (itself a challenging process), to running computerized checks on information to find statistical significance and correlations.

Content analysis, for instance, is a method some journalists use as they

dig through mountains of reports comprising the paper trail they are following at the moment. The computer has done wonders for the ability of
reporters to check facts, correlate information, and spot trends in a hurry.
As more records are put on-line, as more reporters become computer-
literate, and as the price of computer-assisted journalism drops, consumers
can expect more depth and accuracy to reporting. Not all journalists, however, have the skills or resources to delve very deeply into computerized
reporting.

THE SLOWNESS FACTOR

Journalism's need for speed is countered by the fact that truth often takes
a long time to uncover. This is not necessarily the truth associated with
breaking news events such how a traffic accident happened or what the
city council decided in last night's meeting. But it may be the truth associated with *why* that accident happened or *why* the city council voted as
it did. These questions require longer research and often result in issue-
oriented stories, as opposed to the standard daily fare of event-oriented
news.

Each year since 1976 the Journalism Department at Sonoma State University in California has selected a list of stories it believes to be the most
censored stories of the year by the news media. It then presents that list to
a national panel of media experts which shortens the list to the ten best
censored stories. A quick glance at these listings shows that most entries
are issue-oriented stories such as the influence of green-marketing on manufacturing, the government's attack on America's middle class, or the racial
crises in American cities.

The entry voted the top censored story of 1993, for example, revealed
that nine out of ten young people murdered in industrialized nations are
slain in the United States.[2] Other stories on the top-10 list included the
following as labeled by the panel:

- The Hidden Tragedy of Chernobyl. The far-reaching international impact of the
  1986 Chernobyl disaster was censored in Russia, under-reported in America, and
  eagerly accepted by the international nuclear establishment.

- U.S. Army Quietly Resumes Biowarfare Testing After 10-Year Hiatus. Despite
  widespread concern, the U.S. Army has brought biological warfare testing back
  to a site declared unsafe a decade earlier.

- Ecological Disaster Challenges the Exxon *Valdez*. The environmental nightmare
  caused by selenium-contained drainwater makes the Exxon *Valdez* oil spill pale
  in comparison.

- America's Deadly Doctors. A well-documented study revealed that 30,000 to
  60,000 of America's doctors are impaired or incompetent and could be hazardous
  to your health.

It is interesting, in looking at the focus of this book, that at least 40 percent of these top-10 stories deal with public health and/or medical issues, 50 percent if you consider murder a public health story.

But these stories, and the others which make up the list, have something more basic in common. They are issue-oriented stories, and such stories have two things working against them in daily journalism: (1) They take a lot of time to research and report; and (2) Issues are not as breathtaking or sexy as are events and celebrities.

Given these twin problems, it is a wonder that any depth reporting is still being done. But a lot of it is being done, and it will always be necessary. These are the stories that talk about why events are unfolding as they are and what Americans can expect in the future if current trends hold true. It is also the journalism that answers the big question we should have in our minds about news, which is "So what?" It is news you can use in the truest sense of that phrase, athough that message is slow in getting through to the consumer.

Event-reporting, however, is easier and quicker to nail down. Something happens, and a reporter is sent off to answer the who-what-when-where and how questions. It is the bread and butter of daily journalism and is important in and of itself.

Event reporting, however, has also been described as iceberg reporting. Media analyst Maxwell McCombs describes it this way:

Just as radar scans sea lanes for the tips of icebergs portending danger, the news media daily scan the local community and the nation for signs of imminent disruption and danger. That, of course, is part of the job of the press but the unaided human observer unfortunately can describe only the tip of the iceberg. The major portion . . . remains invisible and undescribed beneath the surface. The analogy holds. Public affairs reporting, with its emphasis on discrete news events, typically describes only the tips of our social icebergs. . . . But the capability is available for the profession to render much more valuable service.[3]

Others, like Rosenblatt, argue that the larger truth is not the responsibility of daily journalism. Receiving a daily report of accurate events is all we should ask of the American news media, which are in a bad position to give us the larger truth. Journalism, Rosenblatt argues, looks to where the ball is and not to where it is not. It looks to those events that protrude themselves. Poverty, for instance, is with us all the time. Thus, the subject is hardly news. But when a frustrated, out-of-work father pulls out a gun and shoots a store clerk for $50, then it becomes news.

Rosenblatt suggests looking to books, history, education, nature, and conversation itself to uncover the larger truth. Look to the news media, he suggests, to find only the smaller facts attending distinct events.[4]

The most dedicated of journalists, however, spend a lot of time trying to provide both facts and truth. In their battle, they are up against all the factors that go together to slow down the process of getting at the truth. Chief among those factors is the people problem.

THE PEOPLE PROBLEM

Because journalism relies so heavily on the limited perspectives, vested interests, varying motives, prejudices, and often frail memories of people to get the truth out, the results are sometimes questionable. In fact, given the number of possible contaminating elements in the reporting and writing processes, it is a wonder that most stories emerge as accurately as they do.

Although scholars have tried over the decades to develop a scientific model of the communication process, none has emerged as the standard out of the many that have been offered up. One reason is that there are so many variables that can change either the way the message is encoded, delivered, or interpreted at the decoder end of the scale. The one thing most scholars—as well as journalists—would agree upon is the commanding presence of *noise* along the communication scale and the tremendous influence it has on the accuracy, truthfulness, and perception of the message. It should come as no surprise that this is the case, since the study of communication is the study of how people learn and relate to each other. And people are anything but rational beings. Chief among the people problems which journalists encounter as they pursue truth are the following.

The Desire to Appear Intelligent

There is nothing wrong with a person's wanting to appear intelligent to others. Indeed that can be a useful quality if the person knows what he is talking about. The problem journalists encounter is when a source starts making statements that lie beyond his or her knowledge. Journalists themselves are often accused of speculation and interpretation, but sources do it just as often if not more so. This is one reason why so many different versions of the same story are offered up to reporters by sources. For example, William Rivers found the following varying accounts from sources questioned by reporters in the hours following the 1963 assassination of President John F. Kennedy:[5]

- Some said the rifle used was near the window on the second floor of the Texas School Book Depository, yet others said it was found on the staircase near the fifth floor. Still other accounts had it hidden behind boxes on the second floor. Ultimately, all reports agreed it was found elsewhere—on the sixth floor.

- Some reports on the rifle described it as a U.S. Army or Japanese rifle of .25 caliber, while others said it was a .30 caliber Enfield. Finally, it emerged as an Italian-made 6.5 mm rifle.

- There were several different accounts of how many bullet wounds the president had suffered, and where those wounds were.

- There were conflicting reports on the number of stops Lee Harvey Oswald made in the 14 or 15 minutes between the shooting and his arrival at his room in Dallas' Oak Cliff section. If all these sightings were correct, he would not have had time to do all the things attributed to him.

- At least one radio report told of Vice President Lyndon Johnson suffering a heart attack upon hearing the news of Kennedy's shooting. Obviously, that did not happen.

Some of these inaccuracies could be chalked up to the confusion surrounding the events in Dallas on that November day. But many of these and other inaccuracies were inevitably the outcome of sources passing speculation or hearsay off as actual knowledge about what had just transpired. When that happens, reporters must work overtime to sort out the truth from fantasy, and they must do it on deadline.

The Desire to Look Good

This very human desire is related to the one just discussed because, to look good, one must look intelligent. But there is more at work here. Most reporters would probably agree that sources will sometimes go to great lengths to avoid looking as if they have done something wrong or immoral—and certainly illegal. In fact, these attempts often telescope out to a source's trying to make his or her cause, group, political party, or candidate look good—often at the expense of trashing someone else's reputation. Anyone who has done any political reporting runs into this phenomenon every day, and it is the basis for the well-planned system of leaks in Washington and state capitals around the country.

This is also the basis for much of the secrecy that exists in the country—secrecy which often is hidden behind the rubric of national security. When President Nixon, for instance, refused to turn over the Watergate tapes during the latter months of his presidency, he did so on the grounds of national security. The real reason, as it turned out, was political expediency. To some Washington reporters, in fact, national security is often a euphemism for political expediency in the minds of too many elected officials.

The Source Accountability Problem

Often sources find it easy to embellish the facts, distort them for their own purposes, or just plain lie because they know their identity will not appear in the pages of the newspaper or on the television screen. Probably no other problem has been discussed so much by journalists over the years as the problem of anonymous sources.

Confidentiality is often the carrot extended to a reluctant source to make disclosing information more palatable. The prevalence of anonymous sources was revealed in a *Journalism Quarterly* study which showed 80 percent of all national and international stories in researched editions of *Time* and *Newsweek* magazines contained anonymous attribution. In addition, 33 percent of the stories in the *New York Times* and *Washington Post* used them. More than half of all network newscasts used them as well. In Washington alone, the study found, 30 percent of all interviews done in that district were conducted off the record.[6]

In a national mail survey of top editors at 106 metro daily newspapers in 1994, some other interesting findings surfaced regarding the prevalence of confidential sources.[7] Among them:

- Nine out of ten newspapers use confidential sources and have some kind of oral or written policy regarding when anonymity can be granted and how it is to be granted.

- Fewer than half of those newspapers commit that policy to writing, often for fear that it could be used against them in civil litigation.

- Practically all (98 percent) of the newspapers using confidential sources say they permit them as a last resort in obtaining the truth.

- Most editors questioned say they would never violate a promise their paper made in granting a source confidentiality.

Journalists defend the practice of granting confidentiality to sources because they say many sources would not talk if they didn't receive such anonymity. There are, reporters point out, legitimate reasons for a source wanting to remain anonymous. Those reasons include fear of losing one's job, fear of being ostracized by one's peers, and—in some cases—fear of physical harm. In such cases, journalists say, confidentiality is a legitimate request to honor.

But, as many reporters know, in too many cases the requests are made and granted frivolously. In some of those instances, sources are seeking to hide behind the mask of anonymity so they can make whatever accusations they like without fear of being held accountable for those attacks. In other cases, sources believe granting confidentiality is a standard part of journalism and they would just rather speak off the record than on if possible.

It is the journalist's job to ferret out the legitimate from spurious requests for confidentiality and respond accordingly. Few, if any, reporters would deny that on-the-record statements make for a more credible story. Few would also deny that sources are less likely to lie or distort the truth if they know their name is attached to the statements they make.

Reporters' Routines

Journalists are people, and most people are creatures of habit and routines. Often the reporter's routine is the problem, however, especially if it leads to expedient reporting at the cost of comprehensive reporting.

A study in *Journalism Quarterly*[8] found, for instance, the following results through a sample of metropolitan dailies:

- Reporters do much of the background information retrieval that informs their work, but their focus is very narrow and conventional when they search. In large measure, they look only at their own newspaper's electronic backfiles as they prepare their breaking news stories.

- Reporters still turn to the same official sources as were apparent in more classic newsmaking studies. Even though they use more of these officials in each story, the range of sources has not expanded.

- Reporters are not using external databases enough to help them break out of the "official source" syndrome. In other words, they are still relying on the same sources as always—either by new interview or old backfile—instead of looking beyond their own library to retrieve other sources of information.

In conclusion to this study the researchers note another interesting finding:

The conventions of objectivity appear to be firmly in place. The evidence from this study indicates that journalists are reluctant to openly question statements by interviewees. They may include another source's skepticism about an interviewee's assertions, but the journalists themselves rarely include their own fact statements or interpretations in their breaking news stories. This reluctance persists despite the fact that reporters and editors may have, through the use of electronic information retrieval systems, access to far more information about the topic or issue than the interviewee.[9]

The official-source syndrome mentioned in this study has been a part of mainstream journalism for a long time. The feeling traditionally is that, if you want to know what is going on, you look for the expert. That person is usually the one in charge of the agency, department, or project. He or she usually carries a prestigious title that, it is hoped, will add to the credibility of the statements made. The problem is that, in cases where the department head *doesn't* know what is going on down the line in his or her agency, you then encounter the problem mentioned earlier: someone who is trying to appear intelligent by passing on speculation rather than actual knowledge. You also can encounter the problem of the official source passing on to the public the official *story*. That story may or may not reflect reality, and it may not reflect the actual impact the decision or event could have on the public.

Reporters' Orientations

Journalist Richard Critchfield has written of how he covers news in foreign countries and of how that coverage differs from the traditional, official-source coverage he used to conduct. A former reporter for the *Economist* and the *Washington Star*, Critchfield broke out of tradition when he embarked on his career as a kind of storytelling anthropologist. His goal was to cover what was really happening in Third World countries. He felt the best way to do that was to get away from the national capitals and get out where the people live and work and become involved with them. Critchfield has noted that most of the struggles of the world emanate from the difficult times Third World nations have in adapting to Western technology and ideas. He says the best way to find out how well they are adapting is to talk with the people instead of the government officials. Toward that end, Critchfield spent weeks and, in some cases, months living and working in several villages in Third World Countries, constantly engaging everyday people in conversations—with the help of an interpreter—and taking copious notes each night before he went to bed. What emerged over time, he says, is a chronicle of how a country is changing or refusing to change, as told through the eyes of that country's people. He writes:

I gradually feel my way into getting to know individuals and families. At last, when I sit down to write my story, after typing up as many as 20 or 30 notebooks, I hope that the dialogue I have taken down will reveal the full life and character of a few villagers as persons whose individual destiny appear framed by the setting of the changing culture and technology around them. . . . Because a village is small and simple, not big and complex like a city, it is easier there to see how culture works, how it changes and how this affects the big political stories.[10]

This clash of reporting styles—the traditional official-source syndrome vs. the people-oriented style—was depicted in the movie *The Year of Living Dangerously*. In that film, which takes place in Jakarta in the early 1960s, Australian broadcaster Guy Hamilton learns the secret of truthful and effective reporting from a native photojournalist, Billy Kwan. That secret is to avoid the official story and to instead get the story by observing and interviewing the people whom the government's policies impact.

There are, in fact, several different orientations operating among news reporters today. To cast all journalists into the same psychological profile sharing a common methodology in pursuing the truth is a serious mistake. The mission of most journalists—seeking that truth—may be a constant, but the means of achieving it are varied. A sampling of reporting orientations would include the following:

1. The Joe Friday Approach. This no-nonense, by-the-book detective might be representative of the strictly traditional reporter who believes strongly in the following: strict detachment from the action and people covered; reverence for the basic newswriting format of the inverted pyramid; use of neutral verbiage; avoidance of any subject impressions; a profound belief that objectivity can be obtained; a total devotion to the facts of the story.

2. *The George Plimpton Approach*. Along with the Tom Wolfe Approach which follows, this perspective represents the opposite extreme from the Joe Friday Approach. This is immersion reporting, with the journalist becoming involved in the action he/she is covering to get a more salient taste of that action. It is a quest for greater realism wherein the reporter delivers these sensations first-hand because he or she is actually feeling them.

3. *The Tom Wolfe Approach*. Like the Plimpton Approach, this perspective values how the story is told almost as much as what the story has to say. There is a strong literary tradition found here that often gets reduced to formulaic writing in the Friday Approach. Yet most of the reporters coming to the Wolfe pack do not go as far as Plimpton might in becoming part of the action. Instead, they seek its greater realism through a combination of techniques including:

- Sparing no effort as a reporter in trying to invade the psyche of the person being interviewed. This has sometimes been dubbed imperialistic reporting.
- A recording of the most minute mannerisms of the speaker and people listening to him or her.
- A kind of social autopsy where the reporter paints a scene-by-scene portrait of events relating to the story.
- An abundant use of dialogue, some of which is based on the reporter's informed impressions of what the individual would say, given the chance and his or her personality and similar stimuli.
- Adapting techniques of fiction writing, such as starting with details that lead to mounting action and climax, followed by a neat—and often surprising—ending.

4. *The Scientific Approach*. In this approach, the journalist comes closest to using the methodology employed by the scientist. Championed by such journalistic scholars as Philip Meyer in his book *Precision Journalism*, this approach insists that reporters must have better documentation if their stories are going to mirror reality. The best documentation is found in quantitative research techniques such as those used by social scientists. They include the random sample survey, content analysis, and controlled experiments. By understanding and adapting these methods to reporting, the journalist is better able to explain and predict trends or events happening in society.

5. *The Woodstein Approach*. Popularized in the 1970s by Bob Woodward and Carl Bernstein of Watergate fame, this is the investigative ap-

proach to journalism. It takes a great deal of time, and it takes a lot of money. A second aspect to this approach goes back to the muckraking journalism days of Lincoln Steffens, a reporter for *McClure's* magazine, in the early twentieth century. This involves a somewhat cynical viewpoint of the world. Steffens was fond of saying he would often go into reporting situations simply assuming that corruption was present, and that it was his job to ferret it out. Because of the utter devotion to the story, investigative reporters will often possess another characteristic: a belief that, in many cases, the ends will justify the means of getting the story. Even a casual reading of Woodward and Bernstein's *All the President's Men* will reveal the number of schemes these two journalists used just to get sources to be candid and honest with them.

6. *The Friendly Eye Approach.* To some degree, you might find this approach at the opposite end of the scale from the Woodstein Approach. The reason is that this perspective, championed by such journalists as William Dean Howells, believes that—in balance—the kindlier view of Man is apt to be the truer view. Also, maybe even more than the other approaches discussed, it believes the journalist must do exhaustive homework on an individual before he or she characterizes them in a particular way. Howells believed, for instance, that you should not judge a person by the way they respond to a crisis situation. Instead, he advised, look at the person's life steadily and wholly before categorizing them.

7. *The Pseudo-Journalist Approach.* Daniel J. Boorstin sees too many reporters chasing the bizarre story simply to satisfy a consumer who is yearning for the image of something more exciting and surreal than he thinks he can experience with reality. Boorstin describes a pseudo-event as one that is designed to be dramatic and, therefore, features more flash than substance. It is a planned event, as opposed to spontaneous, and it has little significance on the lives of readers or viewers.

Sometimes a strong marketing or competitive influence is found at the base of this type of reporting as later discussion in this chapter will indicate.

Judgmental Reporting

Semanticist S. I. Hayakawa was fond of discussing the impact of language on our daily lives and on the events surrounding our lives. He noted often that language is not a neutral thing but a catalyst for different types of attitudes and actions among those who hear or read our words.[11] Hayakawa classified language into one of three categories:

1. *Reports.* This is the most objective and neutral form of language and is built upon the premise that everything that is said is verifiable. For instance, if a reporter makes the statement, "Senator Samuel Smith is six feet tall," that is report-style language. You can take a yardstick and measure the senator's height.

2. *Inferences*. When someone makes a statement about the unknown based upon what he or she does know, Hayakawa would say an inference has just been drawn. For instance, if a reporter sees rubber skid marks left in the road, he or she might infer a car had come to a screeching halt there. Much of reporting is inferential or, as some journalists prefer, interpretive. It links one fact to another in an attempt to form a more complete picture of the truth. Hayakawa would say there is nothing wrong with that, depending on how well the inferences are drawn and what data they are based upon.

3. *Judgments*. When a person moves from inferences to writing or saying something which contains a value judgment or opinion, then he has crossed the line into using judgment language. In most cases, writers' opinions—whether emotionally or rationally based—are reserved for the Op-Ed page of the newspaper or a brief editorial at the end of a television newscast. Some media analysts, however, believe many reporters are doing judgmental reporting in their news stories.

One such analyst is John Herbers, a retired reporter and editor with the *New York Times*. Herbers has noted that, around the nation, reporters seem to be going beyond objectivity and analysis (interpretation) to express their feelings. In so doing, they are engaging in judgmental journalism. Writing in an issue of *Nieman Reports*, he stated, "Judgmental journalism is welcomed by many reporters because it gives them freedom of expression they never had under strict standards of objectivity. . . . [Judgmental reporting is a] move beyond analysis into allowing reporters to inject their own feelings or exercise narrow selectivity of subject matter.[12]

Herbers believes one key reason for the change to judgmental journalism is to cater to a generation of younger readers who have become used to the visual imagery and speculation found in television reporting. In competing with television, he says editors feel compelled to "make the news shorter, punchier, less ambiguous, entertaining and, if needed for extra spice, opinionated."[13]

Many journalists, however, believe that injecting emotion and feeling into reporting is valid and falls short of judgmental journalism. They would point out that, if a story is about a people's emotional reaction to a tragedy for instance, then there is nothing wrong in bringing emotions into the telling of the story. It is part of the essence of the story, just as much as the who, where, and when. It is an emotion that any normal person would feel or pick up on if he or she were to wander into the scene being described. In that sense, it is verifiable.

A case in point would be the bombing of the Alfred P. Murrah Federal Building in Oklahoma City on April 19, 1995. From beginning to end, that story was about a people's emotional reaction to tragedy. It was also an emotional drama in which reporters found themselves caught up, as they became an integral part of the downtown scene in the days and weeks following the bombing and during the search and rescue operations. Many of the stories seemed, to some reporters, to cry out for something other than a standard inverted-pyramid treatment. Take, for example, a memorial staged by hundreds of rescuers at the foot of the decimated building on May 5. A standard, objective treatment of that story would probably have focused on what the memorial was for, how many and who attended, and what the mayor and governor had to say at the podium. Yet to many reporters, that was not the story at all. The story was instead the visual and emotional drama lying before them as they stood on bits and pieces of the same rubble that had killed 168 and injured more than 500 innocent people.

It is not surprising, therefore, that one story described the event—in part—as follows:

You stand on Fifth Street in the shadow of what once was the Alfred P. Murrah Federal Building. There is a ceremony under way, but you can't take your eyes off the nine-story carcass in front of you.

. . . You look up and see this monument of man's inhumanity to man; its hollowed-out section of floors and the rubble pile remaining below. Yet you also realize you are staring straight into a tower of love and self-sacrifice.

. . . Everywhere you look you see flowers, wreaths, Teddy bears, and hand-painted signs of thanks. A rose juts its dark red head out of an orange highway cone that is wrapped with duct tape and which appears to have been kicked more than once by a frustrated fireman.

Another rose dangles from a camera tripod belonging to a Reuters TV news photographer.

. . . There are those who insist that, in the battle between the eye and the ear, the eye wins every time. That seems true here today. There is so much to see, so much to take in. There is so much to remember for fear that—if you don't—you may forget your resolve to hate violence in any form.

You realize this is the legacy of violence.[14]

Clearly, a piece like this goes beyond report language and even beyond inference in places. By bringing in an emotional perspective, one could say it enters the world of judgmental journalism. Yet, one could argue, they are emotions that any normal visitor to the scene might be expected to feel by seeing what the reporter sees. In the end, as is the case in all types of journalism, the reader must ultimately trust the reporter's ability to describe an observation or source's statements accurately. The journalist's skill and integrity once again loom extremely important.

ORGANIZATIONAL REQUIREMENTS

Journalism is a business as well as a service, so its idealism is often blunted by the realities of the bottom line. This situation is really no different from any other profession, most notably medicine and law. All three of these professions have considerable public impact, however, so when business considerations get in the way of that idealism too much, the people have a right to cry foul.

When the business side starts dictating what news is covered and by-passed and starts influencing how these stories are covered, both the public and committed journalists alike feel the implied mandate of the First Amendment is being toyed with. That mandate, many feel, leaves the press free so it can perform an important public service of bringing an accurate and comprehensive account of the day's news to the people. Should it remain so free of government checks, some feel, if it is taking its mission too frivolously and substituting titilation for substance; entertainment for news?

Longtime newsman Bill Moyers said recently that the big problem with much of the news media today is that they have, in fact, abdicated their news mission in favor of an entertainment mission. He cited a 1995 extended television interview by Diane Sawyer of Michael Jackson and Priscilla Presley as a classic example of that. He chided ABC for presenting that program "under the aegis of the news division instead of the entertainment division."[15] There is nothing wrong with interviews like that, Moyers said, as long as they are not presented as news.

A few years back, former *Atlanta Constitution* editor Bill Kovach discussed this marketing of the news with Moyers. Kovach said that, while people often think of television as being the chief culprit in mixing news with entertainment, newspapers have fallen prey to the practice, too. He cited *USA Today* as an example of what happens when the marketing department calls the shots at a newspaper, but he said the practice has gone far beyond that one newspaper to include many other dailies as well.[16]

Even in the coverage of a serious beat like the White House, the media—most notably network television—place themselves in the hands of skillful manipulators. One such manipulator, Michael Deaver, was media aide to former President Ronald Reagan. Following Reagan's second term, Deaver spoke of the ease with which his staff was able to dictate to network television which video clips and soundbites would be used in their nightly newscasts and how they could turn negative stories into positive ones for the president.[17]

Since a president's media aide controls the day-to-day access reporters have to the president, then he or she also controls the photo opportunities. Deaver recalled one day when his staff knew some depressing economic news on housing starts was about to be released to the press. To make lemonade out of a lemon—or at least to confuse the two in the public mind—Deaver loaded Reagan on Air Force One and shipped him off to Fort Worth to walk through a large home under construction. Television dutifully followed along to get an unusual shot of the president out in the heartland, and the evening news on all three networks featured Reagan walking through a framed-out home. Although the verbal portion of the story was that housing starts were down nationwide, what viewers saw was the president of the United States touring a new home under construction. To Deaver, in the battle between the eye and the ear, the eye wins every time. Thus, much of the public saw the video and asked, "What is the president doing walking through this home?" On the basis of what they saw, they answered, "Oh. Housing starts must be up."

Business Need No. 1: Advertising

If one were to classify the organizational requirements of the news media, one would seemingly have to begin with advertising. Certainly advertising revenue drives the media machine, even in the case of the print media, which also derive a relatively small percentage of their revenue from circulation. But in practice, it is impossible to separate the need for advertising from the need for consumers (readers, listeners, or viewers), and from the need for appropriate content. All three are related in inextricable fashion, just as breathing, stroking, and kicking are all necessary in order to swim properly.

In essence, advertising is what a media company gets when it has attracted the right kind of audience with the right kind of content and packaging. For a metro daily newspaper, advertising income accounts for up to 80 percent of its income. For a television station or network, it amounts to almost 100 percent. To say, therefore, that advertising exerts clout in the formation of the news product—and thus in the daily snapshot of reality the medium produces—is an understatement.

One of the biggest names in media advertising in the past several decades is Leo Bogart, an internationally known public opinion specialist and former advertising executive. For almost 30 years, Bogart was with the Newspaper Advertising Bureau, where he held the position of executive vice president and general manager. In a paper entitled, *The American Media System and Its Commercial Culture*,[18] the former head of public opinion research for Exxon Corporation made the following key points:

- Though there is much to laud in the rich diversity of the American mass media, there are also serious flaws stemming from their almost complete dependence upon advertising.

- This dependence has led to the commercialization of an American culture "produced for sale to meet marketing requirements."

- Because media managers regard advertisers—instead of the public—as their main customers, advertisers have a strong and often controlling effect on media structure and content.

- This dependence on advertisers who have no stake in media content other than

to use it as a vehicle to promote their product has at least three serious consequences: (1) Advertising becomes a major part of the public's communication
experience; (2) Advertisers affect judgments that shape non-advertising content;
and (3) Advertising considerations decide the fate of individual media.

Bogart argues against leaving American culture entirely to the marketplace and urges that the communications environment get the same kind
of protection as the physical environment. Bogart asks, "Can we preserve
freedom of expression and democracy of taste and, at the same time, make
a national commitment to upgrading the integrity and quality of expression
and taste?"

The first step, he says, is to recognize that a problem does exist and that
market forces alone are not the solution. The second step is to examine
mass communications policy as an "integrated whole," or as one large
system, rather than seeking solutions in the media.

Business Need No. 2: Consumers

Since advertisers are so concerned with using the news media to reach
targeted audiences, media managers see increasing their audience share as
a primary goal. In short, the news media need readers, listeners, or viewers
if they are going to get the advertising. No secret here, but the challenge
presents itself daily to media managers. It often translates into tweaking
the operational definition of news, if not changing it entirely. It also translates into tweaking or changing entirely the way that news is presented to
the users. Case in point: the electronic tabloid news format which a third
of the local television stations have gone to in the United States.

Over the past two decades, several books as well as articles in professional media journals and national news magazines have told the tale of
the winds of change in ideas regarding news. The following titles are in-
dicative of the phenomenon:

• *No Scandal, No Story*
• *If It Bleeds, It Leads*
• *When MBAs Rule the Newsrooms*
• *News from Nowhere*
• *Untended Gates: The Mismanaged Press*
• *The Tyranny of the Apathetic*

Some analysts call it an LCD (lowest common denominator) approach
to bagging an audience. Others call it insulting and say the media vastly
underestimate the intelligence of the American news consumer. Still others
say the media are only giving the public what it wants, and those desires

are reflected every day in the Nielsen and Arbitron ratings charts. Those who look at it in a normative sense see trouble. Bill Baker, president of WNET in New York City, has noted, "To aim only at the bottom line is to aim too low. Our country deserves better."[19]

Business Need No. 3: Marketable Content

Although some readers and viewers turn to the news media for advertising (this is especially true in the case of magazines and newspapers), the great majority of people turn to the media for some sort of information or entertainment. Usually it is this content that draws the users in the first place and turns them into loyal viewers or subscribers. Again, this is especially true for newspapers and magazines. One could make the case, as an untold number of consultants' research studies have, that it is the personality and looks of the on-air talent that are so vitally important for television news. It isn't that content is *not* important; it just often seems that personalities delivering the stories are more so. Go into any television market in the country and start asking people which station they watch most for news, weather, and sports. Then ask them *why* they watch that station. It will be a rare occurrence when they don't give you the name of a lead anchor or on-air reporter as the chief reason.

Newspapers are not immune from marketing considerations, either. Because there is only one daily newspaper in most cities (while there are usually at least three commercial television stations), those marketing considerations may rule newspaper content and packaging to a lesser extent than TV. But they are still important. Angus McEachern, editor and president of the *Commercial Appeal* in Memphis says, "As editor I want to cover all the news that is possible and all parts of our reading area. As president, however, I have to balance that desire with marketing and bottom-line considerations."[20]

McEachern agreed that obtaining the reader demographics that advertisers want will sometimes force a newspaper into downplaying coverage that interests demographics they don't want.

The same marketing considerations that sometimes dictate which stories to cover also have dictated how they are covered. In his essay, *Spicing up the (Ho-Hum) Truth*, John Leo recalled the infamous *Dateline NBC* episode where producers rigged a GM pickup to explode on camera. He also recalled a PBS documentary on how black troops freed Jews from Dachau and Buchenwald that was pulled for review when word arose that some ex-soldiers of the black regiment denied ever being anywhere near either camp.

Leo writes:

In these cases, the question is whether this is inaccuracy or deception. [But] what if it was a preview of what news is destined to become as story line and emotional impact begin to erode the old commitment to literal truth? [Syndicated columnist Richard] Reeves says the old guard has disappeared from TV news, and the business is now in the hands of a new generation whose members don't think of themselves as reporters or producers but filmmakers, with little interest in words and heavy interest in dramatic effect. . . . Obvious competitive pressures have a lot to do with this corner-cutting trend in journalism.[21]

   Newspapers also get into the act of staging pictures or re-creating events at times, such as when *USA Today* ran a staged front-page picture of gun-toting gang members (without noting it was staged) to emphasize the problem chronicled in the accompanying story. To its credit, Leo points out that the newspaper suspended the journalist responsible for the staging.[22]
   So for both the electronic and print media, the marketing department and competitive pressures are as influential as ever in deciding which of the many possible truths the news operation will cover in its area of dominant influence.

WHICH TRUTH TO PURSUE

   The ways in which journalists search for truth will often affect the outcome of that search. There are many truths waiting to be discovered by reporters, and the orientations, methodologies, and different constraints on reporters will influence which of those truths are chased in the first place. It is possible for two journalists to pursue the same story, in fact, and come up with two different and seemingly competing truths about the same event. For instance, a *Boston Globe* writer, writing in July 1995 and looking back on the April 19 Oklahoma City bombing, produced a story headlined, *Oklahoma City Caring Turns to Whining*. In that story, Brian MGrory wrote:

A mountain of good will is beginning to erode into a pile of harsh words, as survivors and family members of those killed in the federal building's bombing are accusing government officials of mismanaging donated relief money. Many victims have complained that the governor and mayor are stalling the distribution of checks sent in by people across the nation.[23]

   The slant, or idea, for this particular story was to probe the feelings of the recipients of disaster aid to see if they were frustrated by the distribution of that money. McGrory found some who, indeed, were upset about it. But his sweeping lead sentence is not supported by anything other than anecdotal comments from two surviving relatives and one personal-injury lawyer. In order for such an overall lead statement to have any real validity, more documentation is needed. There is no doubt that frustration is the true feeling of those interviewed for this story, but there is no reason to suspect that another truth existed for another ad hoc sample that might be interviewed or for the whole population of hundreds of families affected by the bombing deaths and injuries.

For instance, any reporter pursuing the same story could have happened upon several surviving families and victims who had little or no trouble getting their money and who actually praised the distribution system. Such stories were actually done by other news media. In such case, the headlines read something like, *Oklahoma City Caring Turns to Support for Government*, with the lead paragraph being an amplification of that particular truth.

It would have been the same story, with different samples interviewed, resulting in completely different truths which were both valid for the people making the comments. But neither would have been the overall truth for all victims and surviving families. To assess the majority feelings of such a large group, some random-sample methodology would be needed. But such a reporting method is generally beyond the pale of news media doing daily stories. Even if it weren't, many editors and news directors would decry the lack of an individual focus to such trend or survey stories and would insist on a more human focus.

Shedding light on whose truths the various media choose to cover is a 1995 research report entitled *Headlines and Sound Bites: Is That the Way It Is?* Produced by the Freedom Forum Media Studies Center in New York City, the report is a result of content analyses of all articles appearing in the national and international news sections of the weekday editions of the *New York Times, Des Moines Register* and *Atlanta Constitution* from January 3–27, 1995. Concurrently, the content of nightly network newscasts of ABC, CBS, and NBC were analyzed over the same time period.[24] Among the studies' findings were the following:

- The public's reliance on television as a news source continues to grow, while reliance on newspapers is diminishing.
- The three network newscasts are remarkably similar to each other in terms of what stories they cover and how much time they spend on those stories.
- Only about 20 percent of the total news time on each network newscast deals with material that is unique to that newscast as opposed to stories appearing on other network newscasts.

Across the 20 stories that received the greatest amont of coverage during the month of January 1995, the networks provided virtually identical amounts of coverage to all but four stories.

- The network newscasts are "top-heavy," devoting 50 percent of their total news time to the top nine stories of the month.

• There are major differences among newspapers, across a range of factors from size of the national/international newshole to story priorities to top-heaviness.

• The national/international newshole of the *New York Times* is 7.2 times larger than the entire newshole of the network newscasts.

• While there was agreement across the papers as to which set of stories constituted the top four stories of the month, the top story of the month differed for each paper surveyed.

• Network news coverage of several top stories was either comparable to or, in some cases, superior to coverage in the midsize daily papers.

• Demonstrating that the network newscasts can devote significant levels of coverage to serious public policy issues as well as to disasters, in January 1995 *ABC World News Tonight* devoted more words than even the *New York Times* to the coverage of welfare reform.

• While midsize newspapers are able to cover more than twice as many stories as the network newscasts, the depth of most of that additional coverage is very shallow. However, midsize newspapers do provide detailed coverage of about a third more *major* stories than the network newscasts.

• The stories most likely to disappear from network news coverage, given newshole constraints, are continuing international stories.

NOTES

1. Jeff Greenfield, "America Rallies 'Round the TV Set," *TV Guide*, February 16–22, 1991, p. 5.

2. Carl Jensen, *The 10 Best Censored Stories of 1993*, brochure published by Project Censored, Sonoma State University, Rohnert Park, Calif.

3. Maxwell McCombs, Donald L. Shaw, and David Grey, *The Handbook of Reporting Methods* (Boston: Houghton-Mifflin, 1976), pp. 20–21.

4. Roger Rosenblatt, "Journalism and the Larger Truth," *Time*, July 2, 1984, p. 88.

5. William Rivers, *Finding Facts* (Englewood Cliffs, N.J.: Prentice-Hall, 1975), pp. 14–15.

6. K. Tim Wulfemyer, "How and Why Anonymous Attribution Is Used in *Time* and *Newsweek*," *Journalism Quarterly* 62(1) (1985), p. 81.

7. Charles N. Davis, Susan D. Ross, and Paul H. Gates, "Confidential Sources in the Wake of Cohen: A National Survey of Newspaper Editors," research paper presented at the AEJMC National Convention, Washington D.C., August 13, 1995.

8. Kathleen A. Hansen, Jean Ward, Joan L. Conners, and Mark Neuzil, "Local Breaking News: Sources, Technology, and News Routines," *Journalism Quarterly* 71(3) (1994), pp. 566–569.

9. Ibid.

10. Richard Critchfield, "The Village Voice of Richard Critchfield," *Washington Journalism Review* (October 1985), p. 28.

11. S. I. Hayakawa, *Language in Thought and Action*, 4th ed. (New York: Harcourt, Brace, Jovanovich, 1978), pp. 37–38.

12. John Herbers, "Judgmental Reporting," *Nieman Reports* (Winter 1994), p. 3.

13. Ibid.

14. Jim Willis, "Farewell: Emotions Run High at the Murrah Building," *The Edmond Evening Sun*, May 7, 1995, p. A1.

15. Interview with Bill Moyers by Tom Snyder on *The Late, Late Show*, CBS-TV, July 18, 1995.

16. Interview with Bill Kovach by Bill Moyers on PBS' *The Public Mind: Illusions of News*, November 10, 1989.

17. Interview with Michael Deaver by Bill Moyers on PBS' *The Public Mind: Illusions of News*, November 10, 1989.

18. Leo Bogart, *The American Media System and Its Commercial Culture*, Occasional Paper No. 8, The Gannett Foundation Media Center, March 1991.

19. Newton N. Minow, *"How Vast the Wasteland Now?"*, speech at Gannett Foundation Media Center, New York, N.Y., May 9, 1991.

20. Interview with Angus McEachern in Memphis, Tenn., August 7, 1995.

21. John Leo, "Spicing up the (Ho-Hum) Truth," *U.S. News & World Report*, March 8, 1993, p. 24.

22. Ibid.

23. Brian McGrory, "Okla. City Caring Turns to Whining." *Boston Globe* story appearing in *The Commercial Appeal*, July 15, 1995, p. A5.

24. Larry McGill and Andras Szanto et al., *Headlines and Sound Bites: Is That the Way It Is?*, research report by the Freedom Forum Media Studies Center, New York, N.Y., August 1995, pp. 8–9.

3

The Scientist and the Pursuit of Truth

When a scientist sets out to find the truth, he or she pursues a different path and looks for something a little different than does the journalist. The latter is on a daily mission to find truth on deadline and present it in a fashion that will attract the greatest number of readers or viewers. The former is not really looking at all for the particular truths of the journalist or the historian. What the scientist seeks is to systematize knowledge by stating general laws; some may be later revised by newer studies, but the essence of science is that body of general laws rather than the specific truths of the historian or journalist. The researcher cares about the particular only as a building block of a universal principle. As William Rivers points out, the scientist "aims to write sentences that begin with 'Whenever,' 'If ever,' 'Any,' 'No,' and 'All.' Many historians and other scholars have vainly attempted to assert and prove 'laws.' Scientists alone have succeeded. They alone can predict."[1]

Yet it is the relative slowness of research, as well as the different methodology and presentation modes used by scientists, that often frustrates the journalist. Additionally, the different uses made of published medical findings can cause even more misunderstanding between the reporter and the physician or medical researcher. Whether it be a physical scientist, behavioral scientist, medical scientist, or social scientist, the methods used to locate the truth—and how that truth is ultimately defined—make it hard for journalists to mesh their needs with the scientists' needs.

Nevertheless, an understanding of the methods each use can help in facilitating the relationship between the two kinds of professionals.

Some of this understanding has already taken place in the past two decades as graduate journalism schools—and some undergraduate programs as well—have required that their majors take a course or two in research methods or statistics. Additionally, the media's growing interest in surveys and polls have made them aware—to some degree at least—of basic scientific components such as sample size and margin of error. Still, many journalists are still unaware of how the scientist approaches truth. That is the purpose of this chapter.

THE SCIENTIFIC METHOD

Every scientist—whether studying physical or social phenomena—follows the same general guidelines in moving from hypotheses to observations to theory to laws. Those guidelines are found in the scientific method which also reminds scientists that even laws are subject to revision—if not outright refutation—by new research studies. Thus, from the outset, even the basic notion of truth takes on a different cast to a scientist than to a journalist, who may often assume the truth is a more definite and final commodity.

William Rivers notes in his study of fact-finding that natural scientists are not too dismayed when they discover that the "fact" they once respected can no longer be considered valid. In many cases, replacing one fact, or theory, with another is often a cause for rejoicing. New facts and theories that can be trusted depend on a foundation that can be trusted; researchers must work on solid ground instead of quicksand.[2] To be sure, there is always the human element in scientific research, however. No researcher who has built a reputation on developing a usable theory wants to see his or her work depicted as faulty or incomplete by another researcher with a study that disproves his. Still, researchers know that theories only become laws when they are proven over and over again in subsequent studies.

Rivers uses an analysis suggested by Henri Poincare to illustrate the depth and range of the knowledge that a scientist may bring to a problem:

Suppose we have before us any machine; the initial wheel work and the final wheel work alone are visible, but the transmission, the intermediary other, is hidden in the interior and escapes our view; we do not know whether the communication is made by gearing or by belts, by connecting rods or by other contrivances. Do we say that it is impossible for us to understand this machine because we are not permitted to take it to pieces? You know well that we do not, and that the principle of conservation of energy suffices to determine for us the most interesting point. We easily ascertain that the final wheel turns ten times less quickly than the initial wheel, since these two wheels are visible; we are able thence to conclude that a couple applied to the one will be balanced by a couple ten times greater applied to the other. For that there is no need to penetrate the mechanism of this equilibrium and to know how the forces compensate each other in the interior of the machine.[3]

On a much higher level, Rivers notes, this kind of reasoning about hidden mechanisms led to the theory of gravity, the theory of organic evolution, and the theory of relativity.

The scientific method emphasizes the pursuit of knowledge through observation—*systematic* observation. As researcher Frederick Williams points out, "Whatever is said about behavior is reasoned from systematic observation and is tested and retested by observation. In other words, the so-called scientific approach attempts to anchor knowledge in terms of the physical reality it purports to explain."[4]

In using observations as the cornerstone of their methodology, researchers also apply rigorous procedures to guide them in their pursuit of truth. Journalists can find an outline of these procedures in one of their own academic journals: *Journalism and Mass Communications Quarterly*. A typical *J&MC Quarterly* article is divided as follows:

- An introductory statement of the issue and its importance.
- A review of relevant literature which features the results of previous studies conducted in this area.
- A detailed statement of the methodology employed in collecting, observing, and analyzing the data.
- A detailed statement of the results of the study.
- A discussion of the results and conclusions drawn.

Organizing an article in such a rigid fashion is something the more informal journalistic researcher doesn't always appreciate. But to the scientist, this rigor helps insure that the researcher is adhering strictly to the tenets of the scientific method. And to a true researcher, the methodology employed is just as important—if not more so—than the results obtained. For without a flawless methodology, the results become suspect at best.

Validity and Reliability

Two concepts that are extremely important to the scientist are *validity* and *reliability*. Basically, validity of measurement is the extent to which the researcher measures what he or she purports to be measuring. Reliability addresses the issue of whether, using the same measuring instrument, these results would surface again and again in future tests.[5] A reliable test is one which has no internal or external contaminating factors. Breaking these two concepts down, one could use the analogy of a set of bathroom scales. If scales are used to measure your weight instead of some other characteristic such as total fitness, then they are a valid instrument, assuming they are calibrated correctly. You can assume from this validity that they are also a reliable instrument. Validity implies reliability, but reliability does not necessarily imply validity. You could have a reliable set of scales that are calibrated incorrectly and therefore are not valid. If the scales weigh two pounds light, for instance, everyone who gets on them will have a weight showing that is two pounds lighter than they really are. Thus the scales will be consistent, but consistently wrong.

Validity and reliability are important concepts when designing a measuring instrument such as a survey or a field experiment. There are definite rules, for example, in governing the creation of a random sample. If these rules are broken, the sample is not truly random and the measuring instrument is internally flawed or invalid.

Inductive and Deductive Reasoning

To understand the scientific approach to the truth, it is helpful to know something about two other important concepts: inductive and deductive reasoning. Research literature from the social and behavioral sciences is used to emphasize the logic of deductive reasoning, where a hypothesis is stated or implied in the assumptions guiding the project. The resarcher proceeds, then, from the general to the particular. From a set of assumptions, the researcher deduces the hypothesis—for instance, the more aggressive the media content to which persons are exposed, the more likely these individuals are to engage in subsequent aggressive behavior.

This deductive reasoning stands in contrast to inductive reasoning where the researcher moves inferentially from particulars to more general statements. Induction is used continuously, both in problem definition and in interpreting the results. For example, a researcher might observe a case in which a person's tension leads to avoidance of certain communications and, as a result, infer a general relationship between tension and avoidance. Generalizing from measured results is also an inductive process, such as when behavior among a sample of individuals is generalized to a larger population.[6]

In reality, scientists use both induction and deduction, either simultaneously or alternately. One could deduce, for example, that given a set of assumptions about the effects of a certain drug, aggressive behavior might follow its usage. However, consideration of this reasoning might lead to the realization, arrived at inductively, that such a drug might have other consequences as well. The researcher may have observations indicating that a certain drug might produce dependency on it by the patient. Then, generalizing from this observation (an inductive process), the investigator may utilize a new deductive methodology to prove that association.

Basic Steps of the Scientific Method

The scientific method is based upon such concepts as observations, validity, reliability, and inductive and deductive reasoning. Statistics come into play in designing these studies and analyzing the observations that come from them. In general, the steps of the scientific method are as follows:

1. Develop a *research question* that you would like to answer through the process of systematic observation and analysis of data. The research question—or problem statement—is the overall issue you are researching. An example of a research question might be: "To what degree is the drug AZT helpful in slowing the progress of the AIDS virus in a teenage male who has identified the virus at an early stage?"

A few things are important about the research question. First, it must be worthy of the time and cost of investigation. Second, the phenomena composing it must be observable. Third, the observations must be measurable. Fourth, the question must be narrowly focused enough to allow a few variables to be isolated. Fifth, the question must be understandable in operational terms.

To allow the question to be operational, there must be no ambiguities about the terms and concepts that make it up. Therefore, *operational definitions* are established that put any abstract ideas into concrete, observable terms. For instance, in the above research question, the concept of "early stage" must be spelled out. Perhaps it means within the first month of exposure to the virus; perhaps the first three months. In order to test the question, however, the concept must be operationally defined one way or the other.

2. Incorporate in developing the research question a *literature review*. This allows the researcher to see what previous studies have been conducted on the research question or ones similar to it. This review may convince the researcher that a further study is unnecessary, or that one is definitely needed because little has been researched on the issue before. This review could also produce a change in the original research question. Perhaps the literature shows that a more important age grouping for study are those males ages 20–25. The literature review can save a lot of headaches later on by showing the researcher what areas are worthy of further study or whether previous studies are in need of replication.

3. In most cases, various *hypotheses* should be developed from the overall research question. These hypotheses narrow the parts of the study down even more finitely and can yield more data than initially. They also help guide the formation of the research instrument. A survey, for instance, is at its best when the questions asked are ones which address the hypotheses.

Often, hypotheses are asked in a kind of "if-then" format. For example, one hypothesis related to the earlier research question might be the following:

If a teenage male in an inner-city home setting begins taking AZT within the first month of his active AIDS virus, then he will see a weaker restraint on the progress of the virus than if a teenage male in a rural setting follows the same protocol for his AIDS virus during that same time frame.

This hypothesis allows the researcher to isolate just one variable—the patient's home setting—and see if it relates to the effectiveness of the drug AZT.

Research studies often are composed of several hypotheses to measure the possible associations of several distinct variables. And, as in the case of the overall research question, terms and concepts must be defined operationally so everyone concerned knows what they mean and how to analyze them.

4. Select and design the most appropriate research *methodology*. Medical research makes great use of controlled experiments, while social scientists seem to rely more on attitudinal surveys, content analysis, and possibly participant observation. While it might seem to some that this step should come higher in the list, it is necessary that it come after the development of the research question, hypotheses, and operational definitions since they all influence the structure of the measuring instrument.

Controlled or laboratory experiments are some of the toughest measuring instruments to devise. Researcher Hugh M. Culbertson puts it this way:

Experimentalists lead troubled lives. Their training stresses rigor but shows it to be an elusive, many-sided goal. They wind up feeling like the fabled Dutch boy who tries to protect his community from a flood. When he sticks a finger in one hole of the dike, the water threatens to break through elsewhere.[7]

As Culbertson notes, there are at least four such holes:

• Clarifying causal direction.
• Control feasibility.
• Generalizability of the data.
• Precision.

The first "hole" to be filled is to answer the question, "What variable is causing which result?" Communication researcher Bruce H. Westley says that is a hard question to answer, however, so he prefers this approach: Rather than seeking causes, search for necessary and sufficient conditions. If B can occur only in the presence of A, then A is a necessary condition of B. If B occurs whenever A is present, then A is both a necessary and a sufficient condition of B.

At the very least, he says, it is necessary to show (1) concomitant variation and (2) precedence to demonstrate causality. Concomitant variation means that B varies consistently with A. This is what correlation demonstrates. But in showing concomitant variation, Westley notes we are only showing that two variables vary together. We need something more to tell whether a change in A precedes a change in B. So when A and B vary together, and A precedes B in time, we have a basis for saying that A is causally related to B.[8]

The second problem a controlled experiment must address is control. This concept insures that differences in a dependent variable that the researcher attributes to an independent variable are not due to extraneous factors and so remain when these factors are held constant.

The problem of precision is also a thorny one. Precision in design of the experiment reduces the error term or denominator of a statistic. This means cutting down on sources of variation among scores other than experimental manipulations.

The last problem is generalization. This determines the class of persons, situations, and tasks for which an observed relationship appears to be valid. There are really two sides to this problem: defining that class clearly and making it as large as possible.[9]

When designed and implemented properly, the controlled experiment may be the most powerful method of seeking answers to research questions. In fact, the controlled experiment may be the only valid means of answering the question of what causes what.

But the controlled experiment also can take a great amount of time to complete. This is especially the case with longitudinal studies, where variables are measured on the same sample at a minimum of two points in time. These studies are not only very expensive, but also very time-consuming.

Most significant experiments in medical research take time, and answers reveal themselves only in bits and pieces as the experiment moves along from variable to variable.

5. Identify an appropriate, representative *sample* to measure. Whether the sample be composed of humans or animals—in the case of much medical research—extreme care must be taken to develop a sample from which the researcher can generalize to a larger population. Surveys and polls, for instance, usually make use of random samples because these are representative of their populations. Because of this, researchers can make generalizations from them to the larger population. But there are strict rules for constructing a random sample and, if they are not followed, the sample becomes ineffective for making generalizations.

Some surveys, such as quota surveys, are not designed as random samples, because researchers are just interested in obtaining a snapshot of what this particular sample believes about an issue. No attempt is made at generalizing the results to a larger population. The news media's popular "man-on-the-street" survey is a kind of quota sample. The editor tells the reporter to go out and interview six middle-aged men and six middle-aged women about their views, and the reporter might take the first dozen people he or she meets that fit these quotas. But this is definitely not a random sample as formal research methodology knows that concept to be.

6. Conduct a *pre-test* on the sample. This is a safeguard step that helps rid the measuring instrument, such as a survey questionnaire, of any internal flaws. For example, perhaps a researcher asks people to respond to a numerical scale of 1 to 10, but neglects to say which end equates with translated concepts like "very strong" or "very weak." Some respondents might just guess that 1 equates with "very weak," when in fact the researcher meant that end of the scale to mean "very strong." Therefore, the answers from those respondents would be unusable. A pre-test screens for this sort of internal contamination before the real test is done.

A pre-test can also check for some external flaws like the performance of the interviewers in a telephone survey. Perhaps the test will show the need for greater uniformity among the interviewers in the way they ask their questions so as to not skew the responses. External contaminating factors are as important as internal flaws in trusting the final results of the test.

7. Conduct the *test*. Whether it be a laboratory experiment, field experiment, content analysis, or survey, this is the portion of the scientific method which usually takes the most time and money. Some medical experiments take years to complete and can cost millions of dollars. Gathering usable data is the goal of this test. If the proper preparations have been made up to this point, however, the test should run smoothly.

8. *Analyze the data*. With the powerful computers and software programs available now to analyze research data, this portion of the research project runs much faster than in years past. Statistical analysis packages are available today that can perform many intricate jobs and yield mountains of interesting data on the observations made in the test. Many of these packages are also available for personal computers with large RAM capabilities.

It is important to remember that applying the right statistical tests to the data is just as vital as setting up the right experiment to observe the data in the first place. Further, correct interpretation of the data is necessary if a true picture of the results and consequences is to emerge. Journalists must be on guard for any possible "spin" that a vested-interest group might put on such data, so it is helpful for reporters to know enough about statistical analysis techniques to keep from being manipulated.

A large portion of the analysis involves testing the research hypotheses that were originally proposed to see if they can be confirmed or rejected. What researchers actually test for, however, is the *null hypothesis*. The *research hypothesis* predicts a difference will be found between, say, subjects in a control group and those in an experimental group. The null hypothesis, on the other hand, takes that statement and displays it negatively. While the research hypothesis predicts a difference, the null hypothesis makes a statement of no difference. Thus, when the analysis of test data shows there is a statically significant difference, we "reject the null hypothesis," and thus find positive evidence for our prediction.

Researchers must select a *significance level* as a criterion for rejecting the null hypothesis. In other words, if the probability calculated for the null hypothesis is at this level or lower, then we will reject the null hypothesis and accept the research hypothesis. Often a significance level of .05 is taken as a usable level for rejecting the null hypothesis. This level means at least a 95 percent chance of a statistical difference exists between observable phenomena. But there is nothing sacred about this probability level. Sometimes tests will require a lower probability level of, say, .03, in which case the results will be even more believable.

The so-called *margin of error* is derived from this significance level. If you can visualize what is called the *normal distribution curve*, peaked in the center and going downslope on either side symmetrically, then you have the normal range of probable occurrences for observable phenomena. Under this curve is, in effect, 100 percent of the probable occurrences. With a probability level of .05, you are saying that generalizable results will fall within the middle 95 percent portion of this curve. There is an outside chance, however, that your prediction is wrong and that results would be different in the two tails of the curve, each comprising .025 percent of the 100 percent. These are the unknown areas of probability in a test with a .05 significance level, so your predictable results could be off plus or minus .025. In the case of a two-candidate political race, for instance, you could run a poll that has a plus or minus .025 margin of error. That means poll results showing Candidate A holding 48 percent of the vote to Candidate B's 52 percent would be too close to call. Why? Because there is only a 4 percent spread between the results, and your margins of error on either end of the test could total as much as 5 percent.

The same use of margin of error and significance levels is made by medical researchers as they look for the probabilities that certain drugs or medical procedures might aid in the fight against certain diseases.

9. Draw *conclusions*. In this step of the project the researchers interpret the results of what they have just discovered and state their beliefs about the significance of the findings. It is tempting for journalists to rush to this section of the research report and rely totally on it for their story. However, remembering that the conclusions are only as sound as the design of the study and data analysis, the reporter should pay as much attention to the earlier steps in the process.

10. Write the formal *research report*. This is the culmination of the research project, and it is one which cannot be done too hastily. When medical reports go into print, for instance, they become fair game for journalists who may base a lead story on the network news on them. Journalists should also realize that medical research reports are not written for the

casual reader but for other health professionals. Thus, the writing is often somewhat stilted, technical, and jargon-laden. The journalist who understands the vocabulary of medicine will be able to read through all this faster than one who does not.

Medical researchers will also tell you that they are slower to attach finality to journal articles than journalists are. To a researcher, a published article is not necessarily the final word on the subject, but instead offers a tentative conclusion that may or may not be upheld with later research. Thus, where a journalist might see a cure in reading a researcher's conclusions, a physician might see a possible cure or a cure that relates to only a small segment of the affected disease's population.

THE SCIENTIST AND THE JOURNALIST

In his book *Public Affairs Reporting*, George M. Killenberg discusses the conflict that often arises between doctors and journalists. Pointing to the AIDS story, he notes there are several "danger zones" in medical reporting.[10] Among them are:

- the urgency of research in certain areas of medicine;
- the pressure on scientists to secure grants and win acclaim;
- the tendency of journalists to look for "breakthroughs" and "cures."

First, Killenberg explains, reporters must first get the facts right. It is also vital for them to resist the urge—as well as the efforts of others—to exaggerate the importance of medical developments. He concludes, "In all areas of scientific reporting, reporters must proceed with caution and restraint."[11]

As noted earlier, there are a number of scientific and medical journals which carry articles concerning studies done by researchers. Although the public is most familiar with the *New England Journal of Medicine* and the *Journal of the American Medical Association*, there are many others as well. All articles appearing in medical journals are referred or pre-screened by experts who check out the soundness of the studies and conclusions drawn from them. Still, reporters should realize that some articles are more heavily documented than others and some conclusions are built upon studies that have fewer possibilities for error. Knowing some basics about the scientific method, as discussed earlier, will help journalists guide their way through the maze of published medical studies and find the ones which are the soundest and most significant.

Another potential source of conflict between the scientist and the journalist is how the individual case or individual observation is perceived. To a medical researcher, a case is a single unit of observation to be assimilated into myriad other cases, from which some statistical trend may arise. It is that statistically significant trend that is important to the researcher and which he or she writes about. To the journalist, on the other hand, statistics need to be fleshed out in human terms. The readers or viewers, it is felt, will fall asleep if they are presented statistical information. What they want is to know how the problem plays out in individual people. Therefore, most medical stories that appear in newspapers or on television begin, at least, with an individual focus. This single anecdote is developed, detailed, and amplified throughout several paragraphs before the story swings into the phase that discusses the overall trend. Some stories, in fact, make short shrift of the statistical picture and choose instead to stay glued to the individual case being reported on.

This use of *anecdotal evidence* is something most researchers find inappropriate; after all, a single case is just that. You cannot generalize from it with any degree of specificity. To the journalist, however, the focus often is the single case. The conclusion, either direct or indirect, is that this person's plight is typical of many other individuals with the same problem. A classic example is found in the Appendix of this book—the Pulitzer Prize-winning story "AIDS in the Heartland." The story is anecdotal from start to finish, focusing on a male farming couple in Minnesota and the problems they faced with AIDS.

Journalists throughout history have been fond of using anecdotal evidence—the human interest story—to turn the spotlight on societal problems which need solving. These stories are much more moving than the statistical treatises that the medical journals turn out, although the evidence they present for their conclusions is anecdotal and may not be truly representative of the wider population afflicted with a disease. Nevertheless, because these media stories grab the attention of readers and viewers, they also grab the attention of politicians who will often gear legislation to these popularized stories instead of to the more obtuse research articles. Sometimes this is good; sometimes—when the anecdotal evidence is flimsy and totally unrepresentative—it is bad. In either case, however, the research and presentation used by scientists and journalists often differs radically and causes friction between the two camps.

The discussion in the next chapter of how the news media report medical stories will lend more insight into this conflict between the professions of journalism and medicine.

NOTES

1. William Rivers, *Finding Facts* (Englewood Cliffs, N.J.: Prentice-Hall, 1975), p. 9.
2. Ibid.
3. Ibid., p. 10.

4. Frederick Williams, *Reasoning with Statistics* (New York: Holt, Rinehart and Winston, 1968), p. 3.

5. Ibid.

6. Ibid., pp. 22–23.

7. Hugh M. Culbertson, "Statistical Designs for Experimental Research," in *Research Methods in Mass Communication*, ed. Bruce H. Westley and Guido H. Stempel III (Englewood Cliffs, N.J.: Prentice-Hall, 1981), p. 217.

8. Bruce H. Westley, "The Controlled Experiment," in *Research Methods in Mass Communication*, ed. Bruce H. Westley and Guido H. Stempel III (Englewood Cliffs, N.J.: Prentice-Hall, 1981), p. 202.

9. Culbertson, "Statistical Designs for Experimental Research," p. 218.

10. George M. Killenberg, *Public Affairs Reporting* (New York: St. Martin's Press, 1992), p. 268.

11. Ibid.

4

Covering Medical News

Medical news has realized enormous popularity in recent years, partly because the population has been aging, and the baby-boomer generation is well into middle-age with all the health concerns that come with it. Health news is popular for other reasons as well, including:

- A growing emphasis on preventive measures and treatments. Indeed, the leading health magazine in circulation is *Prevention* magazine.
- A strong interest by parents in their children's health and safety.
- The public's addiction to news about new diets and exercise measures designed to reduce body weight and fat.
- Newly identified and extremely threatening viruses such as HIV.
- Innovative high-tech procedures that enhance a young couple's chance of becoming pregnant when traditional procedures fail.
- The increased lifespan of senior citizens brought about by new diagnostic measures and treatments like angioplasties, which have reduced the number of deaths due to heart failure.
- The interest in new medical technologies that makes the subject of medicine more fascinating than ever before.
- The escalating costs of health care services and the government's attempts at controlling those costs.
- The difficulty many Americans have gaining equal access to physicians and hospitals.

For these and many other reasons, medical news is a big seller today for both the print and electronic news media. This chapter will explore some of the trends in covering medical news and some of the challenges involved in it for the journalist.

MEDICAL REPORTING BY THE EXPERTS

Large dailies and many television stations will have one person assigned full-time to the medical beat. One such reporter, Rita Rubin of the *Dallas Morning News* has said she enjoys her job because she believes it helps readers make decisions regarding what to do about their medical problems. "The medical beat is the most personal beat," she says. "It hits closest to home for the readers. Everyone is concerned about their health. It can be extremely satisfying. People have thanked me for helping them."[1]

To Walt Bogdanich of the *Wall Street Journal*, medical news often requires investigative reporting techniques to reach the story behind the story. Bogdanich won a Pulitzer Prize in 1988 for a series he wrote on faulty medical laboratory tests around the country—a story which required more than simply interviewing those in charge. When he began the series, many other reporters were doing superficial stories on how lab tests often yielded inaccurate results. Bogdanich started his probe into questionable lab testing procedures after he had received a wrong finding on his own cholesterol-level test. This faulty result got him thinking about stories he had heard from friends over the years about their own faulty tests. From this experience, Bogdanich said he learned that reporters can often get their most telling information from everyday people affected by medical procedures rather than from the doctors and hospitals administering those tests and treatments.[2]

THE "BREAKTHROUGH"

The concept of a medical "breakthrough" is a troubling one for both reporters and physicians alike. The reason is that this term is used too often to describe a treatment that may, at best, offer limited results. An example was the rush by journalists to report as fact a finding that aspirin can reduce the risk of heart attack by 50 percent if taken every other day. The interesting thing about this story is that it was the *New England Journal of Medicine* that reported the finding as a "breakthrough," not some lay publication. However, two days after that publication in the *New England Journal*, the *British Medical Journal* reported that aspirin "could not, in fact, prevent initial heart attacks; other studies showed that aspirin might, indeed, increase the chances of stroke in some cases."[3]

But the British article was not reported on by many media outlets—subsequent articles and findings often do not receive the same coverage as the initial findings—so many people were unaware of the controversial nature of the aspirin "cure." Additionally, the Food and Drug Administration (FDA) and the Federal Trade Commission asked makers of aspirin to stop advertising aspirin as a possible prevention measure for heart attacks.

REPORTING STAFFS GROW

Because of the popularity of medical news, many newsrooms have increased the size of their medical reporting staffs in recent years. Stephen G. Bloom has reported, for example, that coverage has increased enormously. Over three time periods totaling thirteen months, from September 1993 to November 1994, the *Columbia Journalism Review* and the Kaiser Family Foundation found that there were 3,118 stories on health care reform in five national newspapers—the *Los Angeles Times*, the *New York Times*, the *Wall Street Journal*, the *Washington Post*, and *USA Today*.[4] When the reader considers that such massive coverage did not include articles that concerned medical and health topics other than reform, the amount of newspaper space devoted today to these issues is truly staggering, Bloom says.

A July 1993 Gallup Poll found that when 1,017 respondents were asked whether the media currently gave enough attention to health and medical issues, those composing the largest single category (35 percent) said they would like to see "a lot more." Only 6 percent said a "little less," or "a lot less."[5] The ranks of medical and health care reporters swelled in the mid-1980s. Today, a study of the American Medical Writers Association (AMWA), the leading professional organization for communicators in biomedical and health science, shows only about a third of the members are medical writers, with the rest working in other health communication areas like public relations or health care marketing. Nevertheless, the AMWA reported 1,318 members in 1973 and 4,000 by 1996.[6]

Studying the medical coverage of just one newspaper—the *New York Times*—Bloom notes the huge interest in medical news today. The *Times* has probably the most extensive coverage of medical news of any newspaper in America today. At least six full-time reporters are assigned specifically to the medical and health care beat, and that beat is spread throughout the science, business, and metro departments. The Washington Bureau also gets involved, especially when the government dips into health care reform issues. Starting a national trend, the *Times* added a weekly medical/science section, funded in part by advertisements from physicians, specialty clinics, and hospitals actively seeking patients.[7] "Just about every reporter here sooner or later writes about health-care," said Erik Eckhom, former special projects editor for the *Times*. "We're not just covering the big events; we are doing enterprising, analytical stories explaining why things are happening."[8]

As noted elsewhere in this book, the public's voracious appetite for medical news often dictates that stories be rushed into print or on the air faster than they should be. A 1994 editorial in the *New England Journal of Medicine* noted the following about this phenomenon:

Doctors know that clinical research rarely advances in one giant leap; instead it progresses incrementally. For this reason, the practice of medicine, as well as clinical research, is inherently conservative. But because of the public's keen interest in new medical findings, the media may be less conservative. They are serving a public that believes passionately that the more we can learn about what to eat, or how to live, the longer we will live. And neither the public nor the media are inclined to wait for confirmatory studies. Often the media reports are exaggerated or oversimplified. Even when a report itself is circumspect, headline writers may sensationalize the story.[9]

Larry Thompson, a former *Washington Post* medical reporter and author of *Correcting the Code: Inventing the Genetic Cure for the Human Body*, said certain professional behavior patterns influence what journalists write. He noted that science writers tend to accept the values of the established scientific institutions like the National Academy of Science and the National Institutes of Health. As a result, their stories tend to reflect the norms and interests of the scientific community. The process, he said, determines who is scientifically legitimate and who gets covered, and left out.[10]

Sometimes medical stories are done because of the prominence of the people involved. In fact, often health problems and/or unique medical procedures are spotlighted first because of the status of the patient, then become routine stories in and of themselves. Consider, for example, the evolution of medical news shown by the following incidents:

- NASA's space program of the 1960s brought hundreds of new science writers online at the nations' newspapers. After the moon landing in 1969, however, interest in the space program began to wane, and many of these science reporters turned to medical writing instead, opening new doors in that field.
- Another impetus for medical reporting in the 1960s grew out of the assassinations of President John F. Kennedy, Attorney General Robert Kennedy, and civil rights leader Martin Luther King. The news media did many stories on the paths these bullets took, the damage they caused, and the attempts to revive the stricken leaders.
- In 1964, Surgeon General Luther B. Terry's report on the links between smoking and cancer drew the media's attention to this issue, which has become one of the top health stories in America.
- In 1965, President Lyndon Johnson had gall bladder surgery and showed his surgical scar to the television cameras. Medical news was yanked into the nation's living rooms, and television helped bring health problems into focus.
- Also in 1965, the nation's Medicare program came into existence, and stories began focusing more on government-subsidized medicine for the elderly.

- The growing interest in environmental hazards in the 1970s opened the gate to news connecting ecological and medical concerns.

- Sen. Thomas Eagleton, a vice presidential candidate in 1972, saw his dreams of that office vanish when the press unveiled the news he had received psychiatric care. The jury is still out as to how that kind of news affects a political candidate's chances.

- First Lady Betty Ford disclosed in 1974 that she had breast cancer, a subject that had previously been off-limits for public figures.

- In 1976 the publication *Medical News* invited presidential candidates to submit the results of their physical exams. Sen. Hubert Humphrey, who had cancer, declined. The other candidates complied. This opened the door to the practice of having presidential candidates disclose their medical conditions.

- In 1978 President Carter revealed that he had hemorrhoids.

- President Reagan underwent treatments for skin and colon cancer while he was in the White House.

- In 1991, Sen. Bob Dole developed prostate cancer. Dole's personal medical revelations show how common medical news had become when, in years past, politicians might be reluctant to speak about their health problems. For instance, in 1919, President Woodrow Wilson suffered a stroke, and the White House went to great trouble to keep that news hidden from the public.

- The infamous 1993 Bobbitt case, where a wife cut off her husband's penis, made the use of that word commonplace in the media. Some even went so far as to talk about "Bobbitt Fever." Prior to that time, many media were reluctant to refer to the word penis. A decade earlier, for example, the *Dallas Morning News* carried an in-depth story on circumcision but refrained from using the word until deep into the jumped portion of the story.

- On May 25, 1983, the *New York Times* ran its first front-page story on AIDS, changing the landscape in reporting on that illness. It wasn't until actor Rock Hudson died of AIDS in 1985, however, that it became a commonplace story.

- Medical breakthroughs such as the Jarvik Heart, transplanted successfully in the 1980s, propelled such advances to the front page of the nation's newspapers.

- The trials of Dr. Jack Kevorkian, known by many media as "Dr. Death," brought the issue of physician-assisted suicide into the nation's living rooms.

- The rise of HMOs, PPOs, and managed health care in the 1980s and 1990s has spurred great interest in the coverage of economic aspects of medical treatments and access to hospitals and doctors. Additionally, the proposed legislative reform packages of the Clinton Administration, as well as passage of the Kennedy-Kassenbaum health reform bill, have added great interest to the political reporting of medicine and health care.

In sum, the news media—especially newspapers—have begun treating diseases much more openly. The *St. Paul Pioneer Press Dispatch* story, "AIDS in the Heartland," is a classic case in point. Found in the Appendix, this story won a Pulitzer Prize in 1987 for chronicling the life of a gay farm couple's coping with AIDS. Now newspapers regularly discuss causes of death in obituaries and have brought formerly hushed diseases out of the closet and helped remove the stigmas associated with them. Compelling news is now health-related news about the changes in the quality of life for people struggling with various medical problems. Prevention is also a big story these days and fits in with the media's newfound concept of "news you can use," as people look for ways of living longer, healthier lives.

In the nation's newsrooms, the reality has struck that one-eighth of the country's gross national product goes to health care, so it is big news to the financial and business desks. Nevertheless, only a half-dozen of the country's journalism schools taught medical reporting by the early 1990s.

Bloom is one medical writer who believes that many reporters are too conservative in reporting on medical news. This is a concern that seems to run counter to the worry felt by others that medical reporters sensationalize news about medical breakthroughs. Bloom feels medical writers should get away from reporting so much on established, institutional medicine that has gone through the proper channels and has been written up in the *New England Journal of Medicine* or the *Journal of the American Medical Association* (JAMA). Instead, he feels reporters need to look to doctors who are trying new procedures and spotlight them.[11]

Other reporters like Rebecca Raspberry of the *Jonesboro* (Arkansas) *Sun* believe reporters should proceed more cautiously and moderately in writing about medical news.[12] Reporters, she says, should understand that doctors operate under at least two ethical principles that can be violated in granting journalistic interviews: (1) physicians should not solicit patients; and (2) physicians should not disclose confidences of their patients.

These principles, Raspberry notes, prevent some doctors from being as open and candid as some reporters would like them to be. Additionally, she feels reporters should understand that medical science moves at a snail's pace. Reporters, therefore, must use moderation and discrimination in what they report and write about. Doctors, for instance, think medical reporters make too much of treatments that the average citizen has no access to, and that they also make too much of medical failures.

Television medical reporter Doug Johnson believes in breaking down medical issues into news viewers can use. He says the reporter should answer the questions people don't get a chance to ask when they are at their doctor's office. He also feels medical reporters should cover health trends in major diseases such as cancer and heart disease, tracking who is most at risk, how the problems could be prevented, and where the treatments are headed.[13]

Sherry Jacobson, reporter for the *Dallas Morning News*, worries that news about health care reform is stale in the minds of too many editors who are tired of the issue after the intensity paid it during the first Clinton term. She feels the story of health care reform is now largely a business story and not as consumer-oriented as it once was. "Our stories are now people complaining about the system of managed care: doctors don't like it, patients don't like it, that sort of thing. I'm concerned that we're really forgetting about the problems of the uninsured," she said.[14]

In reporting on the economic aspect of health care reform, economist Dr. Cyril Chang of the University of Memphis has the following advice:[15]

- Reporters should watch out for economists who commit the sin of mixing personal opinion with facts. Economists are scientists, but they are also human, and often reveal their own personal value judgments in with the objective data they've developed.

- Since most economists are trained to conduct scientific research, they are most at ease with questions such as what was, what is, or what will be. They are not as comfortable with judgment questions such as, "What is the best course of action?"

- Economists are horrible communicators. They talk in gobbledygook, and that jargon must be understood by the reporter and then translated to the reader or viewer.

Reporters can also learn from professionals on the other side of the media fence: public relations practitioners. For example, Michael Calhoun, director of corporate communications at Baptist Health Systems in Memphis, sets forth the following observations for use by reporters:[16]

- Reporters and hospital PR people live and work in different cultures and, as a result, operate on different timetables and different missions.

- To a reporter, the basic unit of work is the story, not a book. The pressure is on for brevity. Additionally, most stories are driven by anecdotes.

- In a hospital, however, very little happens in isolation. Anecdotes are connected to other, larger issues that probably caused that anecdote to occur in the first place. "We want the opportunity to explain the anecdote's relationship to other factors," Calhoun says. "If we let you stop at the anecdotal level, we will not get the educational benefit of having our story told in the way we'd like it told. In health care, nothing happens in isolation."

Illustrating this point, Calhoun notes that there are two main divisions, often opposing ones, in any hospital: the business side and the clinical side. Under these two main divisions are four issues which are always present and related to each other. They are cost, access, quality, and choice. "You cannot write about one without discussing the others," Calhoun says. "They're always there, and are underlying every single story. Anytime an issue impacts one, there will be repercussions in the other three."

Calhoun would say, for example, that if a reporter plans to do a story about an emergency room patient who was denied care or had to wait for

that care, he or she must also look at the other issues impacting that incident such as cost, quality, and choice. Perhaps the patient could not pay
for the attention he wanted; perhaps he received a quality of service more
in line with what he could afford; perhaps he showed up at a private hospital not designed to treat indigent persons. Any or all of these factors could
come to bear and should be written about as well as the actual patient
complaint.

One of the basic criteria of news that sometimes requires the reporter to
go easy on the mitigating circumstances is the requirement of conflict. Most
news stories are built upon some kind of overt or covert conflict ranging
from an outright physician conflict, to an emotional conflict, to a conflict
of ideas or ideals. A news story is at its strongest when that conflict is
polarized at its widest. A hospital, which should be known for its caring,
makes an indigent patient wait for hours for treatment. Readers and viewers are outraged that a hospital could be so cold and heartless. But if the
reporter brings in the mitigating details and tells the hospital's side in too
great of detail, that polarization is compromised; there is a reason for the
hospital's behavior and it is understandable. Now in most cases, the story
is not front-page any more. Reporters are well aware of this unscripted
newsroom scenario, and as a result they love stories with great conflict.

Writers Henry Schulte and Marcel Dufresne note it is no coincidence
that many of the important medical stories reported in the nation's newspapers and television newscasts appear on Thursdays. That's the day the
New England Journal of Medicine reaches its subscribers. Informed observers of medical matters have come to expect interesting, important, and
sometimes offbeat medical stories in their local newspaper each Thursday,
thanks to the *Journal*. The wire services like the Associated Press generally
stay abreast of the leading medical journals, and a myriad of local newspapers pluck these stories off the wires and use them, sometimes localizing
them for their communities.[17]

Schulte and Dufresne note that much media coverage focuses on research
that holds the promise of helping people improve their lives. While many
stories require a direct, serious tone, writers sometimes take a lighter approach when the subject warrants, such as the following story shows:

Science has found an explanation for one of the obvious effects of drinking too
much: the beer belly.

Swiss researchers report that when people drink alcohol, their bodies burn up fat
much more slowly than usual. And any fat that is not burned is stored in the
paunch, the thighs, or other places where people put on weight.

The study was based on an experiment in which people were put on a diet that
included about 3 ounces of pure alcohol a day, the equivalent of about six shots
of whiskey, or six beers. That much alcohol reduced their bodies' burning of fat
by about one-third.[18]

In telling the story this way, the reporter called upon a good technique: explaining scientific theories or procedures with familiar examples. For instance, comparing three ounces of alcohol to six glasses of beer gave readers a simple and concrete image they could use to evaluate the study's relevance to their own drinking habits.[19]

Every so often, medical researchers take their findings directly to the public by issuing news releases or scheduling press conferences before the study is published in research journals, creating a certain degree of controversy in research circles because they bypass the normal peer review process. Sometimes, in fact, the American Medical Association (AMA) uses news releases to focus attention on specific health problems. For example, in September 1996, the AMA published results of a major survey it did on media violence. The survey showed 75 percent of parents disgusted with media violence, gave a long list of facts concerning media violence, and presented a set of guidelines to help doctors and parents reduce exposure to media violence.

Reporters should exercise care in covering news conferences to announce research findings. Several years ago, a professor of journalism from New York University conducted an experiment to see how gullible journalists might be in covering such events. Promoting himself as a medical researcher, he sent out a press release informing the media of his press conference and stating he had discovered a cure for infertility among women. At the press conference, which was attended by the wire services and several other reporters, the professor made some outlandish claims regarding his "medical breakthrough," none of which were true. Nevertheless, several news outlets across the nation published the story as if it were true. Later the professor announced that it had, in fact, just been an experiment. He chided the journalists present who wrote the story and urged others to exercise more caution in the future.

Alternative medicine is a story that is getting more play in the 1990s. One of the best-known examples of a big alternative medicine story was carried in the 1980s when actor Steve McQueen, suffering from cancer, eschewed traditional medical treatments and went instead to Mexico to receive Laetril treatment for awhile. Many people have grown frustrated with the limited abilities of mainstream medicine to ease their pains and stop the progress of diseases, some of which may be fatal. Some of the forms of alternative medical help sought are acupuncture, herbal medications, biofeedback, spinal manipulation, colonic irrigation, meditation, homeopathy, neuropathy, hypnotherapy, music therapy, folk medicine, guided imagery, and Shiatsu massage, to name a few. Writer John Langone has reported about these new therapies:

In addition to thousands of lay practitioners, an estimated 3,000 American physicians have begun to incorporate acupuncture into their practices, and hundreds more are taking courses in its use. In Europe, the trend is overwhelming: out of 88,000 practicing acupuncturists, 62,000 are medical doctors. . . . A third of adult Americans . . . spend an estimated $13.7 billion a year out of their own pockets on a bewildering array of breakaway treatments.[20]

Obviously, alternative medicine is looked upon with deep suspicion by the established medical institutions like the AMA, which characterize many of the therapies as pseudo science and placebos. Some studies published in the *British Medical Journal*, however, indicate that homeopathic remedies are actually more effective than placebos, and a number of reports document their efficacy in treating hay fever, respiratory infections, digestive diseases, migraine, and a form of rheumatic disease.[21]

As in the case of all medical reporting, reporters should exercise caution in writing about alternative therapies, searching for the documentation that shows the effectiveness of these treatments.

With greater frequency, newspapers and magazines are taking longer, more in-depth looks at the status of various medical diagnostic measures and treatments. A special *Dallas Morning News* series, "Understanding Mental Illness," published in April 1996, is a prime example of this kind of detailed reporting. The series dissects the challenges of mental illness. A portion of it is found in the Appendix.

Another example is a series done in July 1996 by New York's *Daily News* called "Medical Menace." It is an investigative series that discovered scores of untrained, unlicensed charlatans posing as doctors in New York's Chinese community, preying on immigrants and leaving some patients disfigured and near death. A passage from the series reads:

A thriving subculture of medical charlatans is preying on New York's Chinese immigrant community and inflicting serious harm on a growing number of victims.

Posing as doctors and pharmacists, these hucksters have deprived patients of the use of their limbs and sight and plunged one into a coma. They have caused brain damage, disfigurement and paralysis. They have subjected women to botched, nearly fatal abortions.

They perform amateur surgery, administer prescription drugs and give injections of unknown substances. They sell their patients toxic potions banned by the U.S. Food and Drug Administration.[22]

The *Charlotte Observer* published another investigative series, also in 1996, concerning the slow response time of ambulances in Mecklenburg County which left some victims dying while they waited for the ambulances. Among the problems which the series brought to light were:[23]

- Roughly one of every eight patients in the Charlotte region waited more than 15 minutes for an ambulance. Scores of those patients have died.
- The Mecklenburg and Gaston County EMS squads took longer than 10 minutes,

on average, responding to cardiac arrest calls. After about 10 to 12 minutes without a heartbeat, a patient is all but certain to die.

- Mecklenburg County dispatchers sent ambulances to 20,000 people who didn't need to go to the hospital, diverting paramedics who would otherwise be available for real emergencies.

As a result of this series, editor Jennie Buckner said county commissioners made the biggest improvements to the ambulance system in its seventeen-year history and agreed to purchase thirteen new emergency vehicles and hire 76 new paramedics. They also turned over the county's emergency medical service to Charlotte's two hospital groups to speed service.[24]

In 1988, the *Indianapolis Star* won a Pulitzer Prize for a series which it spent a year researching detailing examples of medical malpractice in the state. That followed by a year the series on the gay farm couple confronting the reality of AIDS that won a Pulitzer Prize for the *St. Paul Pioneer Press*. Obviously, medical reporting is seen as extremely important subject matter by some of the toughest media judges in the world.

Not to be outdone are the magazines. A solid example of in-depth magazine reporting on medicine was a special issue of *Time* in September 1996 on "The Frontiers of Medicine." The lead article in that issue was written by Sherwin B. Nuland, who is a physician as well as a writer. Nuland is a clinical professor of surgery at Yale University School of Medicine. He wrote the best-selling book, *How We Die*, and followed it up with *The Wisdom of the Body*. His article in *Time* was called, "An Epidemic of Discovery," and discussed the extraordinary wave of medical advances that raise new expectations, but also problems and costs.

Other articles featured in that 90-page special issue focused on cancer, genetics, stroke, fertility, alternative therapies, mental disorders, technology, plagues, AIDS, managed care, transplants, and aging.

Investigative reporting of medicine is not easy to do. To begin with, reporters are up against a subject and language that is foreign to most of them, putting them at an immediate disadvantage in trying to uncover whatever a doctor or hospital or HMO is trying to keep covert. Also, many reporters are intimidated by physicians who might take a superior attitude at times toward journalists. Reporter Robert L. Peirce, for instance, has observed:

The first time I tried to investigate a doctor, he asked disdainfully whether I was aware that the liver has five systems. Health care specialists are not easy subjects to interview. Hospital administrators sometimes claim that their private businesses are as legally sheltered from prying reporters as are General Motors' auto design plans for the (future). At a medical center, many researchers have no use for television and newspapers; they all seem to have favorite stories about some ignorant reporter who nearly ruined their lives with a misquote or oversimplification. The recognition important to their careers normally comes from publishing in their own professional journals; not in newspapers. . . . But despite discouragement, the medical community is not impenetrable; the hunting is good and the stories important.[25]

Peirce offers these pointers for reporters wanting to investigate some aspect of medicine or the medical community:[26]

- Since the government pays about 40 percent of the costs of health care in the United States, many medical records are now open to the public. That is good news for the journalist.
- Using these records, a reporter can examine a hospital's finances, study the fees charged by doctors in a community and track their increases, and get clues to which hospitals are underutilized and which are devouring money for unnecessary new wings or equipment.
- Information is becoming available for the first time in some parts of the country on death rates and medical complications in hospitals.
- The plaintiff-index file at the civil court building could lead a reporter to malpractice suits, providing a fascinating journey into the dark and bloody corners of area hospitals.
- A reporter can check to see if area schools are adequately protected against the onslaught of some disease by studying the percentage of students who are properly immunized.
- State inspection records of nursing homes and state institutions might reveal fire hazards in hospitals that remain uncorrected year after year.
- The nurse on the ward or the health inspector in the field can both provide tips regarding problem conditions.
- Never underestimate the pull of human nature. Within the breast of the great healer could beat a heart scarred with such common human emotions as jealousy and ambition.
- A reporter should not be intimidated by the reputation, education, or ego of the physicians with whom he or she is dealing. Instead a reporter should think about what is motivating them as human beings. The reporter should ask, "How can I use those motives to gain the information I want?"
- A reporter should find out how things work in the local hospital and medical center. Which committees control how work is done and money is spent, and who is on these committees?
- A reporter should check out how the health care is delivered in the community and who gets left out.
- A reporter should find out how the quality of physician training programs at the area medical school is evaluated. If the reporter is not competent to judge the value of medical research at a university, he or she should find out who is and interview him or her about it.
- Read. A reporter must develop a basic understanding of medicine and medical terms in order to investigate the medical field.

• As far as the vocabulary goes, it is not as difficult as it initially seems. Once a reporter knows the prefixes, suffixes, and word roots of medical terminology, he or she can figure out what a medical term means even he/she has never seen the word before.

Much of the medical reporting done by laypersons in the mainstream press is surprisingly accurate. To investigate how accurate one segment of the media (consumer magazines) is in covering one major health problem (breast cancer), two Rutgers researchers studied 232 articles in magazines which don't publish original research. The research, published in August 1995, discovered that science magazines contained the lowest number of errors compared to other types of consumer magazines studied, and that errors of omission were more common than errors of commission in all types of magazines studied. Moreover, omission of sources and omission of relevant information about results were the most common errors, especially in women's and alternative magazines.

The following passages provide an example of the kind of material that was not sourced that makes several alarming claims:[27]

If 45 percent of the 48 million American women 40 years of age or older had yearly mammograms, the estimated number of abnormal mammograms would be more than four million per year, and the proportion is even higher in younger age groups.

And:

Xenoestrogens raise the creepy possibility that if toxic chemicals are estrogens in disguise, personal-risk factors might actually be the result of environmental exposures. . . . Breast-feeding is a protective factor, and it also shifts toxins from a woman's breast tissue into her breast milk.

The lessons for journalists should be obvious: attribute all important and/ or seemingly new information to credible sources. Leaving statements such as these without attribution leaves readers wondering if such claims can be believed, or gives them the false sense that they are credible when, in fact, they might not be.

The researchers conclude about this issue:

Whatever the reason for omitting sources, the result is a disempowering of the reader. Sourcing allows the reader to challenge the article's contents. Coincidentally, health books—whose articles rarely omitted sources, as compared to all other magazines—were among the few magazines to address directly the notion of reader empowerment. *Prevention*'s media kit, for example, said, "*Prevention* does not merely report—it guides, motivates, and empowers readers to achieve higher levels of well-being, fitness, and personal fulfillment."[28]

A large percentage of health reporting today deals with diet and fitness topics. A scan of several months' worth of *Prevention* magazine, for instance, showed nine out of ten cover stories dealing with these subjects. Reporting on evolving diet and related health science issues presents a particular challenge for journalists as the public's thirst for this information grows and news reports influence daily food and lifestyle choices. Compounding the issue, according to the International Food Information Council (IFIC), surveys show consumers rely more on the news media than on doctors and dietitians for food and nutrition information.

To find out how the media are covering these issues, the IFIC Foundation commissioned the Center for Media and Public Affairs to conduct a three-month content analysis of diet and health reporting across 37 broadcast and print media outlets. In examining the findings, Sharon M. Friedman, director of the Science and Environmental Writing Program at Lehigh University's Department of Journalism, said, "The good news on nutrition and food safety is the media are covering it and bringing that information to the public. There are many issues related to public health in other areas that are never discussed because the media pay no attention."[29]

Among the findings of the study were the following:[30]

- A wide range of newsworthy events spanned the spectrum from research on pesticides in baby food to controversies over meat safety and food labeling regulations to the discovery of a "fat gene" and its implications for dieters.

- The research clearly demonstrated the popularity of diet and health topics in the media. Both print and broadcast media gave these topics considerable attention.

- The most noticeable omissions in quality of nutrition reporting were a lack of context for dietary recommendations, putting foods into "good food/bad food" categories.

- A simplification of the science-based details does not allow consumers to judge the relevance of information to their own diet, lifestyle, and nutritional needs.

- Local media outlets gave food safety and nutrition news more play than did national outlets. For example, the *Rocky Mountain News* carried four times as many articles and almost twice as many column inches of text as The *New York Times*. Local television stations averaged four times as many stories on their evening news shows as the networks did.

- Fat consumption attracted twice as much coverage as any other nutritional topic. Nearly half of all media reports mentioned some aspect of the need to reduce dietary fat intake.

- The media accurately reflect scientific consensus on dietary fats as an important risk factor in chronic disease. But such massive coverage seems disproportionate to the role any one factor plays in diet and health.

- Disease prevention finished second only to dietary fat on the list of leading media topics. Preventing illness through proper diet was a major theme of the coverage, especially in the women's magazines.

- Many articles treated individual foods as magic bullets rather than components of a balanced diet that is conducive to good health.
- Beyond providing food content information, the media offered frequent advice on food choices and their health effects. News reports featured nearly 2,500 assertions about the harms and benefits of particular foods and dietary choices.
- Overall, the media provided far more advice on foods to seek out than on those to avoid. But the positive association of food choices with good health was balanced against frequent warnings about the dangers of foodborne illnesses and, to a lesser extent, man-made food additives and contaminants.

The IFIC Foundation research was conducted by S. Robert Lichter and Daniel R. Amundson and was published in February 1996.

One medical story that has received heavy coverage in recent years is the emergence of acquired immune deficiency syndrome, or AIDS. Indeed, it is probably the most talked about and reported medical subject, aside from health care reform. Much is written elsewhere in this book about AIDS coverage, and the story "AIDS in the Heartland" is featured in the Appendix. But the coverage is put into perspective by a joint report issued by the Henry J. Kaiser Family Foundation, Princeton Survey Research Associates, and *Columbia Journalism Review* in July 1996. Providing a history of AIDS coverage in America, the report points to an August 8, 1982, story in the *New York Times* as the first time the term acquired immune deficiency syndrome, or AIDS, appeared. Over the next several years, the report asserts, the news media confronted the challenge of reporting on a deadly and mysterious new health problem in a responsible manner—to inform but not inflame, to educate but not alarm.[31]

The study's findings generally speak favorably about journalistic performance in covering the AIDS story during the 1980s and 1990s. The researchers concluded:

Overall, what the press did best was to maintain broad-based coverage—AIDS did not become a political story or a story focused solely on homosexuals or I.V. drug users. Instead, AIDS coverage tended to examine the disease's impact on multiple groups and communities; or put a human face to the disease to demonstrate AIDS' impact on individuals and their families.[32]

The report notes the tremendous influence of the death of Rock Hudson in 1985 and the revelation in 1991 that Magic Johnson had tested positive for the HIV virus. The 1990 death of young Ryan White and the 1993 death of Arthur Ashe from AIDS were other milestones in the coverage of the disease, as was the 1996 revelation that boxer Tommy Morrison tested HIV-positive. In establishing a principal news topic, the press most often concentrated on activities of celebrities (25 percent), followed at a distance by prevention/protection issues (12 percent). The story of tainted blood supplies, international AIDS conferences, and the response by entertainers to AIDS also drew heavy coverage.

A University of Florida researcher, Kim Walsh-Childers, examined the issue of newspaper influence on health policy development in the United States. Reporting in a 1994 article, Walsh-Childers' study focused on an *Alabama Journal* series on infant mortality and of subsequent changes in related state health services. The series was called "A Death in the Family," and ran in the Montgomery daily of 20,000 circulation. Her results show that the series helped increase public support for policy changes to reduce infant mortality and created pressure on the governor and legislators to make those changes. She concludes:

Factors that seem to have affected the series' influence include expert agreement on solutions, the existence of supportive private citizen groups and public officials, Alabama's political situation, the newspaper's location in the capital city, widespread distribution of series reprints, editorial and reporting follow-ups, and publicity when the series won a Pulitzer Prize.[33]

The findings of this study seem consistent with reports coming from other newspapers and television stations which have done enlightening stories on health problems. The *Daily News* series on quack doctors, discussed earlier, resulted in stern government action that produced a number of reforms. For instance, the city Consumer Affairs Department launched a false advertising crackdown, and the offending ads for unlicensed doctors dropped off sharply, according to managing editor Arthur Browne. Also, state licensing authorities and criminal justice officials formed a task force that included Chinese-speaking investigators. At last count, they had opened 63 criminal investigations.[34]

In another example, noted previously, the *Charlotte Observer*'s series on slow ambulance response time resulted in the hiring of 76 new paramedics and the purchase of thirteen new ambulances by the county.

These stories are not isolated examples of the influence that medical reporting has on public health policy. Good, hard-hitting reporting on serious problems almost always results in some kind of government reaction if the readers are disturbed enough by the stories.

REPORTING ON HIGH-TECH MEDICINE

It is as important for reporters to report accurately on new drugs and high-tech diagnostics and treatments as it is for them to report accurately on health risks themselves. Sometimes, a wrong drug or a drug with a potent side effect can be a risk in and of itself. Since the Food and Drug Administration lifted its ban on direct promotion of drugs to the public, pharmaceutical firms are increasingly advertising in the media. Medical writers have interviewed and quoted authoritative health care experts on drugs newly approved by the FDA. In some cases the reporting is too hurried, and reporters may not look for possible ties between these experts and the drug manufacturers.

In addition, reporters should focus more attention on high-tech medicine and medical procedures. This is for two reasons: First, the boundaries of traditional medical procedures are expanding and, second, these high-tech procedures are quite expensive. It is this expense, in fact, that is fueling much of the costs of U.S. health care. Changes in medical technologies tend to account for more than 50 percent of the long-term growth in U.S. health care costs, according to many policy experts.[35] Some innovative medical technologies are cost-decreasing, however. Compared with standard exploratory surgery, for example, locating gall stones with ultrasound and crushing them with lithotripsy is more cost-effective and promotes the quality of the patient's life.[36] Further, since the mid-1980s, most administrative technologies in hospital pharmacies and nursing stations have been cost-effective.[37] Some other technologies, however, are extremely expensive without being cost-effective. Therefore, balanced reporting on high-tech medicine is vital.

To deal with the increased health problems coronary heart disease poses (it is the leading cause of death for men in America, regardless of race, and is increasingly so for women over age 70), the FDA approved the drug Redux in 1996.[38] This is an anti-obesity drug and was the first one approved in more than 20 years. Redux fools the stomach into thinking it has had enough to eat. As such, it warranted in-depth coverage. What it got, however, was rather anemic. In many cases, it was carried as a short business news item rather than as a health care or medical news item. Missing from much of the reporting was important information on cost-effectiveness in clinical testing, contraindications, and any potential complications from short-term or prolonged usage. Many reporters also ignored the fact that health insurers are unlikely to cover the cost of Redux, especially in the period immediately following its FDA approval.

The FDA also approved in the Liposorber LA-15 system in 1996, a medical device that selectively extracts 73 to 83 percent of LDL—or bad—cholesterol from the blood of patients with an LDL-cholesterol reading of 200 mg/dl or more and documented heart disease.[39] Diet and maximum tolerated drug treatments are ineffective therapies in these groups of patients.

Two new high-tech medical treatments have received good coverage, and that coverage indicates the kinds of things reporters should include in their stories about new procedures.

One story concerns the newly approved device known as Prostatron, a breakthrough medical device that shrinks excessive prostate tissues with microwave heat and offers the hope of reducing prostatic cancer deaths. A

1996 editorial in the Memphis *Commercial Appeal* carried the news of Prostatron. The coverage included its improved effectiveness in treating the disease symptoms (it may help 75 percent of patients), the significant treatment cost-reduction, the way the device operates, and the improved quality of life it offers patients.[40] This editorial contained most of the salient facts of potential value to patients, especially the data on costs and medical benefits expected from the Prostratron treatment. A similar story appeared in the *Wall Street Journal* which gave information on the sample tested in the United States and Europe.[41]

The second medical treatment is an experimental one that had not yet received FDA approval in 1996. It is Dermagraft, a bio-engineered skin developed from the foreskin of circumcised male babies. It is reported to be the world's first off-the-shelf bio-engineered human tissue skin replacement product.[42] The "skin" is useful for burn and chronic diabetic foot ulcer patients. However, a story in the *Commercial Appeal* noted its possible use, compared expected marginal benefits and costs to other current treatments, and discussed its possible use as cardiovascular tissues in heart attack patients.[43]

High technology in medicine varies from diagnostic and therapeutic treatment equipment to the use of computers and electronics in the production of medical care. One example is the sterile preparation of biotechnology drugs for administration in hospitals. But the difficulties inherent in medical technology assessments could be leading to higher health care costs. High-cost, innovative technologies significantly increase the cost of treating breast cancer and myocardial infarction patients, for example.

One critic has argued that the public perception of medical technologies tends to be clouded by "headline-grabbing" innovations such as organ transplants, open-heart surgery, renal dialysis and scanners. More recently, this had included MRIs and genetically engineered medicine.[44]

Technical changes in medicine tend to be unique in the following ways, compared with those in the other manufacturing sectors of advanced economies:

1. Patients can influence the efficiency with which high-tech medicine is translated to improved health status.

2. Medical technologies fuel and permeate each level of the dynamic health sector. These technologies change constantly, due to the competition for profits by the economic agents. Where innovation and competition are low, prices and wages are likely to rise faster if the demand is less price-sensitive. The pace of technical change in the individual economic sector, therefore, tends to explain the rate of technical advances in the entire economy.

3. The process through which innovative medical technologies are adopted tends to be regulated more closely by the government. The FDA approval process for new drugs and medical devices is a classic case. Currently in America, assessing

a new medical technology requires the demonstration of efficacy and/or safety. Gastric freezing, MRIs and CT scanners were, however, adopted before their efficacy testings.

4. Rapid growth of medical technologies such as genetic engineering comes with several complex ethical and legal issues attached. Schools of law and business increasingly provide legal and business training to health care professionals, most notably doctors.

5. New medical technologies such as MRIs are usually more expensive in the short run because of high initial capital investment costs relative to use. Given a sufficiently large market size, however, a large-capacity MRI can achieve a lower unit cost efficiency compared with the older radiological method. If MRI confers more added benefits than the additional costs over its life cycle, then the investments in MRIs are more cost-justified. Further, the MRI, ultrasound, and other imaging techniques are potentially substitutable procedures for the detection of breast cancer. If MRI-detected lesions are not detected through other imaging methods, then it provides more information. But is the additional information cost-justified?

How does one determine if, in fact, the new technology confers more benefits over costs? It is important to know that if direct and indirect costs and benefits are accounted for, a new therapy is decidedly cost-increasing if it is more expensive than current treatments and offers no potential for significantly improved outcomes. The United States Congress in 1989 created the Agency for Health Care Policy and Research (AHCPR) to assess the proper use of new technologies and therapies. AHCPR reports on scientific research, looking at outcomes and effectiveness and development, and promotes practical guidelines on the appropriate use of selected medical technologies.

Additionally, the U.S. Office of Technology Assessment (OTA) established a formal system for assessing medical technologies composed of three parts: efficacy, cost-benefit and safety, and effectiveness. Technology assessment is a powerful tool for gathering information that could assist doctors in optimal selection among alternative care technologies.

In this era of rapid growth of managed care systems, a more careful choice of medical technology can be a strategy for minimizing the cost of care while protecting provider profit margins under capitation. If prices are competitively determined under capitated payments, the newer for-profit HMOs in particular are more likely to provide minimal medical services without sacrificing quality to retain most of the capitation payments. Given limited resources, controlled use of expensive medical technologies and procedures is more likely to intensify under managed care. Utilization reviews are a proven strategy for accomplishing this.

Here are some guidelines for reporting on high-tech medicine:

1. Balanced coverage should include not only the physician's opinions but also those of the health economists, including pharmaco-economists if the story is

about a new drug. This is because scientific norms tend to constrain a physician's willingness to speculate. The economist is less constrained.

2. Reporters should relate the reported technologies to financing arrangements and access, and how the emerging concepts of medical arrangements (notably, managed care HMOs) are likely to accommodate the new technology.

3. Reporting on medical technologies entails scientist-journalist interactions. These two groups engage in the transfer of information to the public. However, as is discussed elsewhere in this book, reporters and medical researchers operate on different agendas and often for different goals.

4. Reporters should monitor the follow-up events of initial technology breakthroughs and report on how well the new treatments or diagnostics are actually working.

5. Reporters should go beyond simply reporting on the latest findings and present a broader analysis of the previous studies of specific medical interventions. The Internet affords medical writers infinitely more information than ever before to do this backgrounding.

6. Reporters should take continuing education courses in the science, economics, and politics of medicine and technology assessment. Doing so will help them improve their communication with doctors, medical equipment manufacturers, health economists, and political scientists.

7. The print media should complement their verbal reporting with schematic diagrams that are easy to understand. These graphics should compare existing procedures and treatments with new ones and show their advantages and disadvantages, if any.

8. Reporting of health care and other public policy issues should be more outcome-based. This ties in with the notion of public journalism and suggests that the media organizations conduct focus groups for each of the stakeholders in health care. Audience-based outcome reporting could automatically expand the market for newsworthy public policy health care issues, as the media learn how well new technologies work or don't work and come to understand what consumers are interested in.

NOTES

1. Ralph S. Izard and Marilyn S. Greenwald, *Public Affairs Reporting* (Dubuque, Iowa: William C. Brown, 1991), p. 291.

2. Ibid., p. 294.

3. Ibid., p. 295.

4. Stephen G. Bloom, "The Legend of the Potholes," *The Pharos* (Summer 1996), p. 2.

5. Ibid.

6. Ibid., p. 5.

7. Ibid., p. 6.

8. Ibid.

9. M. Angell and J. P. Kassirer, "Clinical Research—What Should the Public Believe?", *New England Journal of Medicine* 331 (1994), pp. 189–190.

10. Larry Thompson, "Communicating Genetics: Journalists' Role in Helping the Public Understand Genetics," in R. F. Weir, S. C. Lawrence, and E. Fales, eds., *Genes and Human Self-Knowledge: Historical and Philosophical Reflections on Modern Genetics* (Iowa City: University of Iowa Press, 1994), p. 104.

11. Stephen G. Bloom, comments to the Society of Professional Journalists National Convention, St. Paul, Minn., November 8, 1995.

12. Rebecca Raspberry, comments in the seminar "Understanding and Communicating the Health Care Story," the University of Memphis, Memphis, Tenn., May 25, 1996.

13. Doug Johnson, comments in the seminar "Understanding and Communicating the Health Care Story," the University of Memphis, Memphis, Tenn., May 25, 1996.

14. Sherry Jacobson, comments in the seminar "Understanding and Communicating the Health Care Story," the University of Memphis, Memphis, Tenn., May 25, 1996.

15. Cyril Chang, comments in the seminar "Understanding and Communicating the Health Care Story," the University of Memphis, Memphis, Tenn., May 25, 1996.

16. Michael Calhoun, comments in the seminar "Understanding and Communicating the Health Care Story," the University of Memphis, Memphis, Tenn., May 25, 1996.

17. Henry H. Schulte and Marcel P. Dufresne, *Getting the Story* (New York: Macmillan, 1994), p. 384.

18. Ibid., p. 385.

19. Ibid.

20. John Langone, "Challenging the Mainstream," *Time* (Special Issue) (Fall 1996), p. 40.

21. Ibid., p. 42.

22. Molly Gordy, "Quacks Prey on Immigrants," *Daily News*, July 18, 1996, p. 2.

23. Jennie Buckner, editor, in a letter to the Associated Press on the Ames Alexander series on emergency response systems, June 24, 1996, p. 1.

24. Ibid.

25. Robert L. Peirce, "Health Care," in *The Reporter's Handbook*, ed. John Ullmann and Steve Honeyman (New York: St. Martin's Press, 1983), p. 394.

26. Ibid, pp. 395–396.

27. Christine Morrongiello and Barbara Straus Reed, "The Accuracy of Breast Cancer Reports in Consumer Magazines," *Research Report No. 95–45*, School of Communication, Information & Library Studies, Rutgers University, Princeton, N.J., p. 22.

28. Ibid., p. 19.

29. Jennie Buckner, editor, in a letter to the Associated Press on the Ames Alexander series on emergency response systems, June 24, 1996, p. 1.

30. S. Robert Lichter and Daniel R. Amundson, *Executive Summary of Food for Thought: Reporting of Diet, Nutrition and Food Safety*, Center for Media and Public Affairs, Washington, D.C., February 1996.

31. *Covering the Epidemic: AIDS in the News Media, 1985–1996*, the Kaiser Family Foundation's AIDS Media Monitoring Project; designed by the Foundation and Princeton Survey Research Associates, and conducted by Princeton Survey Research Associates. Supplement to the July/August 1996 issue of *Columbia Journalism Review*.

32. Ibid.

33. Kim Walsh-Childers, " 'A Death in the Family'—A Case Study of Newspaper Influence on Health Policy Development," *Journalism Quarterly* 71(4) (Winter 1994), p. 820.

34. Arthur Browne, in a letter on the Molly Gordy series, "Medical Menace," to the Associated Press, July 1, 1996, p. 2.

35. David Cutler, "A Guide to Healthcare Reform," *Journal of Economic Perspectives* (August 1994), pp. 13–29.

36. D. P. Doessel, *The Economics of Medical Diagnosis: Technological Change and Health Expenditures* (Brookfield, Vt.: Avebury Press, 1992).

37. Steven Eastaugh, *Health Economics: Efficiency, Quality, and Equity* (Westport, Conn.: Auburn House, 1992).

38. Bloomberg Business News, "Fat-Drug Approval Spurs Share Rise," *The Commercial Appeal*, Memphis, Tenn., May 1, 1996.

39. Benita Whitehorn, "Liposorber Removes LDL Cholesterol from Blood," *Memphis Health Care News*, May 3, 1996, pp. 1, 6.

40. Editorial, "FDA Approves Microwave Prostate Treatment," *The Commercial Appeal*, Memphis, Tenn., May 6, 1996.

41. Laurie McGinley, "FDA Approves Nonsurgical Alternative from EDAP to Treat Enlarged Prostate Cancer," *Wall Street Journal*, May 7, 1996, p. B6.

42. Jaan Van Valkenburgh, "Circumcision Yielding Skin for Ulcerous Feet," *The Commercial Appeal*, Memphis, Tenn., May 7, 1996, pp. B5, B9.

43. Ibid.

44. Anne A. Scitovsky, "Changes in the Use of Ancillary Services for Common Illnesses," in S. H. Altman and R. Blendon, eds., *Medical Technology: The Culprit Behind Health Care Costs?* (Washington, D.C.: National Center for Health Services Research, 1979), pp. 39–56.

5

Covering
Environmental Risks

Of the many types of stories conveying risks, probably no other type affects so many potential victims as environmental hazards. From stories on nuclear waste, to groundwater contamination, to acid rain, to the deteriorating ozone layer and the diminishing size of the rain forests, environmental stories are all around us and affect us all in one way or another.

With this in mind, it is surprising that the environmental beat ranks as low as it does among many news media in considering which stories are most deserving of coverage. Television's Sam Donaldson was candid in commenting on the lackluster nature of environmental reporting when he said upon leaving the White House beat to co-anchor ABC's *Prime Time Live*, "It's not like I'm being fired or sent to cover the ecology beat."[1]

CRISES, CONTROVERSIES COUNT

A recent study supports the belief that the environment is not usually a front-page story. As in most cases, it takes a crisis or a controversy to bring an issue to the forefront, as that study will show later. An example is the oil spill by the Exxon tanker *Valdez* in Alaska's Prince William Sound, which brought the hazards of oil sea transport home to the public. Another example from the 1980s focused on the Environmental Protection Agency (EPA) itself when its then-director, Anne Burford, was cited for contempt of Congress during an inquiry regarding potential conflict-of-interest practices in the EPA. The amount of time the television networks devoted to the EPA over a two-year period shows what a difference a controversy makes. A mere 16 stories were done by the networks in the first year. In the next, 28 stories were done until December when things started breaking in the congressional inquiries of the EPA and Burford. Some 18 stories were done on the EPA in that month alone. Then, during the first three months of 1983, the three networks did a whopping 116 stories on the EPA. Six months later, the networks were back to their nominal treatment of the agency as if nothing important were happening in the environment.[2]

Part of the reason for the scant attention Washington reporters pay the EPA arises from the fact that few journalists can decipher complex and confusing chemical information regarding toxic wastes, pesticides, and air and water pollution. Also, as in the case of the myriad governmental agencies in Washington, there are just not enough journalists around to produce daily stories and still do the deeper enterprise pieces that can result in proactive journalism. As a result, the twenty or so regular reporters covering the EPA generally focus on the more obvious stories, like budget wrangling with Congress and the White House. The press often seems to focus more on the size of the EPA budget cuts than on the nature and impact of those cuts. If these questions go unprobed, however, reporters are easier prey for White House and congressional officials who insist the cuts will have no negative impact on environmental standards. Nor is it enough for this probing to go only as far as official press conferences conducted by environmental organizations or the EPA itself. Rather, systematic, in-depth reporting is required.

Too many Washington environmental stories focus on the give-and-take of accusations from official advocates representing each side of an issue. In terms of fairness, the media don't do a bad job. But in terms of trying to verify which side is more accurate, journalists face a more difficult challenge. Too often, reporters adopt the classic technique of reactive reporting, of waiting for press conferences or formal statements and then reporting their contents without investigating the charges themselves. Such was the case with the Burford EPA and its coverage in the 1980s, and things haven't improved much since then.

In reporting on environmental issues, journalists face the same sort of challenges other beats can present. Chief among them are people and agencies with vested interests who try to sway journalists into buying their view of an issue or the laws and practices surrounding that issue. Attempts at media manipulation are alive and well among both EPA officials and environmental groups which are often at odds with the government over issues of ecology. It is the job of the journalists to not only present each side, but also to try and discern which side is more accurate with its view.

Sometimes various not-for-profit agencies publish guides that can help journalists in understanding their subject matter and getting at the truth. One such agency is the National Safety Council's Environmental Health Center (EHC). In 1989 it published *Chemicals, The Press, and The Public*, which is a journalist's guide to covering chemicals in the community under the federal "right-to-know" law. Formally that law is the Emergency Planning and Community Right-to-Know Act, passed as Title III of the Super-fund Amendments and Reauthorization Act (SARA). The purpose of this reporter's guide was to help journalists derive the full potential from the plant- and community-specific chemical information mandated under the law. The press guide followed publication of the EHC's *Reporting on Radon* journalist's guide. Among the contents of the chemicals guide are chapters showing reporters how to research and write about a chemical emergency, and how to access and use electronic databases on toxic chemicals and their release. Among the questions it suggests reporters ask about chemical emergencies are the following:

- Is there an LEPC (Local Emergency Planning Committee) in the area?
- Had risks at the facility been previously identified?
- Who are the experts to contact?
- What is the chemical involved in the incident?
- Is it a gas? Liquid? Solid?
- What are the public health implications?
- What quantity was released? Was the release accidental or routine?
- By what routes are humans exposed to the chemical?
- What are the current temperature, humidity, and wind conditions? What are their implications for public health concerns in spreading this chemical?
- What is the short-term forecast for changes in weather and how will that affect the chemical?
- What is the nature of the area in which the chemical incident occurred?
- Are there nearby population centers such as schools, hospitals, or shopping centers that might be affected?
- Are health risks associated to duration of exposure or concentrations?
- Does the chemical interact synergistically with other chemicals or factors in the environment?
- What preparations did the carrier—if it was a transit accident—make for such an accident?
- What preparations has the community made for such an accidental leak?

Press guides can be extremely helpful, especially given the lack of knowledge of general-assignment reporters about specific health hazards they have never covered. But a word of caution: some of the agencies publishing press guides may indeed have a vested interest in the industry producing the health hazard or be biased in their anti-industry stance. Sometimes environmental groups fall into this latter category, while companies like Mobil Oil—which has produced many advocacy "editorials" over the past two decades championing the values of petrochemicals—fall into the former category.

RISK, DRAMA, GEOGRAPHY, COVERAGE

A recent study done by four communication researchers showed that sudden, violent risks get more coverage than chronic risks which are of equal consequence. It noted that the power of television to shock the American conscience by showing images of helpless birds coated with oil struggling to survive coastal oil spills dwarfs the impact of any other medium. Indeed, television is especially suited to present dramatic stories, which are the ones most Americans tend to recall. Seventy-three percent of Americans get environmental news from television, compared to 62 percent from newspapers, and only 37 percent from magazines. The same is true for health information.[3]

However, if the visual media are somewhat responsible for the public awareness of environmental and health problems, they may also be partly responsible for the public's confusion about the relative risk of different types of hazard. The researchers note:

Government, corporate and environmental group representatives criticize television's tendency to concentrate on the visual and dramatic—that is, spectacular scenes, crises, conflicts, heroes and villains—and to ignore familiar but deadly health and environmental hazards. When the mass media cover environmental risk issues, they pay relatively little attention to the scientific degree of risk. Even the assumption that the most visual and dramatic risks are covered has been challenged.[4]

Instead, history seems to indicate that, for television, the physical and financial hurdles involved in getting crews and equipment to news locations are two key factors in whether a story gets covered, or how much attention it gets.

A study by Michael Greenberg, David Sachsman, Peter Sandman, and Kandice Salomone focused on every environmental risk story aired by ABC, CBS, and NBC on their nightly news broadcasts during a 26-month period. It examined the extent to which the relative degree of risk affected coverage, compared to the availability of dramatic visual images and the distance from the crew's starting point to the news site. Among its findings are the following:[5]

- The major networks presented 564 environmental risk stories during the study period, an average of five a week. Altogether, environmental risk news consumed 13.8 hours, or 1.7 percent, of total nightly news air time.

- Forty-five percent of the stories were 30 seconds or less, while 5 percent were 40-60 seconds, 43 percent were 70 seconds to four minutes, and 7 percent were longer than four minutes. Half of the stories had no field reporters, and 46 percent had one. Four percent used two or more.

• One-third of the stories were aired without sources, one-fourth had one, and 42 percent had two or more.

• As expected, there was much greater coverage of airplane accidents, the Bhopal chemical spill, and the Mexico City earthquake than of asbestos, smoking/tobacco, acid rain, and endangered species. The networks showed about 11 ½ hours of airplane safety and accident stories, or 482 stories. They showed only 3.7 hours of smoking, asbestos, acid rain, and endangered species stories. In fact, there was almost as much coverage of airplane accidents as of all environmental risk stories combined—482 stories versus 564.

• To a great degree, environmental stories were "readers" (no tape used), while airplane, earthquake, and Bhopal stories were mostly taped packages or live shots.

To put this coverage in perspective, the researchers noted that an estimated 350,000 Americans die annually from smoking tobacco, and 9,000 from asbestos exposure. The average annual number of deaths from all airline accidents in the United States in 1975, 1980, and 1985, was 220. If coverage matched risk, as measured by total number of deaths, then there should have been 26.5 minutes on smoking and 41 seconds about asbestos for each second devoted to airplane accidents. Instead, reverse proportions were discovered.

Hazardous waste sites were chosen as the barometer to show the influence geographic locations of news sites have on coverage of risks. Eighteen hazardous waste stories and 86 oil/gas release stories reported environmental risks at specific locations. These 104 news items represented 18 percent of the environmental risk stories. The results showed that, in their coverage of environmental risk, the networks are more heavily guided by the cost and convenience of accessing these stories than by the risk the stories depict. The researchers concluded:

The networks are (also) guided more by the traditional determinants of news and the availability of dramatic visual images than by the scientific degree of risk of the situation involved. . . . The American public was well served by television's film images of birds coated in oil from the Santa Barbara spill. Nevertheless, the disproportionate coverage—from the scientific perspective on risk—of chemical incidents, earthquakes, and airplane accidents probably reinforces the public's well-documented tendency to overestimate sudden and violent risks and underestimate chronic ones. The public needs a steady stream of stories on the hazards of asbestos, smoking, alcoholism, and even sunbathing.[6]

Environmental author Bill McKibben believes that if the predictions come true about impending global environmental alteration, then we are likely to see a lot more environmental stories. Thus, the idea of a "stable, normal nature" may start to disappear and be replaced in our minds by the reality of living in a shifting and unsettled environment. McKibben feels this environmental shift is already occurring and notes:

The best example is the greenhouse effect. Current forecasts call for increases on the order of 4 degrees Fahrenheit in global average temperature during the next century, as carbon dioxide traps heat near the planet that would otherwise radiate back out to space. In other words, the amount of energy in the earth's physical systems will increase considerably. In everyday terms . . . this extra energy will be felt in more and greater natural disasters. Hurricanes, for instance, draw their power from the warmth of the sea surface. . . . An increase of only a few degrees in sea surface temperature could mean hurricanes with winds 50 miles an hour higher.[7]

Additionally, McKibben says, summer heat waves should become more frequent and intense in the nation's cities. Dallas, for example, could go from 29 to 75 days above 90 degrees. With more heat comes the likelihood of greater drought. Heat and drought, in turn, have a devastating effect on agriculture, and the successive layers of impact go on.

If McKibben is right, then environmental news may one day become the key beat in most newsrooms. Until then, however, the ecology often languishes as a largely uncovered story as environmental shifts take place on a simple incremental basis. The danger of ignoring the story at this point, McKibben believes, is that journalists may be leaving the nation largely unprepared for what lies ahead. He uses the analogy of the United States falling behind Japan and other countries in their standard of living and in being the world's dominant trader nation. Americans now realize that the power of their nation, in a global sense, is not what it used to be. But that realization did not come because of some startling and revealing Pulitzer Prize-winning series on America in decline. Instead, it came from the day-in-day-out coverage of the deficit and the poverty rate and the manufacturing trouble in Detroit, the length of the Japanese schoolday, the quality of German appliances, and many other stories noting the incremental shifts in the power of America vis-à-vis other nations. To be sure, there have been benchmark investigative stories done along the way such as the *Philadelphia Inquirer* series, "America: What Went Wrong?" But by and large, it was the daily reporting on international business trends by crack business reporters that let Americans know where their country was headed.

If Americans are to be prepared for the same kinds of shifts in the environment, McKibben says, then there must be more day-to-day solid environmental reporting on the incremental changes. He concludes:

The relationship between people and the earth, and the changes we are almost certainly causing, is an even bigger story. . . . But we are so used to thinking of nature as background, as static and unchanging and in news terms unimportant, that we run the risk of missing this story entirely, or covering it only when, like Hurricane Andrew, it demands coverage. We lack a grammar for journalistic writing about the natural world. The people who find it, who develop the vocabulary and the techniques, will be the great enlighteners of the next century.[8]

According to at least one recent study, the media can influence public opinion about the environment. Researcher Joel J. Davis explored the relationship of media message framing to the public response on three environmental issues: conservation, recycling, and buying environmentally safe products ("greenshopping"). His conclusions were as follows:[9]

• Message framing does influence response to environmental communications and subsequent intentions by the public to participate in environmentally responsible behaviors.

• Individuals were most favorable toward (and most influenced by) a communication which emphasized the negative consequences of their own inaction on themselves and on their own generation.

• Public intentions to participate in environmentally responsible ways are best fostered through communications which present simple, clear, and understandable actions and which show how the individuals will be negatively affected if they don't behave responsibly.

WHERE WE GET ENVIRONMENTAL NEWS

Where does the public get most of its news about environmental risks and hazards? The Greenberg study cited earlier clearly indicated that, in the 1980s, television was the dominant source of information. That was still the case a decade later, and the respondents added that they found TV to be a helpful source, although they also believed there was too little environmental news covered.

A 1995 nationwide survey by a Denver-based public relations firm showed that television is the hands-down winner as the public's "most useful source" of environmental information. When asked to name the news medium that helped them the most to understand environmental issues, 64 percent of 1,014 adults interviewed said TV, while 18 percent said newspapers, and 8 percent said they relied on magazines to clarify the information.[10]

Included in the sample for this study were 224 environmental journalists and 179 corporate public relations (PR) executives, in addition to members of the general public across the country. Here is a summary of the key results:

• Seventy percent of the journalists and 56 percent of the adults believe there is too little media coverage of environmental issues.

• Sixty percent of journalists say their news organization is doing either an excellent or good job of reporting environmental issues. However, only 30 percent of the public and 22 percent of the corporate PR executives agree.

- Fifty-eight percent of journalists feel the quality of environmental reporting within their own news organizations has improved over the past few years, whereas only 29 percent of corporate communicators say the quality has improved.

- Aside from environmental specialists, 57 percent of journalists report that reporters are not prepared enough to cover environmental issues, while 74 percent of PR executives agree.

- Forty-six percent of reporters say they were not prepared enough when they first began covering environmental issues.

- Nine in 10 journalists say additional training in either environmental law and regulations (91 percent) or the natural sciences (90 percent) would be helpful. Journalists also report that additional training in environmental economics (87 percent) and health risk assessment (86 percent) would be useful.

- Ninety-one percent of journalists believe academic and professional journals are credible, including 47 percent of environmental journalists who say they are very credible.

- Fifty-three percent of reporters believe business executives are credible when it comes to environmental issues.

One key to discovering where environmental news comes from may be found in the area of so-called information subsidies. For instance, researchers Robert J. Griffin and Sharon Dunwoody analyzed 373 daily newspapers in the Midwest in 1994 and found that information subsidy from an environmental group affected press coverage of a story about pollution from industrial toxins.[11] In other words, promotion of environmental stories by environmental groups can have some effect in obtaining media coverage. In this study, a press kit the group sent to newspapers appears to have influenced the papers to run a story on industrial toxic releases, although editors used the information as a springboard to send their own reporters out to cover the story.

The ability of various groups to access important information about the environment was enhanced in 1986 when Congress passed the Superfund Amendments and Reauthorization Act, which gave the public access to information about the release, storage, and possible health effects of toxic chemicals in their communities. A portion of the law required manufacturers to report annually the amount of hazardous chemicals they have released into the environment. The EPA then makes this data available to the public through its computerized database called the "Toxics Release Inventory" (TRI).[12]

When special-interest groups compile press releases or information kits to send to the media, they are, in effect, providing the media with information subsidies. Researcher Oscar H. Gandy believes that the price of securing information will affect its use by the news media, and that those who "subsidize" the news media by providing them this information free will increase the chances of journalists covering the stories they want covered.[13] The Griffin and Dunwoody study generally supported this conclusion. They conclude:

[I]nformation about health risks and related problems stemming from local contaminators in a community is sensitive information and is treated carefully by local media. In particular, daily newspaper use of information subsidies seems to be affected by a cost-benefit tradeoff that takes into account the ease of gathering the information as well as anticipation of the effects of that information on the social and economic workings of the community of which the paper is a part.[14]

HISTORY PROVIDES INSIGHT

Journalists covering the environment must first wrestle with the issue of stance as detailed in an earlier section of this chapter. Whether they choose to take a traditionalist or advocacy stance to the craft, however, all journalists must realize that conclusions flow out of facts. Therefore, exhaustive research is needed before going into print or onto the air with news about the environment. In that sense, environmental journalism is no different from any other type of nonfiction writing.

The muckrakers of the early twentieth century were the forerunners of the environmentalists today, and history is always a good teacher. Interesting lessons can be found in reading about the practices used by such reform-minded journalists during the decade of 1902–1912. It was Theodore Roosevelt who adapted the term muckraker to journalists, drawing his figure from the Man with the Muck-rake in *Pilgrim's Progress*, who would not look up from the filth on the floor even when a celestial crown was offered him. [15] Leading publications in the movement were *Collier's, Cosmopolitan, McClure's, Everybody's,* and the *Arena*. Prominent among series of magazine articles during these years were Ida M. Tarbell's "History of the Standard Oil Company," and Samuel Hopkins Adams' "The Great American Fraud," an exposé of the patent medicine business. Although some of these efforts were seen as sensationalistic, a lot of fact-finding went into the published reports, and the crusading spirit behind them seems to permeate much of environmental journalism today, for better or worse.

It is perhaps revealing that the height of this environmental muckraking coincided with the presidency of Theodore Roosevelt, himself an advocate of conservation.[16] Environmental developments were covered after that era, but there appeared no special concern over conservation issues until a book, *Silent Spring*, by Rachel Carson, called public attention to the effect the pesticide DDT would have on wildlife. "Out of the ensuing national debate, a new consciousness was created about the precarious nature of man's

estate on earth," wrote journalism educator John Hohenberg.[17] It was also
a time when the public began paying attention to the historical warnings
about such issues as pollution, overpopulation, and diminishing natural
resources. Eventually, the press seized the issue, and the modern concept
of environmental journalism was born.

The efforts of environmental journalists have not been lost on Pulitzer
Prize juries over the years. Among stories winning the coveted prize was
one by the Winston-Salem (N.C.) *Journal and Sentinel* on blocking a strip-
mining operation that would have caused irreparable damage to the beautiful hill country of northwest North Carolina. Other Pulitzers have gone
to the *Milwaukee Journal* for its successful campaign to stiffen the laws
against water pollution in Wisconsin, and to the *Louisville Courier-Journal*
for its attacks on the Kentucky strip-mining industry. The *Christian Science
Monitor* took home a Pulitzer for its critical examination of the future of
the American national park system.

Illustrating the involvement strategy, several papers have helped lead
movements to save the environment. The Bend (Oregon) *Bulletin* once de-
fended a great national resource, Rock Mesa, from use by mining interesst.
The Casper (Wyoming) *Star-Tribune* took great pains in reporting the long
effort to halt the slaughter of eagles by ranchers. The Durango (Colorado)
Herald fought against the pollution of the massive Colorado plateau. In
the battle against oil pollution and drilling in Santa Barbara Channel in
California, the Santa Barbara *News-Press* has been a devoted crusader. On
the East Coast, such papers as *Newsday*, the Newark *Star-Ledger*, and the
Providence *Journal-Bulletin* have campaigned against both oil spillage and
the dumping of sewage in coastal waters.[18]

Other efforts have followed suit. The *Chicago Tribune*, with disclosures
of the contamination of drinking water, succeeded in forcing the adoption
of new standards for drinking water in the Chicago area. The Manhattan
(Kansas) *Mercury* instituted a "Product Patrol" of reporters who examined
products on the shelves of local stores. The *Christian Science Monitor* at-
tacked the illicit traffic in prescription drugs, and the *Washington Star* and
Wall Street Journal disclosed the danger in using the pesticide Kepone.[19]

As history shows, environmental journalism and crusading journalism
have often been synonymous. In the more recent past, however, some environmental journalists have wondered where the line should be drawn
between crusading—almost advocacy—journalism, and objective, scientific
reporting of the facts.

OBJECTIVISTS OR ADVOCATES?

Not all journalists are unified on how environmental reporters should
orient themselves to their craft. Many believe the environmental beat
should be handled no differently from any other one a reporter approaches.

They believe a strict objective stance is a necessity, with the journalist taking care not to take sides in the issues covered. This is the long-held traditional view of American journalism, and it has the reporter assuming the role of painstaking researcher and impartial observer and chronicler of the issue at hand.

Other journalists believe environmental reporters should assume the role of advocates for cleaning up the environment, and making sure the government notices the problems and takes steps to solve them.

As is the case for most specialty reporting areas, there is an organization of environmental writers that has proposed guidelines for appropriate reporting. This is the Society of Environmental Journalists (SEJ). Founded in 1989, its membership now exceeds 1,000. While many of these remain dedicated to objectivity, some critics such as syndicated environmental writer Alston Chase see the SEJ as more concerned about marketing the environment and hyping environmental problems beyond the actual risks associated with them.[20]

The SEJ sees potentially huge risks involved in such issues as nuclear waste disposal, hazardous spills and waste disposals, and the hole in the ozone layer. Like most avid reporters, they are deeply concerned about the problems they write about and feel closer to them than the general public. But Chase believes this leads to a paradox. He writes:

By hyping environmental problems, society is often less than tolerant toward those who doubt the severity of these putative crises. Its meetings are largely love feasts. And this conformity tends to make the field both boring and irrelevant, negating the promotional efforts of the faithful. Like much environmental press coverage, SEJ's national meetings have become exercises in orthodoxy, where true believers reign and dissenters are denigrated.[21]

Chase believes environmental journalism is caught in a "downward spiral, where fear of declining popularity motivates reporters to hype stories, thereby ignoring debate and falsely creating the impression that issues are simplistic contests between good guys and bad guys. In this way, they bore and misinform."[22]

Chase chided the SEJ's 1995 national meeting for missing the point of analyzing some important environmental issues. Conference Chair David Ropeik told the newsletter *Environment Writer*, "We're trying to put the environment on the political agenda of the United States."[23] But Chase notes the agenda offered panels on "the environment and spirituality" and "building a sustainable society," but none on deregulation, the Endangered Species Act, risk assessment, cost-benefit analysis, ecosystems management, abolishing the EPA, national parks closure, national forests, or grazing and mining reform.

Panelists for the fifth annual meeting included environmental activists Ed

Begley, Jr. and recording artist Don Henley, who led a panel on the media's role in saving a local nature preserve from developers. Members of the Penobscott tribe explained the Indians' fight for land rights. Organizers said the conference paid special attention to Republican-led congressional attacks on environmental protection laws, including the Clean Water, Superfund, and Endangered Species acts.

Nevertheless, Ropiek told United Press International, "The purpose of the conference is cross-fertilization, the exchange of ideas. We are not green; we are not environmentalists."[24]

Chase sees problems.

Such is the mischief caused by treating environmental journalism as a distinct profession: It inevitably transforms practitioners from disinterested reporters into salespeople promoting their trade. . . . Since one's career advancement depends on the continuation of the catastrophe in question, it transforms scribes into advocates of doom. So I prefer to see myself as an observer of popular culture; a task that includes covering attitudes toward, and policies concerning, the environment.[25]

Chase's comments didn't sit well with the SEJ. In rebutting his criticism, SEJ President Emilia Askari said the organization is committed to improving the quality, accuracy, and visibility of environmental journalism. She said Chase selectively highlighted portions of the 1995 agenda that could be interpreted as bolstering his theses, omitting other portions that would have given his readers a more balanced and fair view of the gathering.[26]

If Chase represents the traditionalist view of objective reporting, one well-known environmental journalist who strikes an advocacy pose is Dr. Michael Frome, former conservation editor of *Field and Stream*, columnist for the *Los Angeles Times*, and author of several books on the environment.

Frome believes environmental reporters should "write from the heart," and believes the motivation should be to show the intangible values of the human heart and spirit and how living in harmony with nature can only lead to living in harmony with each other.[27] Frome points to journalists like the late Ed Meeman of the old Memphis *Press-Scimitar*, who made conservation a front-page story and who crusaded for creation of the Great Smoky Mountains National Park. Frome says:

The environmental journalist begins with hope that things can be better. We must reawaken the environmental consciousness we all inherit. The inverted pyramid is not enough. The environmental journalist looks at the whole, examining all the interlocking aspects of life from politics, to religion, to ecology. The environmental journalist should be like a scientist while writing independently, letting the chips fall where they may, with consequences to follow. I just found a lot of bastards screwing up the environment. A journalist's job is to expose the bastards. We need to get some good advocates and journalists to shake up the place. But I consider myself a journalist first. Environmentalism is my specialty. The issues are what fire my belly. Journalism is my way of venting that fire.[28]

Frome takes his inspiration from early-twentieth-century muckraker Lincoln Steffens who crusaded for better city governments while working as a reporter for *McClure's* magazine. But he also likes to get involved in the issues he is covering, a practice which a traditional journalist decries. For instance, when government officials in Memphis decided to route a section of Interstate 40 through the city for better traffic flow, Frome's help was sought by a neighborhood opposition group. It seemed that the path of the interstate would result in the near wrecking of the city's famed Overton Park, which is 400 acres of a little forest in the middle of the city. Frome responded to the call of the Friends of Overton Park. "As a writer, the more I become involved in real-life issues, the better writer I am," Frome says.[29] So he wrote about the issue and went to the U.S. Supreme Court with a handful of local advocates to help save the park. The result: the interstate was re-routed around the city instead of through it.

Many environmental journalists like Frome find promise in alternative media outlets to ply their particular brand of environmental journalism. Numerous magazines catering to environmentalists now populate the newsstands. One of the more unique ones is *Garbage*. Founded in 1989, *Garbage* looks at the problems of waste and recycling. A typical issue, for instance, carried the following articles:

- *Visionaries: The Future of Garbage*. A story about entrepreneurs who are turning garbage into money by burning it and transforming it into fuel.
- *A Petrochemical Primer*. Makeup and potato chips can be had oil-free, but there's no such thing as an oil-free life.
- *Getting Rid of Batteries*. They're hard to recycle, and a lot of people don't even want them collected.
- *Theatre of the McServed*. The environment has center stage in the burger wars drama about what to do with styrofoam burger containers.

The founding editor of *Garbage*, Patricia Poore, is an example of a conservationist who decided she would start a magazine crusading for the environment. She was a member of the Sierra Club at 18, walked to work every day, never even owned a car until 1991, and was a vegetarian and avid backpacker.[30] She parted company with the more militant of the environmentalists, however, over the issue of disposable diapers, which she—as a mother—confessed to using. Following that confrontation with her readers, Poore took an unusual tack for an editor of a environmental magazine. She began talking about the "dark side" of the environmental movement in which green "vigilantes" enforce unquestioned compliance with liberal environmental orthodoxy. The experience caused the editor to change her own ideas of the environmental movement and to reposition her magazine dramatically.

She told the *Boston Globe* she actually has come "180 degrees" to the point where she actually places greater trust in industry—in major chemical companies—when seeking environmental information than she does in major environmental organizations.[31] The new *Garbage* has included stories defending nuclear power and questioning whether the ozone depletion is a scam or a legitimate crisis. In one article, Poore criticized both the environmental movement and the journalists who cover environmental issues:

It's taken me a while to realize that many writers accept the platform of national environmental organizations as not only infallible but also sacred. I have pulled my punches, so to speak, to avoid alienating the well-meaning people who support environmental causes. . . . I have seen our sources, our writers, our editors, even our advertisers be affected by political correctness. The overwhelming pressure to be pro-environment has resulted in media bias, a distrust of business, and scientists who won't talk because they refuse to be quoted out of context.[32]

Poore believes major environmental groups like Audubon, Greenpeace, and the Sierra Club harbor assumptions she thinks are wrong. One of those assumptions is that most Americans are wasteful. Another is that our quality of life is going downhill; that we're fouling our own nest.

Other assumptions, she wrote, may be found in the standard environmental curriculum that "contains oversimplification and myth, has little historical perspective, is politically oriented, and is strongly weighted toward a traditional environmentalist viewpoint." That viewpoint, she says, emphasizes limits to growth, distrust of technology, misinformation concerning waste management, and gloomy scenarios.[33]

Another environmental magazine is *National Wildlife*. It was a 1993 article in *National Wildlife* on the Exxon *Valdez* spill, in fact, that won the Trudy Farrand/John Strohm Magazine Writing Award for outstanding reporting on conservation. The writer, Rick Steiner, is a biologist and fisherman—not a professional journalist. Still, the magazine wanted a unique voice and found it in Steiner, who proved a very good writer.

Such magazines as these take much more of an advocacy stance on issues, while, at the same time, build their point of view on exhaustive research of the subject.

In commenting on his newfound writing abilities, Steiner echoed Frome's view that important writing comes from the heart. Steiner said, "This was a compelling subject. This was the Exxon *Valdez*. I think many people here could do the same."[34]

Concluding his own views on environmental journalism, Frome says:

The big problem in America is greed. I'm not saying growth and development are evil, but they ought to be recognized for what they are. I've been criticized a lot for my stance. People say, "What you say is all right, but don't you think you're being idealistic?" I say, "I hope so." We need to save the wild to show there's more out there than humankind. But we also have to show that saving the environment is good business.[35]

Another environmental journalist, Kevin Carmody, sees Earth Day 1990 as marking the apex of the "amateur hour" in environmental reporting.[36] He looks at this event and sees a media circus where countless numbers of publications and television news shows rushed to join the bandwagon and get their pieces on recycling and the hazards of ozone depletion published or aired. The problem, Carmody feels, is that journalistic objectivity got trampled in the process.

Columnist John Leo provided an example of Carmody's thesis in a 1993 *U.S. News & World Report* essay entitled, "Spicing up the (Ho-Hum) Truth." He writes:

And now, another announcement from NBC's dynamic and expanding department of apologies. It's about those dead fish from the Clearwater National Forest in Idaho that NBC Nightly News showed on January 4. These powerful pictures were meant to show how clear-cutting by the timber industry fouls streams and kills fish. NBC has now learned that the dead fish weren't from Clearwater and the Clearwater fish weren't dead. They were stunned by forest officials to count them and check their health. Sorry about that.[37]

Leo discounts the idea that this and other such stories have been journalistic lapses. He believes they may signal a disturbing trend in television news and fears it's what news is destined to become as images, story line, and emotional impact begin to erode the traditional commitment to literal truth. Syndicated columnist Richard Reeves believes the "old guard has disappeared from TV news," and the business is now being run by a new breed of people who think of themselves not so much as reporters or producers, but as filmmakers with a commitment to dramatic effect.[38]

Leo likens the Clearwater fish story to the infamous exploding GM pickup truck story, also carried—as well as staged—by NBC on its *Dateline NBC* program. In this story, a GM pickup was rigged to explode on camera at just the right moment to dramatize the potential problem if the truck were hit in its gas tanks.

Some might call this new style of journalism virtual reporting, as opposed to literal reporting. It's as if some journalists believe it is okay to stage or re-create an event or two in order to show what probably would happen on its own if conditions were right. In other words, the essence of the point made is correct; it is just not literally correct. The GM truck did not explode on its own this time without help from NBC.

Is the thrust of environmental reporting moving in a different direction now? Looking at the approach of Earth Day 1995, Carmody said the pendulum in environmental reporting seemed to be swinging in the opposite direction: toward questioning and challenging the extreme views of many environmentalists. He writes:

[A]rticles in The *Economist* and The *New Yorker* took pokes at those environmentalists, as The *Economist* put it, whose "efforts to scare the world over global warming seem not to have worked." The *New Yorker* piece . . . embraced conservation measures, but other journalists are trumpeting the views of a loose network of anti-environmentalist "citizens" groups. While attracting people who genuinely believe American life is over-regulated, many of them are fonts for industrial polluters or have ties to radical-right organizations, including the John Birch Society and antigovernment militias. . . . In newsrooms throughout the country, the hot story is the "high cost of environmental regulation," not the people or resources harmed when that regulation fails.[39]

Timothy Noah, environmental reporter for the *Wall Street Journal*, agrees with Carmody's assessment. He notes that, in 1990, there was too little objective reporting in covering environmental issues. But by 1995, Noah said, "there is a faddish, unthinking knee-jerk reaction in the other direction. The truth is in neither extreme."[40]

Carmody believes that there are still scores of good, objective environmental reporters plying their craft in America. But he also believes that there is a large contingent, led by national news organizations, "whose approach tends to be broad-brush coverage by nonspecialist reporters and general-assignment reporters elsewhere."[41]

Some news media, like the *Los Angeles Times*, ABC News, and the *Chicago Sun-Times*, were adopting the stance in the mid-1990s that Americans were being scared unnecessarily about perceived environmental risks. And the gremlins doing the scaring were the news media, they said. Some journalists, for instance, believe Americans were being scared about relatively minor risks, like pesticide residues on foods, while often not getting the full story on more serious health hazards like alcohol consumption and nutritional risks. The series done by the *Los Angeles Times* called "Are We Scaring Ourselves to Death?" is a classic example of that kind of journalistic soul-searching with regard to environmental reporting.

RECYCLING ENVIRONMENTAL NEWS

Some environmental stories never seem to die, even though decades may pass between episodes of coverage. Then, when these stories do resurface, they are often approached from different perspectives altogether. Two such examples are the United States government's injection of five Americans with plutonium between 1945 and 1947, and the evacuation of Times Beach, Missouri, in 1983 because of dioxin contamination.

It was not until November 1993 that Eileen Welsome, a reporter at the *Albuquerque Tribune*, was able to publish a three-part series detailing the plutonium injections that had occurred almost 50 years earlier as part of the government's pioneering projects in nuclear radiation in the New Mexico deserts. Apparently, the government wanted to know how much bomb-grade plutonium a human body would retain over time. She had seen a footnote on a report while researching another story in 1987, and her six-year journey began to find documentation and amplification on the plutonium story. Welsome's stories joined a growing host of other stories about federal radiation experiments that began appearing in 1976 in special-interest magazines. But outside of a few congressional inquiries and reports, none of the stories generated much media attention. Several reasons for the scant attention have been offered and include the following:[42]

- The media had other big stories to contend with when Congressman Ed Markey's report was released in 1986 detailing government malfeasance and human tragedy. Among them were the upcoming congressional elections, Ronald Reagan's Iceland summit with Mikhail Gorbachev, and the president's approval of an $11.7 billion budget reduction measure.

- Nuclear proponents, according to Markey, did what they could to distort and sap credibility from his committee's 95-page report. They claimed the report was "old news," and a "one-day story," he said.

- The Reagan Administration debunked the Markey report. There was concern that if the story broke big, it would hinder the progress of the government's nuclear arms negotiations with the Soviet Union.

- Markey was known in some circles as a publicity hound.

So it was in 1987 that Welsome stumbled onto her footnote and began the six-year research project on 50-year-old government plutonium injections. Among all the stories done to that point on radiation experiments, it paid off the biggest. It resulted in 44 pages being devoted to the series and, ultimately, a response by Secretary of Energy Hazel O'Leary, who announced a pledge to declassify Department of Energy documents, acknowledge that human radiation experiments had taken place, and promise to "right the wrongs" done to the victims.

The dioxin story was another interesting case of an old story resurfacing and taking on a different spin. In March 1993, *New York Times* reporter Keith Schneider began a five-part series on misdirected policies of the federal government concerning the environment. In it, he reported that billions of dollars are wasted each year in combating ecological problems that are no longer considered that serious.[43] As environmental writer Vicki Monks points out, the front page article cited only one example of such a substance that may not impose such a big risk after all: dioxin.

Dioxin is a chlorine-based chemical which is unintentionally created during the manufacture of paper, herbicides, and other products, including some household cleaners. It can also enter the air in the fly ash from incinerators, and has been found in rivers downstream from some factories.[44]

Until the early 1990s, most stories done on dioxin had portrayed the chemical as health hazardous. Stories about Agent Orange in Vietnam, a defoliant containing dioxin, were done en masse in the years following that war, as veterans began complaining of health problems. In 1982 the Centers for Disease Control found some of the highest levels of dioxin in the town of Times Beach, Missouri. But it took a flood the next year to spread the contamination and force evacuation of the town's 2,000 residents.

Some critics of revisionist ideas regarding dioxin warn that the substance is still dangerous. Monks says the new conclusions are flat wrong:

Many experts in and outside of the federal government say there is no scientific basis for suggesting that dioxin is less dangerous than previously thought. . . . (EPA specialist Dr. William) Farland says the latest research has raised concerns that dioxin may cause immune and reproductive system problems even at the minute levels found in the general population.[45]

Other reporters who attended the same symposium that Schneider did came away with different conclusions about the danger of dioxin. Among those were reporters from *Newsday* and the *Wall Street Journal*. [46]

Schneider told the *American Journalism Review* that, despite some scientists at the symposium challenging his interpretation, he is simply "bucking conventional wisdom," and decried what he sees as a press held captive to environmental groups:

What drives the national environmental groups is not necessarily the truth. Environmental journalists have to regard environmental groups with as much skepticism as we have traditionally regarded polluters. We haven't done enough to to look at the other side of those issues. We haven't done as good a job to find those scientists who are skeptical.[47]

Whichever side is right in the dioxin debate, the case serves to point out some of the different perspectives the passage of time can generate and the difficulty of even finding environmental reporters who agree how best to cover the dangers and rank order the risks to human health.

NOTES

1. R. Jeffrey Smith, "Covering the EPA, or Wake Me Up if Anything Happens," *Columbia Journalism Review* (September/October 1983), pp. 29–34.

2. Ibid.

3. Michael R. Greenberg, David B. Sachsman, Peter M. Sandman, and Kandice L. Salomone, "Risk, Drama and Geography in Coverage of Environmental Risk by Network TV," *Journalism Quarterly* 66(2) (Summer 1989), pp. 267–276.

4. Ibid.

5. Ibid.

6. Ibid.

7. Bill McKibben, "Uncovered: The Changing, Natural World," *Nieman Reports* (Winter 1992), pp. 27–28.

8. Ibid.

9. Joel J. Davis, "The Effects of Message Framing on Response to Environmental Communications," *Journalism and Mass Communication Quarterly* 72(2) (Summer 1995), p. 295.

10. Jerry Walker, "Public Finds Useful Green News on TV," *Boston Globe*, September 28, 1995, p. 3.

11. Robert J. Griffin and Sharon Dunwoody, "Impacts of Information Subsidies and Community Structure on Local Press Coverage of Environmental Contamination," *Journalism and Mass Communication Quarterly* 72(2) (Summer 1995), p. 271.

12. Ibid.

13. Oscar H. Gandy, Jr., *Beyond Agenda-Setting: Information Subsidies and Public Policy* (Norwood, N.J.: Ablex, 1982), p. 61.

14. Griffin and Dunwoody, "Impacts of Information Subsidies," p. 282.

15. John Hohenberg, *The Professional Journalist*, 4th ed. (New York: Holt, Rinehart, and Winston, 1978), pp. 504–505.

16. Ibid.

17. Ibid.

18. Ibid.

19. Ibid.

20. Alston Chase, "Do Environmental Journalists Really Exist?" *Detroit News*, August 31, 1995, p. 8.

21. Ibid.

22. Ibid.

23. Ibid.

24. "Conference Examines Environmental Issues," United Press International, October 26, 1995.

25. Chase, "Do Environmental Journalists Really Exist?"

26. Emily Askari, "Rebuttal: Chase Criticism of Journalists Unfounded," *Detroit News*, October 10, 1995, p. 9.

27. Michael Frome, "Let the Presses Roll—Green!", speech at the University of Memphis, Memphis, Tenn., April 17, 1996.

28. Ibid.

29. Ibid.

30. Charles Kenney, "Trashing Garbage," *Boston Globe*, November 30, 1993, pp. 61, 64.

31. Ibid.

32. Ibid.

33. Ibid.

34. "Oil-Stained Legacy: The Exxon *Valdez* Oil Spill," *National Wildlife* (August-September 1994), p. 37.

35. Ibid.

36. Kevin Carmody, "It's a Jungle Out There," *Columbia Journalism Review* (May 1995), p. 40.

37. John Leo, "Spicing up the (Ho-Hum) Truth," *U.S. News & World Report*, March 8, 1993, p. 24.

38. Ibid.

39. Carmody, "It's a Jungle Out There," p. 40.

40. Ibid.

41. Ibid.

42. Debra D. Durocher, "Radiation Redux," *American Journalism Review* (March 1994), pp. 34–35.

43. Vicki Monks, "See No Evil," *American Journalism Review* (June 1993), pp. 18–20.

44. Ibid.

45. Ibid.

46. Ibid.

47. Ibid.

6

Covering Disasters

Among the stories journalists write that convey the element of risk are ones about various kinds of disasters, both natural and man-made. In the 1990s alone, these stories have ranged in type from the earthquakes which struck Los Angeles and San Francisco, to the bombing of the Alfred P. Murrah Federal Building in Oklahoma City. On an international level, they involve the horror stories from such places as Bosnia and Rwanda.

Disaster stories represent a serious challenge for risk communicators. E. W. Brody notes they are different from the traditional crisis story, because a crisis develops in a relatively predictable fashion and can be described as a decisive turning point in a condition or state of affairs. This condition is often gradual and allows journalists time to acclimate themselves to the story as it unfolds. A disaster, on the other hand, is often that unpredicted, breaking event that triggers a crisis.[1] Disasters can include human error as well as natural disasters, together with disasters secretly planned and carried out by societal deviants. Although the news media can, and should, develop disaster coverage plans, it is impossible to tell when those tragedies will actually occur and in what shape.

WHAT TO LOOK FOR

Michael Killenberg advises journalists covering disasters to concentrate on five distinct stages of reporting:[2]

1. Determining the dimensions of the disaster.
2. Providing the public with safety information and advice from officials.

3. Alerting the public to current and potential dangers.

4. Calming the public by emphasizing positive aspects of the disaster, such as courage and the outpouring of support from others.

5. Assessing the situation as to causes and, if complications that contribute negatively to the crisis arise, determining who is responsible for those complications.

Because of their devastating nature, disasters often require the call-up of special units not normally found at the scene of accidents and other tragedies. Among these are the National Guard, police and sheriff's reserve units, state emergency management agencies, the Federal Emergency Management Agency (FEMA), out-of-town police, fire units and ambulances, the Red Cross, the Salvation Army, civil defense agencies, and other relief organizations such as local churches.

All of these units provide additional manpower, as well as additional sources for the journalist. Most of the personnel from these agencies are allowed closer to the disaster site than reporters often are. Because of the large number of rescue and relief workers, they may work in shifts and rest on the perimeter of the site when not working. These off-duty personnel often take the time to talk to reporters, tell what they've seen and done, and answer questions.

Among the facts reporters should pursue in covering disasters are the following:

• The number and identity of the dead.

• The number and identity of the injured.

• The total number of people affected or in danger because of the disaster.

• The cause of death for those fatally injured.

• The cause of the disaster.

• Eyewitness accounts.

• Property loss to homes, office buildings, businesses, land, and public utilities.

• Rescue and relief operations, including evacuations, rescue of victims, search operations for bodies, acts of heroism, unusual equipment used or unique rescue techniques, number of official personnel and volunteers and where they are from, and names and identities of those interviewed.

• Human-interest stories associated with the disaster and concerning people who may have been directly victimized by the tragedy.

• Acts of looting or rioting.

• Warnings issued by officials from agencies like police and fire departments, health departments, public utility agencies, and so forth.

• Number and type of spectators.

• Investigations, suspects sought, and arrests made.

- Insurance stories of uninsured losses.
- Stories of pending lawsuits relating to the disaster.

Reporters should remember that eyewitnesses may have developed an emotional attachment to the event and people involved, or may have even been traumatized by what they saw. Therefore, journalists should exercise caution in believing everything that is said by witnesses and should try to verify the information provided by these people. Other things being equal, eyewitness accounts offer some of the best documentation available, but they are not always 100 percent accurate. Researchers have often found the testimony of eyewitnesses to be incomplete and wrong.

Some suggestions for interviewing at the scene of disasters are:

- Ask the eyewitness to reconstruct the incident "in general." Ask the witness to describe the scene. This will stimulate recall.
- Tell the witness not to hold back just because he or she thinks the detail isn't important. Report everything.
- Tell the witness to recall the event in a different order. "Now that you have told it from the beginning, start with the most impressive incident, or start at the end."
- Have the witness change perspectives. "Think about the event from the view of others who were there."

A unifying characteristic of all disaster stories is human interest. In many of these stories there is also the continuing element of risk or danger. In the weeks after the bomb exploded at the Alfred P. Murrah Federal Building in Oklahoma City, rescue workers and searchers combing the rubble faced constant danger from huge overhanging concrete slabs swaying in the Oklahoma winds. Reporters should remind readers and viewers of the dangers faced by such rescue workers.

Disaster stories are also action stories and contain a great deal of detail concerning exactly what happened and how it happened. These details must be presented in some sort of logical order—generally chronological—so readers and viewers understand clearly what happened, when it happened, how it happened, and possibly even why it happened.

Additionally, disaster stories offer the writer a greater opportunity for descriptive and innovative writing than most other stories. Even with the visual descriptions supplied by still and video photographers, there is still plenty of description available with words, as shown by the examples in the following section.

THE OKLAHOMA CITY BOMBING

Among recent disasters that could serve as a textbook on the challenges facing journalists in covering tragedies, the bombing of the Alfred P. Murrah Federal Building in 1995 heads the list.

The case of the Oklahoma City bombing provides an example of the kinds of risks associated with disaster coverage.

First, there is the element of risk for the reporters and photographers themselves. On the morning of April 19, 1995, several reporters and photographers arrived at the scene along with—and a few before—the emergency personnel from fire and police departments. As the chaos of the first hour unfolded, photojournalists were making their way through the rubble at the base of the swaying building's carcass. There were even reports that other bombs might still be awaiting detonation in the nine-story building. It was, by all accounts, an unsafe area even after the last of the sections of concrete flooring had fallen. One rescuer, nurse Rebecca Anderson, lost her life when she went back in to assist survivors.

Journalists at the scene faced the same dangers from falling debris and possible unexploded bombs as all others present. It was some time before all non-emergency personnel were removed from the area and yellow police tape went up.

Rescuers at the scene described the area around the building as "organized chaos." An Oklahoma City police officer, Sergeant Jerry Flowers, was one of the first on the scene. He wrote the following about the blast site:

Black smoke was shooting in the air. People, both old and young, were covered with blood. Some were holding towels and clothing articles against their bodies trying to stop the bleeding. Babies and adults were lying on the sidewalk. Some appeared to be dead. . . . Everywhere I looked was blood, misery and pain. I saw a car hood buring in the top of a tree. Debris, rocks, bodies, burned cars, glass, fire, and water covered Fifth Street. A large hole about thirty feet in diameter was where a small circle drive used to be in front of the Murrah Building.[3]

This was the quintessential breaking news story, and it is hard to restrain reporters who are able to arrive on the scene early enough to capture the initial action and drama. Yet reporters must realize the dangers involved and understand that they are not trained to deal with the hazards of these disaster sites. No story is worth a reporter's losing his or her life over.

Second, there are the risks faced by rescuers in the days and weeks to follow. In the case of the Oklahoma City bombing, rescuers faced danger as they continued to climb through the stacks of rubble looking for survivors and/or bodies. It was the job of reporters and photographers to convey these risks realistically, avoiding either underplaying or overplaying them to readers, viewers, and families of those sifting through the rubble for bodies.

One story of the rescuers' risks began as follows:

Searchers in the devastated Oklahoma City federal building played a giant, dangerous game of Jenga Saturday, where pulling out the wrong block could send tons of rubble crashing onto workers below.

"You have to be careful, because all these pieces are connected to each other," Maj. John Long of the Oklahoma City Fire Department said. "You pick up one piece, and something else moves."

It may well have been such an incident that caused a huge concrete slab of flooring to dropslide two stories Friday, endangering workers in the pit below. That dangling threat and others like it suspended work in the central crater area, in which six to eight bodies were found last week.[4]

Journalists covering such events should remain aware that friends and families of these rescuers may be among the readers of these stories. No one is asking the reporter to soft-pedal the dangers faced by these searchers, but overstating them will needlessly worry loved ones.

A third element of risk lies in telling such stories to friends and families of victims of the disaster. In the case of the Oklahoma City bombing, nearly 700 people were injured or lost their lives. That translates geometrically to tens of thousands of family members and close friends who may hang on every word written and spoken about the blast, its victims, and the search-and-rescue efforts.

Reporters can expect to find certain hurdles to story-telling as a result of such considerations. In Oklahoma City, for instance, the nearby First Christian Church served as headquarters for families of the victims. It was a place for them to gather and to hear official word about the progress of the rescue efforts. This was the scene of much emotional agony, and photographers were barred from shooting anything or anyone on the grounds. Reporters were also kept at arm's length from families and were not allowed in the areas reserved for those families.

Back at the blast site, photojournalists had to make many decisions regarding the graphic nature of their shots. Should corpses be covered before photographing them? How far should I intrude into an injured victim's agony? Should I respect the privacy of someone who has just lost a co-worker and friend or depict their grief publicly?

Reporters and photographers are always asked to balance a truthful portrayal of the disaster scene with minimum intrusion on people's grief. In Oklahoma City, that was an especially tough balancing act since so many people were affected by the terrorist blast. Still, this was a story that virtually everyone was intensely interested in, and many journalists who covered it realized the vital service of the media in providing an information conduit to people who truly do want to know.

A fourth type of risk associated with disasters such as Oklahoma City is that of copycat occurrences. Several phone threats were received at other federal facilities around the country after the Oklahoma City attack became front-page news. None of these other threats actually materialized into bombings, but officials nevertheless had to take precautions. Some callers were identified and arrested. Among other burdens journalists bear is the knowledge that the simple telling of a story like the federal building attack will probably give rise to other such threats in other cities. Copycat criminals do exist and often feed off the news reports of the tragic.

Police and other law enforcement officials are concerned when the media provide too much information on how bombs were made, planted, and detonated for fear they may provide a kind of inspiration, as well as instruction manual, for other radical minds. Journalists, on the other hand, must provide details of the crimes they are covering to answer the obvious questions readers and viewers have. Therein often lies one source of conflict between police and the press: how much to tell versus how much to omit in the interest of public safety.

Many journalists believe that news reports constitute the main information lawmakers have to help them construct safeguard legislation. Absent those details, legislators may not know how best to pinpoint or focus future laws to help prevent such attacks.

In covering the Murrah Federal Building bombing, journalists faced many challenges. Ed Kelley, managing editor of the *Daily Oklahoman*, explained that his newspaper found itself educating a large portion of its readers about the nature of terrorism.

The crime took its toll on the city and the state. Most of our readers and readers across the country are not familiar with terrorism. This was not a traffic accident or a post office shooting. This was terrorism. To give you a sense of just how powerful 5,000 pounds of oil fertilizer can be, at 9:02 A.M. we heard what could be called an old-fashioned sonic boom. Our building (eight miles away from the bomb site) shook so hard we thought we had been bombed. It was obvious we needed the help of every staff member. Everyone got a piece of the story including retirees, some of whom volunteered to work for free.[5]

Kelley said the newspaper immediately dispatched as many people as possible to the crime scene. Extensive coverage of the event called for long hours from the *Oklahoman* staff. The staff worked more than 150,000 hours of overtime, and 70 additional pages were produced within one month to tell the story.

The story was deemed too big for the city desk alone, so editors called upon all members of the newspaper team. Each editor was assigned an aspect of the coverage such as crime, damage, casualties, and community and family support. One person alone was assigned the casualty list and, for 28 days, did nothing but obituaries and life profiles.

Some of the paper's best work came from its sportswriters, who according to Kelley, said they knew best how to write about people.

The *Oklahoman* also tested the skills and limitations of its graphic artists. The paper placed a copy editor to act as a liaison between the artists and the editorial side.

The first edition after the blast came the next morning, with an additional 50,000 copies printed. It was not enough. Some paper owners were getting $5 and $10 apiece for copies.

The *Oklahoman*'s extensive coverage catapulted the paper into a world-wide media spotlight. Days two and three were the tough ones for the staff, because they were distracted by the outside world. The paper received calls from television stations in Germany and newspapers in Norway and Sweden, and 22,600 letters from all 50 states, every Canadian province, and eleven other countries. There were also immediate pleas from magazines and the foreign press for the *Oklahoman*'s pictures.

The *Oklahoman* also dealt with the story in a number of unconventional ways. They established Audiotex, a type of information line to give people a place to call and talk about the bombing. Some 130,000 calls were received, with 65,000 coming in the first six weeks after the bombing.

The paper included three regular feature stories, artwork by Oklahoma's children, and the Newspaper in Education Program which allowed teachers to use the paper in helping children deal with the tragedy. In addition, all proceeds from *In Their Name*, a Random House book containing stories and photos by the staff, were donated to the Recovery Oklahoma City Project.

Kelley concluded the following about the staff's work:

I wish a lot of readers who at times are so very critical of our profession could have seen what I did. Powerful, precise stories, photographs and graphics that were written and developed with a collective soul from a group of talented and very caring people. There was no blueprint for what we did. There was no way to measure ourselves. There had never been a disaster like this one before. Hopefully, there never will be again.[6]

But the *Oklahoman* was only one of a score of papers covering the disaster. The bombing also showed what a small daily could do in covering the scene as well. Actually, the first newspaper into print with the story was the *Edmond Evening Sun*, a 10,000-circulation daily in a northern suburb of Oklahoma City, about 10 miles away from the blast site. When the bombing occurred at 9:02 A.M. on Wednesday, April 19, the concussion was so huge that it shook the suspended ceiling in the *Sun*'s newsroom, shaking dust particles loose that came drifting down onto the staff below.

Checking with emergency officials, the *Sun* learned that the Murrah Building had been bombed and moved rapidly into action, dispatching a reporter and photographer to the scene. The *Sun*'s normal pre-noon deadline was extended to allow the paper to convert its entire front page to photographic and textual coverage of the bombing. That afternoon, the readers of the *Sun* got a graphic look at what had happened just a few hours ago.

The bombing and the ensuing search-and-rescue operations became huge news for Edmond, because 21 of the 168 people killed in the blast came from this city. Many other Edmond residents, working or conducting business at the federal building, were injured.

The paper proceeded on three fronts over the next several weeks:

1. Each day, from the bombing to the building's implosion in May, the *Sun* had at least one reporter/photographer on site covering the search-and-rescue phase of the operation and producing daily stories of the attendant events.

2. Each day at least one reporter and photographer interviewed friends and family members of victims living in Edmond, doing grassroots, people-oriented features on how the bombing affected the lives of these people. As extensive as this coverage was, the *Sun* adopted a policy of not covering funerals of the victims unless they were asked or permitted to do so by family members. The paper felt that to do otherwise would have been to invade the privacy of the grieving loved ones.

3. Through the *Sun's* wire services, the paper covered the national manhunt underway for suspects in the bombing, together with the arrests of Timothy McVeigh and Terry Nichols.

The lessons learned by reporters covering the blast and aftermath in downtown Oklahoma City included the following:

1. Small dailies can compete with metro dailies and television in covering disasters if they are staffed by capable people who are not intimidated by the presence of celebrity reporters and well-known daily staff members. Reporters at disaster scenes are not necessarily let in or kept out because of the size of the news operation they represent, except in cases where government officials allow only designated pools of reporters inside the lines.

2. Official press credentials that carry photo identification and the name of the newspaper or television station are imperative at disaster scenes. For breaking events, police and fire officials don't have time to create special, uniform press passes and accept every variety of press credential as long as they carry the name of the reporter, the organization for which he or she works, a photo of that person, his or her signature, and the signature of the editor or news director.

Sometimes, however, during a planned portion of the disaster's aftermath—such as the implosion of the Murrah Building—the government agency in charge will issue a special press pass which must be applied for and worn by all journalists covering the event. Even here, however, the reporter is wise to also carry his or her own personal press pass.

In all cases, it is best to have these passes laminated and worn on a long chain around the neck so officials can quickly identify them at the police lines.

3. In the case of prolonged disaster cleanup or search-and-rescue efforts, officials will undoubtedly establish regular, daily briefings at a designated

place near the site. Heads of various agencies represented in the aftermath operations will use these briefings to explain officially the progress of the operation. Reporters and photographers should plan on attending each of these briefings to receive the latest overall information.

4. Having said this, journalists should realize their best stories may not come from these official briefings but from observations and interviews conducted with the rescue officials at the disaster scene. This is where the human face of the story comes through, and these are the people who are probably feeding the information to their superiors who turn around and filter it to the media at the daily briefings.

Journalists must remember to let these people do their jobs and not interfere. Often, however, in the case of Oklahoma City, firemen coming off a shift on the rubble pile would collapse on a street curb to rest and take questions from any reporter who happened to want to interview them. Some rescue workers seemed to feel a cathartic effect at unloading some of their emotions on reporters.

At other times, rescue officials or relief workers would wander back to the site during their off-hours to see what was happening after taking a few hours to sleep. In these cases, they were eager to talk with reporters to find out how the operation was going.

5. Often there will be informal briefings held at the disaster site by one or two designated officials. In the case of Oklahoma City, these informal briefings were on an ad hoc, but fairly regular, basis and were conducted at the yellow police tape separating the press area known as Satellite City from the blast site. Officials conducting these informative briefings were members of the Oklahoma City Fire Department's Public Education Team, led by the ubiquitous and very helpful Assistant Fire Chief Jon Hansen.

6. Only part of the disaster story concerns itself with what is happening at ground zero. Many stories are waiting for discovery away from the immediate site, and can be uncovered by interviewing business people and store owners in the greater area who are directly affected by the damage done to their buildings as a result of the disaster. Lying in wait are stories of what it was like to be nearby when the disaster struck, what dangers these people faced, what they lost in the process, and how they plan to rebuild their businesses and their lives.

7. Reporters and photographers can, and often do, cooperate with each other in exchanging information and expediting each other's reporting processes. In Oklahoma City, for instance, reporters talked freely among themselves about their different observations and interviews, facts they had gathered, and people they found interesting to interview. Sometimes one television station that had hired a tall crane and elevator cage would make it available to a photographer from another news operation who wanted to give a high, overall shot of the disaster scene.

8. Generally, defying police rules is a mistake at the scene of a disaster.

In Oklahoma City, some reporters and photographers who sneaked across police lines to get closer views of the carnage paid for their derring-do by earning bad reputations among the police and having harder times getting information from these officials in subsequent days. In a few cases, offending members of the press were banned from the scenes altogether.

This advice could be relaxed, however, if rescue officials are being too unreasonable in censoring information, or inaccurate in describing the scene of the disaster, or keeping reporters too far from the action.

9. Look for the opportunity to create and join small pools of reporters and photographers who are led into the ground-zero area by rescue officials for brief periods to get a closer view of the aftermath. This is a much better way of getting closer than risky, freelance ventures that go against the established rules of procedure.

10. Trained observation is extremely important at disaster scenes, and reporters should learn to take as much in as humanly possible. Don't forget, also, to turn around occasionally and look at what is behind you or out of the crowd's line of sight. What you find is often surprising. One wrenching photo from Oklahoma City, for example, showed a team of hard-hat workers peering out of a darkened window of the *Journal Record* Building at the towering hulk of the Murrah Building during an emotional memorial being conducted at its rubble-filled base. The scene would have gone unnoticed if the photographer had not taken his eyes off the main center of attention—the ceremony—and pivoted to see what was happening behind him.

11. Observation should also extend to the minute details often hidden in the nooks and crannies of the disaster scene. The handwritten, get-well notes written by school kids, sent in and posted on the windows of Salvation Army food kiosks; the floral sprays with messages like "Our Prayers are With You," sent in by a neighboring rescue agency; the handpainted sign across the rear windshield of a police cruiser reading, "We Will Never Forget"; the rose protruding from the tripod of a Reuters cameraman at a memorial scene.

These and countless other images await the trained observer and beg to be conveyed to the reader and viewer.

12. Remember that much of the story is about human emotions. Often these types of stories do not lend themselves to traditional story structure and beg for innovative and creative structuring that reflect the personality of the individual reporters and how they are themselves moved by the scene and people involved. Some interesting reporting coming out of Oklahoma City was emotionally charged and told in the second person. As long as the emotions are a true representation of those at the scene—and therefore are factual emotions—then they are appropriate. Emotional overtones are inappropriate when they are add-on, or hyped, emotions. The second-person viewpoint is often a good technique to transport readers to the scene

of the disaster by making them feel they are there with the reporter who is describing it. Reporters should channel the emotions they feel at the scenes of these events and let them flow appropriately through the story.

13. These free-wheeling techniques, coupled with descriptive narrative, can produce a kind of verbal picture that rivals—and certainly amplifies—the visual pictures presented.

The following excerpt from the implosion of the Murrah Building embodies some of these techniques:[7]

Amid an immediate family of much older siblings, the teenager died just after dawn today.

Mortally wounded by assassins' explosives just over a month ago, the Alfred P. Murrah Federal Building was finished off by fewer than 150 pounds of charges that were detonated about 7 A.M.

Some 4,800 pounds were used on April 19 to turn most of the nine-story building into twisted and hollowed-out carnage.

The inanimate giant, which has come to life over the past five weeks, survived that firing squad. But today, it seemed to await a single officer who stepped forward, pulled a pistol and put a bullet in its brain. When the end came, it was swift, sure, and surprising even to those trained observers who had been glued to their vantage points since 5:30 A.M.

The Murrah Building was 18 when it died. Nearby at its death were downtown's more venerable buildings like the *Journal Record*, Downtown YMCA, and the old Southwestern Bell buildings to the north. Under a partly-cloudy sky and with a brisk wind blowing from the south, the explosive charges ignited. The warm spring air was filled with several short, loud reports, and the building was gone within the few seconds predicted by Controlled Demolitions International.

It seemed much quicker, but the operation was surgically precise and was carried out as planned. The sound seemed as fitting a memorial as Oklahoma City has witnessed yet. The several short, curt blasts came within nano-seconds of each other.

They formed a sound strangely similar to a 21-gun salute.

When the smoke had cleared five minutes later, the building had disappeared. It was like watching magician David Copperfield in a television act where he jerks a jetliner or the Statue of Liberty from your conscious view.

But this was no stunt, and the Murrah Building is no more.

Among the many reporters covering the Oklahoma City disaster was NBC's Tom Brokaw. Praising the people of Oklahoma for their alert response to the tragedy and for the great help they provided the rescuers, searchers, and media during the aftermath, Brokaw said journalists had to set aside their personal feelings and cover the story:

The shock and bewilderment gave way instantly to the work to be done. . . . By the morning after the bombing everything but the rescue efforts seemed to have slowed to half-speed. People spoke in low voices or silently greeted each other with spontaneous hugs. Various configurations of ribbons began to appear for the dead, the children, the families.[8]

Brokaw also spoke of the Pulitzer Prize-winning photograph of infant Baylee Almon who lay dying in a rescuer's arms.

Newspapers and magazines around the world had published a photograph taken moments after the explosion. It was a policeman handing a dying baby to a rescue worker. The amateur photographer told me he spent the night in prayer and that he hoped the child's parents wouldn't be upset with him for such a heartbreaking image. The rescue worker . . . said that at the end of his long shift he called his wife to say he was okay and asked to talk to his son. He just wanted to hear his voice. We both had to pause before continuing the interview.[9]

Brokaw's recollections provide an insight into some of the challenges, both physical and emotional, facing journalists who cover the scenes of such devastating disasters.

The face of each disaster changes to reflect the particular incident that has occurred. Still, the guidelines for coverage that came out of the Oklahoma City bombing are universal and can be applied to all disaster reporting.

COVERING AIRLINE DISASTERS

One of the more common types of disasters that reporters are called upon to cover are airline crashes. The loss of lives in just one such disaster can be enormous, and the details are often sketchy on how the accident occurred. The cause of some airline tragedies, like the crash of the U.S. Air flight in Pittsburgh in 1994, were still under investigation in 1997.

Reporters face a special set of challenges in covering airline crashes. To begin with, access to the crash site is extremely limited as reporters are usually kept at a long arm's length from the scene until all bodies have been removed and investigators have a chance to pore through the wreckage for clues. That is a process that can take days or weeks, or even longer.

The explosion and crash of TWA Flight 800 over Long Island Sound in the summer of 1996 is a classic case in point of just how long it can take investigators to literally piece together clues to the cause of the disaster. This nighttime tragedy which killed all 230 passengers and crew aboard brought a bevy of journalists from near and far who were looking for at least some answers by deadline. Absent answers, they were looking for interviews with airline officials and federal investigators, eyewitnesses, friends and family of survivors, search and rescue personnel combing the dark waters off Long Island, or anyone else who might have something to say about the horrors of that night. But with the airplane scattered in small pieces deep beneath the water's surface, there were few facts. In their place was a tremendous amount of speculation and a number of theories for the cause ranging from on-board bombs, to an accident that caused a fuel tank to explode, to the possibility of someone shooting the plane down with a ground-to-air missile. Months after the tragedy, the speculation continued, even after the flight data recorder and cockpit voice recorder were recovered.

With the absence of hard facts, the temptation was always there to go instead with the theories and speculation, as many journalists and their media organizations did. Even though it was understood that these were theories and speculation, the public airing of them over television and in the newspapers sent shudders through the airline flying public, many of whom wondered about the next flights they would be taking.

So, as in the case of all disasters, journalists must engage in calm, accurate reporting. If they don't, they run the risk of adding to the confusion and putting friends and loved ones at needless emotional risk. Trauma runs high at the scene of these tragedies and in the homes of loved ones waiting word on survivors, and journalists must respect this fact and report appropriately.

James Holton, an expert on emergency management, has encouraged reporters to check and recheck information before publishing it or airing it. He says, "Official sources often disagree with one another. They often lack the overall picture. There may not even be an overall picture."[10]

Joseph Scanlon, another expert in emergency response, cautions reporters to be patient.

Rather than harass already over-burdened officials with demands for precise information—how many injured, how many dead, what's the extent of the damage—the media should understand even the best planned response effort will take time to learn precisely what has happened and what needs to be done.[11]

Michael Killenberg advises reporters to be as understanding as possible about the emotional state of survivors and others involved. For example, when the United Airlines plane crash-landed in a Sioux City (Iowa) cornfield in 1989, many survived but 111 perished. Some survivors who fled the burning wreckage felt guilty about the fellow passengers they couldn't help and whom they left in the wreckage. Also, secretaries who had the grim task of typing body-identification tags were so emotionally traumatized that they required assistance from psychologists who were brought to the scene.[12]

Among the items on a reporter's checklist in covering airline accidents are the following:

• Time, location, and official cause of the crash (see later discussion on difficulty of establishing cause quickly).

- Airplane flight number.
- Destination and origin of flight.
- Number and identification of dead and injured.
- Any prominent people aboard.
- Type of aircraft, including its number of engines and the company manufacturing it.
- Condition of the injured.
- Exact cause of death of those killed (often it is smoke inhalation instead of the impact itself).
- Where the dead and injured were taken.
- Weather at the time of crash and general flying conditions.
- Altitude and location where pilot first reported trouble.
- Rate and angle of descent.
- Communications between pilot(s) and tower; last words.
- Number and kind of police, fire, and rescue units at the crash site.
- Amount of preparation evidenced by rescue team(s) and the professionalism in which they conducted themselves.
- Any individual or team acts of heroism in rescuing survivors.
- Possible deaths and destruction on ground resulting from the falling aircraft.
- Coverage area of aircraft's debris.
- Challenges faced in getting to it and the victims.
- Whether the flight recorder was recovered and its shape.
- Comments from the National Transportation Safety Board (NTSB) and Federal Aviation Administration (FAA) investigators.
- Previous crashes involving this type of plane.
- Previous crashes in the same area.
- Funeral and obituary information of deceased.

Some confusion arises among reporters as to who is actually in charge of investigating crash sites. There are two main agencies at work here: the NTSB and the FAA. John Bures, aviation inspector for the FAA, explains.

A lot of media get our two agencies and their jobs confused. Basically, the FAA is a regulatory agency, and the NTSB is the investigating agency that determines probable cause. The government says you can't have an agency that does the regulating also do the investigating, so that's the reason for the division of functions.[13]

In practice, however, Bures noted that the FAA is often asked to help out on investigations, because the NTSB staff is often stretched too thin to handle all the work. In such cases, the FAA inspectors make their reports to the NTSB, and the NTSB is the agency that delivers the official probable cause to the public.

The crash of United Flight 232 in Sioux City illustrates what happens at the scene of an airline crash and how determination of probable cause is made. In that incident, a piece of the plane's center (No. 2) engine came apart, ripping holes in the tail section and severing all hydraulics in the aircraft. Since the DC10 depended solely on hydraulics for controls, the pilot had virtually no traditional control mechanisms left and had to resort to methods that were not in the book to get the plane down. In large measure, he was steering by boosting the power of one wing engine while cutting back on the other. He was controlling the altitude by either boosting or cutting back on both engines at once.

When the plane landed, it was descending at several times the normal rate of descent and was traveling much faster than a plane would on a normal approach. Adding to its problems was the fact that the pilot could not steer to the appropriate runway and had to use a much shorter one not designed for large jets.

The result was a severely hard landing that drove the left wingtip of the plane into the runway's apron. That, in turn, sent the plane into a tumbling motion, ripping apart the fuselage and sending pieces of it into adjacent corn and bean fields. The cockpit itself was driven upside down into the ground.

Although 111 passengers died, the miracle was that more than half of the plane's passengers and crew survived, including both the pilot and co-pilot. Bures credited this to the resourcefulness, skill, and courage of the cockpit crew.

To determine the probable cause of the accident, investigators first recovered the so-called black box, which is actually painted orange, from the plane's tail section. "The black box is installed in the tail section on the theory that no plane ever backed into a mountain," Bures says.[14]

From that flight recorder, investigators began a long journey toward establishing the probable cause of the crash. Along the way, however, the pieces of the plane had to be collected, and the whole plane was virtually reassembled to find out what actually went wrong.

In discussing why the FAA and NTSB are reluctant to make quick calls on probable cause to the media, Bures notes that—on his own flight to the Sioux City scene—he was surrounded on the plane by "pinstriped suits worn by lawyers." Litigation is an immediate concern in airline crashes, and no one wants to make quick, public judgment calls in an environment like that, when his or her words could be used to convince a jury that the airline should or should not pay someone millions of dollars.

The FAA, however, dispatched a memo in 1995 to its top management that directs agents to be as open and cooperative with the news media as possible, Bures said.

EARTHQUAKE STORIES

Like commercial airline accidents, earthquakes are big news. Also like airline crash stories, reporters are dealing in events which convey the possibility of future similar disasters. Survivors of major earthquakes report there is nothing more frightening than feeling the ground below your feet start cracking and moving. There is little that can be done when that happens except hope that the quake ends soon. Inside a building, the terror can be amplified as things above and below start giving way and you are caught in the middle.

California is most vulnerable to earthquakes, and residents have learned to live each year with a series of tremors and minor quakes, praying that none escalates into a major one. But other areas of the country are also susceptible to earthquakes. Not many people realize, for instance, that the lower Mississippi Valley is host to a major fault line. Researchers there have been predicting that a major quake might strike anytime.

While predicting future damaging earthquakes is not easy, indications have shown this area is overdue for a medium-magnitude quake and could be facing a severe one, according to Dr. Arch Johnston, research director for the Center for Earthquake Research and Information at the University of Memphis. In discussing the New Madrid Fault Zone, he says understanding the past helps researchers to make sense of the present and future activity of the zone.

The New Madrid Fault Zone runs north and south in eastern Arkansas, part of the bootheel region of Missouri, and northeast Tennessee. It is named for a series of severe quakes that ravaged the Mississippi Valley area in 1811–1812.

Earthquakes of a magnitude 7 or 8 are considered disastrous, and the nineteenth-century earthquakes in this region reflected these magnitudes. In fact, Johnston has called the most severe 1811 earthquake the greatest continental earthquake in North America.[15]

Not only would the Memphis area sustain considerable damage should such a quake strike again, but many cities in the Midwest and South would also be damaged from a magnitude 7 or 8 earthquake. These could include St. Louis, Nashville, Little Rock, Indianapolis, and even Chicago, Dallas, and Atlanta.[16]

The historic behavior of the zone gives a glimpse of what to expect from the New Madrid Fault. That average behavior pattern shows how active the zone is, because some 50 earthquakes of magnitude 2 are recorded annually along the fault line, Johnston said. From five to ten magnitude 3 quakes occur every year, and magnitude 4 quakes occur every one to two years.

Earthquakes registering magnitude 5 represent the threshold of damaging quakes, and they occur every ten to twelve years along the New Madrid

Zone. The last one, however, was in 1976, and that means the region could be overdue for one of this size. A recent major scare in the region occurred in 1991, but the predicted damaging quake never materialized.

The troublesome statistic is this: a magnitude 6 earthquake occurs every 70 to 90 years, although the last one was in 1895. This was the so-called Missouri Earthquake. Again, the historical pattern shows the region may be overdue for such a damaging quake.

The New Madrid history is unique and doesn't follow the classic single main quake/aftershock sequence. That uniqueness makes its future activity nearly impossible to predict with any degree of accuracy. For instance, between 1811–1812, there was actually a series of quakes, with some aftershocks interspersed. The current activity along the New Madrid Fault could, in fact, be long-delayed aftershocks from those nineteenth-century quakes.

In covering earthquakes, reporters should remember that people usually want to know what happened and what will happen next. Scientists are pretty good at telling what happened and why. But telling people what to expect next is harder to do.

Reporters should also be ready to probe the readiness of the area to withstand future tremors and quakes and to deal with any disasters that do occur. Detail is very important in disaster stories, and most newspapers go to great lengths to cover these tragedies. Dozens of reporters and photographers may be sent to collect as much information as is humanly possible. Usually one or two editors back in the newsroom are assigned the task of assimilating all of the gathered stories and raw facts into some sort of coherent coverage of the disaster.

In the case of the Los Angeles area earthquake of January 17, 1994, the *Los Angeles Times* actually published several special sections over time which looked at every aspect imaginable of the earthquake, from cause, to what the future holds, to how the region put itself back together.

The San Francisco *Chronicle* pulled out all stops in covering the Bay Area earthquake in October 1989. The opening paragraphs of the first-day story by Randy Shilts and Susan Sward contain great detail, and signify great reporting:[17]

A terrifying earthquake ripped through Northern California late yesterday afternoon, killing at least 211, injuring hundreds more, setting buildings ablaze and destroying sections of the Bay Bridge.

The quake was the strongest since the devastation of the great 1906 shock. Yesterday's tremor measured 7.0 on the Richter scale and shook the state from Lake Tahoe to Los Angeles.

The temblor erupted from the treacherous San Andreas fault and was centered in sparsely populated mountains 10 miles north of Santa Cruz.

Late last night, Lt. Gov. Leo McCarthy estimated damage at "well over $1 billion" and predicted, "It will climb much higher in the light of day."

The Los Angeles-area earthquake that struck five years later on January 17, 1994, also drew quick response from the area media as well as national press. The 6.6 quake drew massive coverage from Los Angeles media who had been called upon in the months preceding the quake to cover high-risk events like major rioting and destructive brush fires.

Even though the quake's most devastating damage was focused in the San Fernando Valley where it was centered, virtually all other areas of the Los Angeles basin were hit hard. Freeways collapsed and hundreds of businesses, homes, and other buildings were shaken by the temblor. A week after the quake, some 51 people had been counted among the fatal victims of the earthquake.

Editor & Publisher magazine reported that the Los Angeles *Daily News'* headquarters in Woodland Hills and its Santa Clarita Valley production facility were hit so hard that editorial and production staffs were evacuated from the building. The ceiling caved in on the newsroom, and power went out. For the first-day story, editor Robert Burdick and his staff set up an emergency newsroom at the *Santa Monica Outlook* and printing was done at the *Torrance Daily Breeze*, both Copley, Los Angeles newspapers.[18]

By the second night, the news staff had moved to the *Pasadena Star-News* and published out of the West Covina plant of the San Gabriel Valley Tribune Inc. By January 19, the Woodland Hills facility was declared safe by inspectors, and operations resumed there under a newsroom banner that read "Home Sweet Home."[19]

The *Daily News* responded to the earthquake with a twelve-page, ad-free special edition the first day, nine pages the second, and 30 the third day. Single copies were a sellout, and bundles of papers were dropped off free at shelters for displaced residents.[20]

Among the hurdles to coverage during the hours immediately following the quake were power outages. Computers went dead, and phone lines could not handle all the traffic coming across them. So for several hours, the *Los Angeles Times* staff worked out of the plant's parking lot, using cellular phones.

Altogether, the *Times* drew upon the resources of 120 reporters, editors, and photographers for the story. Like many other newspapers, the *Times* has an emergency plan on paper. But metro editor Leo Wolinsky said, "When it comes down to dealing with a disaster, you use your wits and fly by the seat of your pants. Plans are not predictable."[21]

Drawing upon its own planning, the Los Angeles Bureau of the Associated Press had rented downtown offices in building owned by ARCO, which contains a huge backup generator. The power outage affected it for only a short time, and the AP quickly had the power it needed. A key aid was AP's direct phone line to the wire service's New York headquarters, where the first-day story was assembled.

The AP also brought in extra reporters and photographers from Chicago,

Boston, and other cities. A year later, when the Oklahoma City bombing occurred, the AP bureau there also imported reporters and editors from other cities.

Editors of smaller metro and suburban newspapers also reported high energy levels and many hours of overtime among their news staffs. There was much to be covered in these residential areas, and residents hung on every word they could hear or read about the earthquake and the cleanup efforts.

Spot news photography is vital in chronicling disasters, and Agence France-Presse (AFP) Los Angeles staffer Carlos Schiebeck, awakened by the quake in his south Los Angeles home, responded as many other photographers did. He says, "I had Washington on the phone before the quake stopped shaking. I knew right away this was a big one."[22]

AFP's deputy director, Jonathan Utz, began alerting staff photographers from around the country to head for the city to assist in coverage. As the magnitude of the damage was realized, AFP's Bob Pearson was called in from Miami to assist in coordination and coverage. With power out at AFP's bureau in downtown Los Angeles, a few staff set up a transmission center at one of their homes in the San Fernando area. Schiebeck shot aerials of damaged buildings and collapsed highways from a helicopter while his partner, Hal Garb, shot the damage from the ground.

Other AFP photographers were summoned and were positioned at other strategic sites to shoot the hardest hit areas of Northridge and Granada Hills. Special attention was given the Northridge Meadows Apartments and to area parks and community centers where thousands of people, fearful that another quake would trap them in their homes, were setting up camp outside.[23]

The second day of the quake's aftermath found victims trying to get back into their property and into their routines. The AFP staff hit the streets and airways again, just as they did for the remaining days of the coverage.

SEVERE STORMS

The United States has more natural weather disasters than any other country in the world. Conditions are more favorable in the United States for natural weather disasters. Because of this, the National Weather Service (NWS) uses the National Oceanic Atmospheric Administration (NOAA) Weather Radio Network to disseminate quick and reliable weather warnings to the public. The weather service also relies heavily on mass media for disseminating weather warnings.

"Without the news media, we would not be able to get information out to the host of people who need to know what risks to expect," says Ric Coleman, former area manager for the National Weather Service operations in Tennessee.[24]

A great innovation for the NWS in predicting the track of severe storms is doppler radar. Doppler radar is capable of picking up and registering moisture, dust particles, and winds within 20 miles of the antennae. By using radars across the area, meteorologists are able to have a good feel of what the winds are doing. This is extremely important if there is a grass fire—or even just a building fire—in the area of high winds. The weather becomes a key factor in working other accidents and disasters as well, such as the Murrah Building bombing in Oklahoma City. Much of the danger faced by rescuers working the rubble below the heavily damaged building was caused by the nine-story building's swaying in steep Oklahoma winds. Video cameras were mounted across the street and big orange dots were painted on the remaining building columns to show how much the building was swaying and when workers should be evacuated.

Every weather situation, however, may not show up on radar, and journalists need to be aware and prepared for unexpected outbreaks of severe storms. Some smaller, yet potent, storms may just sneak through the radar.

Coleman encourages journalists to carry a small NOAA radar with them on the job if they are in the business of reporting on severe storms. The NOAA radar is a link to the weather station 24 hours a day. If severe weather occurs, an alarm will sound.

In areas of repeated outbreaks of severe storms, trained weather reporting becomes even more important. The so-called Tornado Alley corridor through Texas, Oklahoma, Kansas, and Arkansas is fraught with the possibility of spring and summer tornadoes. Similar winter twisters occur in Tennessee, Mississippi, and Alabama. Reporters in all news media in these states could tell many stories about chasing twisters or, in some cases, being chased by them. Other areas, such as the Gulf Coast and eastern Florida—as well as the coastline of the Mid-Atlantic states—face the ubiquitous hurricanes that form at sea and move in menacingly close at times, several times a year. Some of them make landfall and do tremendous amounts of damage, as in the case of the Homestead (Florida), hurricane several years ago and others approaching its severity since then.

Agencies responding to such disasters include FEMA, the Red Cross, the Salvation Army, the National Guard, and local police and fire departments. Command centers are always set up to deal with the aftermath of these storms, and they serve as the locus of activity for many journalists covering the events.

As always, journalists need to be mindful that they don't hamper rescue and relief efforts in the course of their coverage.

HAZARDOUS WASTE SPILLS

Every city or town in the United States with an interstate highway or rail lines passing through faces the possibility of hazardous waste spills following wrecks of carriers. Some cities are ground transportation hubs because of their strategic location. In the case of Memphis, for instance, the city has the only rail bridge spanning the Mississippi River for many miles up or down river. A lot of cargo passes through these cities, and some of it is hazardous.

"People sometimes don't realize the potential for accidents in this area," says Charles Bryant, regional director of the Tennessee Emergency Management Association (TEMA). "In West Tennessee alone, nine of the 21 counties have 131-plus miles of interstate and one out of every ten trucks carries hazardous materials."[25]

Bryant said that TEMA probably fields more calls than most other state emergency management agencies, but that all are kept hopping with calls of real or potential disasters. He pointed to the first eight months of 1995 when TEMA's headquarters at Nashville responded to 837 weather missions, 32 search-and-rescue operations, several hazardous materials missions, four calls about earthquakes, and 8,610 general assistance calls.

For most cities, the most common type of major accident is the hazardous chemical spill. In 1994 alone, for instance, TEMA responded to 76 accidents in West Tennessee involving hazardous materials; 49 of those released hazardous materials into the air. Altogether in that year, some 914 different companies and other facilities reported they were transporting hazardous materials across the state.

Tennessee is similar to other states in its resources to handle such accidents. For example, in West Tennessee alone, four local governments have hazardous materials response teams, and one private company has one. One of the functions of TEMA is to train individuals who respond to emergencies, and several clinics are held for this and other purposes.

In one accident involving a hazardous chemical spill, a train derailed and sent dangerous gasses spewing into the air. Before the cleanup was over, eight firefighters and one television camerman were killed.

"Sometimes the media is going to be at the site long before we are," Bryant says. "That is why it is important they have some idea of the potential danger existing there."[26]

To help the media better understand this potential, state emergency management agencies hold workshops on disasters and the media to clarify the conditions facing reporters and photographers who might be covering them. For example, regarding chemical spills, it is important that all observers be kept at a long arm's length from the crash site until the dangerous fumes are capped.

When an accident does occur, TEMA and other state emergency management agencies stage similar responses. An Incident Command System swings into action, and the incident commander is often the first TEMA official on the scene and is responsible for supervising rescue and cleanup operations, planning, logistics, and finance. To deal with reporters better,

the incident commander will often appoint a public information officer or
handle that task himself or herself, depending on the extent of the disaster.

In larger disasters, an emergency management agency will set up an entire
Emergency Operations Center (EOC) instead of designating just one individual to supervise the operations. Part of that EOC is a Joint Information
Center where all the public information officers from the different operating
groups and rescue agencies come together to talk to the media.

It is from these Joint Information Center briefings, similar to the daily
ones held in Oklahoma City during the bombing aftermath, that most official information will emanate. When possible, these briefings will be held
at the scene where most of the reporters are.

A GUIDE TO MEDIA DISASTER PLANS

Like all other major companies, the news media should develop a disaster
plan in the event that a tragedy like the ones described in this chapter befall
the market area. While there is no way of knowing what kind of disaster
might strike (except in areas with a strong storm or earthquake history) or
when such a tragedy will occur, the news media can enhance their readiness
to deal with such events.

The Disaster Audit is the tool used to create such a state of readiness. It
is simply a probe into potential disaster situations which can affect the area.
Often it is based on educated guesswork, but the record of history is also
available to tell which kinds of disasters are most likely. The guesswork is
a deliberate process of anticipating all possible disasters that could occur
in the market area. The process of worst-case planning takes place when
managers draw up a list of all possible disasters and work up a disaster
plan to respond to them.[27]

Even with all the brainstorming a company might do, however, it may
take the actual occurrence of a specific disaster before the organization will
give such an event serious thought. So it is important for organizations to
monitor the disasters affecting other news media and other cities. As Lloyd
Newman states, "The challenge is in training executives to think the un-
thinkable."[28]

Once a media organization comes up with potential catastrophes that
could strike the area, planners must do three things: (1) develop disaster
management plans; (2) put those plans through trial runs; and (3) challenge
and update those plans as conditions warrant.

Disaster plans, also called emergency response plans, should include detailed instructions regarding who in the organization does what, both in
immediately responding to the disaster and when the initial response winds
down. Often, follow-up communication is required as in the case of employees who may be suffering emotionally from the disaster's effects. Such
was the case in Oklahoma City, where numerous reporters received coun-

seling for emotional trauma resulting from the search-and-rescue portion of the federal building bombing.

Many governmental agencies such as FEMA, as well as any private businesses that can expect media attention during disasters, realize the most important thing company spokespersons can do is to be available to the news media for interviewing about progress in the aftermath of the disaster. A splendid example of a public affairs officer who was always available, night or day, is Assistant Fire Chief Jon Hansen of the Oklahoma City Fire Department during the aftermath of the federal building bombing. More than any other individual, Hansen facilitated the telling of the bombing story accurately and speedily. His availability, responsiveness, and courteousness won him the respect of worldwide journalists covering the disaster, and created an immensely positive image for the Oklahoma City Fire Department.

Whether or not journalists have the kind of sources that Hansen represents, they are still required to get to the bottom of the incident they are covering. In the case of disasters, that is not always easy on deadline, given the volatile nature of the circumstances and the threat to human life that still may exist. The journalists who understand what happens at the scene of such crises, and who deal sensitively with the people involved, are those who will be most successful in their reporting.

NOTES

1. E. W. Brody, *Managing Communication Processes* (New York: Praeger, 1991), p. 4.

2. George M. Killenberg, *Public Affairs Reporting* (New York: St. Martin's Press, 1992), p. 198.

3. *In Their Name: Oklahoma City. The Official Commemorative Volume* (New York: Random House, 1995), pp. 34–35.

4. Jim Willis, "Concrete Slab Threatens Workers," *Edmond Evening Sun*, April 26, 1995, p. A1.

5. Ed Kelley, comments to the seminar "Understanding and Reporting the Disaster Scene," November 8, 1995, University of Memphis, Memphis, Tenn.

6. Ibid.

7. Jim Willis, "Blast Fells Murrah Building," *Edmond Evening Sun*, May 12, 1995, p. A1.

8. *In Their Name*, pp. 104–105.

9. Ibid.

10. Killenberg, *Public Affairs Reporting*, p. 199.

11. Ibid.

12. Ibid.

13. John Bures, comments to the seminar "Understanding and Reporting the Disaster Scene," November 8, 1995, University of Memphis, Memphis, Tenn.

14. Ibid.

15. Arch Johnston, comments to the seminar "Understanding and Reporting the Disaster Scene," November 8, 1995, University of Memphis, Memphis, Tenn.

16. Ibid.

17. Randy Shilts and Susan Sward, "Hundreds Dead in Huge Quake; Oakland Freeway Collapses; Bay Bridge Fails," *San Francisco Chronicle*, October 16, 1989.

18. M. L. Stein, "Covering Another California Disaster," *Editor & Publisher*, January 19, 1994, p. 11.

19. Ibid.

20. Ibid.

21. Ibid.

22. Bob Pearson, "AFP Mobilizes Staffers to Cover Quake," *News Photographer*, June 1994, p. 19.

23. Ibid.

24. Ric Coleman, comments to the seminar "Understanding and Reporting the Disaster Scene," November 8, 1995, University of Memphis, Memphis Tenn.

25. Charles Bryant, comments to the seminar "Understanding and Reporting the Disaster Scene," November 8, 1995, University of Memphis, Memphis, Tenn.

26. Ibid.

27. Deborah J. Walton, *A Study of Components and Variables Comprising Corporate Crisis Communication Plans*, unpublished Master's Thesis, University of Memphis, 1993, p. 3.

28. Ibid.

7

The Influence of TV, Movies, and the Internet on Health Perceptions

Television and films set the public's perceptions about many issues in American life. Among these perceptions are health risks associated with everything from sexual intimacy, to alcohol, tobacco and drugs, to the level of violence in society, to various types of illnesses, to perceptions about physician competency.

If the agenda of the news media is to seek out and portray, as close to the truth as possible, the health risks society faces, the agenda of the entertainment media is to dramatize these risks as much as possible for maximum viewer effect. In so doing, many of the the depictions of these risks on TV and in the movies become slightly or greatly exaggerated. The depictions wind up becoming part of the landscape of public perception about health risks. This chapter will look at just a few of the portrayals that television and film producers offer the American public, and the impact that some of these depictions have on sectors of the public.

THE PERCEPTION OF PHYSICIANS ON TV

Baby-boomers readily remember when doctors became stars on television. Like law enforcement agents, it happened in the early years of the medium as the public became captivated by the doings of *Medic*, young *Dr. Kildare*, *Ben Casey*, and, later, *Marcus Welby*. If the first three images were ones of dash and daring, then the fourth was one of the good family doctor as we would like to remember him. There were few female physicians seen on television, and even fewer bad doctors. America was in love with the good doctors.

Compare these images to the ones conjured up on the television landscape in shows like *Chicago Hope*, *E.R.*, *Picket Fences*, and earlier shows like *St. Elsewhere*. While physicians still win the day, they are often female and often have to fight through a bevy of personal problems, some difficult doctors who may not have the right attitudes or necessary skills, and a lot of personal questions about whether a procedure was done correctly. A classic example of this kind of medical show was the long-running *M*A*S*H*, which featured the bumbling, problematic Frank Burns.

Reflecting some of this updated imaging was a study published in 1995 by Michael Pfau, Lawrence J. Mullen, and Kirsten Garrow. The content analysis looked at the influence of television viewing on the public perceptions of physicians. Specifically, the study looked at the manner in which prime-time network television programming depicts physicians and the medical profession in general. It also studied the influence of these images on public perceptions. Briefly, the results seemed to indicate that network prime-time TV programming depicts physicians as more likely to be female and young, and as more imbued with interpersonal communication style, physical attractiveness, and power, but less imbued with character traits. These are also the features described by heavy prime-time viewers when asked how they perceive physicians.[1]

Historically, studies of media depictions of doctors have shown them to be "consistently positive, offering an idealized view of physicians contributing to a cultural predisposition to hold the entire medical profession in . . . awe."[2] Some studies found TV doctors to exhibit power, authority, and knowledge, and to be more fair, sociable and warmer than other professionals.[3]

A 1984 study found these images contributed to a generally positive public perception of doctors. In fact, approval ratings of physicians have consistently run at or above 80 percent, according to the Center for Health Services Research and Development.[4]

But the 1995 study indicated that some of these more positive images have diminished in the 1990s. About this possibility, the researchers note: "here is the possibility that network television's depictions of physicians have changed for the worse, and that these less flattering images may exert an influence on public perceptions of physicians just as the nation begins to focus its attention on the adequacy of the health care system."[5]

In discussing their findings, researchers concluded that:

- Television's depictions of doctors clearly influence public perceptions, and these depictions, and thus perceptions, are often negative. While so-called "frontstage behaviors" were positive (at worst, benign) on television, the "back regions" are also exposed by the medium, revealing occasional uncertainties in diagnosis and mistakes in treatment, as well as exposing "unflattering personal traits including adultery, arrogance, and avarice."
- Some researchers suggest that this backstage imaging undermines trust by the public in the medical community.

- Compared with physician perceptions of the profession, TV depicts doctors—and the public buys the image—as more powerful, imbued with higher salaries, status, and strength.

- TV also depicts physicians as lower in character, meaning less moral, right, unselfish, good, and honest.

- The present images stand in stark contrast to past imaging of physicians, once portrayed as "super-doctors," who were role models for young people. Past programs also generally ignored issues about the political economy of modern medicine and related concerns over who pays for, and who benefits from, medical care.

- Some researchers maintain that trust underlies the medical practice. Given this, the current TV imaging of doctors could harm the profession and the relationship of patients to doctors.

This last conclusion could have been drawn from a policy perspective in *JAMA* (the *Journal of the American Medical Association*) in 1995. Entitled the "Patient-Physician Covenant" and signed by eight medical doctors, it states in part:

Medicine is, at its center, a moral enterprise grounded in a covenant of *trust*. This covenant obliges physicians to be competent and to use their competence in the patient's best interests. . . . Today, this covenant of trust is significantly threatened. From within, there is growing legitimation of the physician's materialistic self-interest; from without, for-profit forces press the physician into the role of commercial agent to enhance the profitability of health care organizations . . . medicine is a special kind of human activity—one that cannot be pursued effectively without the virtues of humility, honesty, intellectual integrity, compassion, and effacement of excessive self-interest. . . . Our first obligation must be to serve the good of those persons who seek our help and trust us to provide it. . . . Thus we honor our covenant of trust with patients.[6]

Other analysts surveying the television physician scene have discovered that current medical shows do deal to some extent with changes in the medical field. Among them are the prevalence of health maintenance organizations, the existence of hospital review committees, and the dominant role of insurance companies. These changes, however, are often at odds with, and therefore subservient to, the major "doctor-show formula" that features young, good-looking doctors pulling patients through medical and/or personal catastrophes.[7]

Nancy Signorielli has noted the major discrepency between how accessible physicians and nurses are to patients in TV shows as compared to the ratio in real life. She observes:

These studies consistently show that the world of television has a large number of doctors and nurses even though characters are seldom physically ill on television, and mental illness is often used as a way to justify violence and killing. A special analysis . . . revealed that between 1973 and 1985 among the major characters there were 103 doctors, 13 psychiatrists, and 28 nurses for 228 physically ill and 88 mentally ill characters. This is a ratio of one doctor for amost every two patients, one psychiatrist for every seven mentally ill patients, and one nurse for every eight physically ill patients . . . in the world of network prime-time dramatic programming there is roughly 1 doctor for every 30 characters.[8]

In contrast to these television depictions, the real figures showed that in 1990 there were 198 patient care physicians for every 100,000 people, or 1 doctor for every 500 people, and 1 nurse for every 150 people.[9]

In contrast to the Pfau study, Signorielli finds other literature showing about 9 out of 10 television doctors are male as opposed to female. They are also white, and young or middle-aged.

When daytime serials are taken into account, an even starker contrast is shown between the ratio of real-life doctors and patients with television's version of the scenario. One study showed some 68 percent of all professionals depicted on daytime TV are in the field of medicine, and another found that about 80 percent of all the male characters are doctors. As far as women doctors are concerned, there are plenty of them in the soaps and they are seen as strong and long-suffering characters "whose professional sacrifices are often at the expense of personal happiness." Signorielli concludes:

Overall the media present a very troublesome image of the medical world. The image of the physician is dominated by traditionally masculine traits, even if the doctor happens to be a female. Nursing, on the other hand, is dominated by traditionally feminine traits and practically every nurse is a woman. . . . Physicians are glorified, the all-important healers who need very little help from others. Nurses are helpers with very little autonomy. . . . The dominant media images . . . thus do little to provide adquate and useful information about what to expect from the medical profession.[10]

TELEVISION NEWS AND MEDICINE

Not all depictions of the medical community and medicine come from the entertainment arm of broadcasting. Many come on a regular basis via television medical news reporting. Done both at the local and network levels, medical reporting has been called a "tight fit for the television screen."[11] The reason? While the medium reaches more people than any other, it is in many ways the least capable of covering the bulky health care story adequately. Still, viewers repeatedly cite medicine as one of their favorite subjects on television newscasts when they respond to viewership surveys. In the world of television news, health sells. David Howell, news director at KTSP-TV in Phoenix, said in 1992, "health stories are very promotable, particularly one that reaches a broad audience."[12]

The problem is that the complexities of medical news and the exigencies of the scientific method do not lend themselves to the traditional brief treatment of television news stories. Also, given television's need for visuals and the fact that many health stories don't offer good video, some important stories never get aired or get aired as readers. Also, an illness or medical procedure has to be among the "hot" categories to warrant much time on the air.

Adding to the problem of converting medical stories to the television format is the need to have doctors reduce their terminology to sound-bite proportions. This leaves the door open for those physicians who are articulate and can craft short nuggets for the microphone, but who may not be the most skilled physicians. "If you give a cliché, you know it can be quoted," says Dr. Joseph Painter, former American Medical Association (AMA) president and vice president for health policy at the University of Texas M.D. Anderson Cancer Center. "I think our emphasis on bites leaves a lot to be desired in the sense of really communicating to the public."

CBS Evening News medical correspondent Edie Magnus tells of another problem TV medical reporters face: discerning among hype, self-interest, and legitimate news. Sometimes, she says, it's best not to do a story at all, citing a press conference in 1992 by the Physicians Committee for Responsible Medicine, a group promoting vegetarianism. At the press conference, which featured pediatrician Benjamin Spock, leaders of the committee spoke about the dangers of eating and drinking dairy products. "Here is a group with a particular axe to grind, dedicated to taking meat and cheese out of the American diet, telling us that a staple of the American diet is bad," she says. "Do we do a story that leads with all of these charges that undoubtedly are going to be very unsettling?"[13]

One former television medical correspondent with CNN, Gary J. Schwitzer, discusses other problems in television health reporting:

I wanted to be at the forefront in predicting and reporting trends in health care. It was clear that the incentives in television news were going in the other direction. On any given day, if you didn't have the same story reported in the same way as everybody else, you were actually called into question: "Why didn't you have what USA Today had in three inches on the front of their lifestyle section? Don't tell us you've got this innovative report. Don't tell us about that investigative story."[14]

Nevertheless, some stations—and all television networks—have added physicians to their reporting staffs. Some see this as a plus, just as most sports commentators today are former professional athletes themselves. They understand medicine better than a layman would. Others, however, see problems associated with the practice. Professional journalists say they may not know medicine as well, but they do know how to find the information better than doctors do. And when they access it, they know how to put it together better. The television doctors often must rely much more on producers and writers than do professional journalists.

TELEVISION'S PORTRAYAL OF ALCOHOL USE

As is the case of television's portrayal of doctors, the medium's portrayal of such medical issues as alcohol abuse results in particular beliefs by the viewing public about that use. A report prepared by Janet Bridges, Christine Price, and Terri Breaux studied health belief messages about alcohol consumption in network television entertainment programs.[15] In it, the researchers noted that the social costs of alcoholism in America are more than $116 billion annually, and alcoholism, the country's third most serious health problem, impacts about one-fourth of all homes in America. The report explains, "Entertainment television, an integral part of most individuals' environments, can provide subtle messages about appropriate behavior and consequences of behavior in terms of beliefs about the effects of alcohol."[16]

This research complements similar studies which note that:

- A child will watch someone take a drink on TV an average of 100,000 times by the time he or she turns 18. Some characters in late prime-time programs will take a drink on the average of once every 20 minutes.[17]

- National Opinion Research Center data on whether an individual uses alcohol are modestly and negatively correlated with television use. However, controlling for sex, age, education, income, and race makes the relationship positive and statistically significant.[18]

- A study of adolescents concludes that drinking on popular television programs was done by the "good guys," sending a message to teenagers that drinking is a desirable behavior.[19]

- One study found only four negative, long-term consequences of drinking over a 120-hour period of one year's prime-time television programs.[20]

- A report by the National Institute of Mental Health (NIMH) found alcohol use during evening hours of television averages 1 ½ incidents per program, and increases to three drinking acts per program in later prime time.[21]

- While studies on daytime serials found more women than men characters to be problems drinkers, studies of prime-time programs find more men to be problem drinkers.[22]

- The NIMH study found that almost half (48 percent) of the women starring in adventure and/or crime programs are drinkers.[23]

Overall, while research indicates there are no direct links between drinking behavior depicted on television and drinking in real life, it does suggest that television offers an "indirect learning environment for heavy viewers, who tend to perceive life and the world more like the world as shown on television than like real life itself.[24]

Nevertheless, there is some support for a connection between television use and belief formation, and between beliefs and the formation of intentions to perform certain behaviors.[25]

The Bridges study, published in 1995, analyzed the drinking behavior depicted on 56 half-hours of prime-time continuing programs and 47 half-hours of daytime serials. It concluded the following:

- The most frequently depicted health belief about alcohol in the programs was that alcohol affects social enhancement.

- The second most frequent message was that alcohol use is associated with relaxation.

- The third association connected alcohol use with assertiveness.

- No significant differences between daytime serials and prime-time programs surfaced on the association of social enhancement and assertiveness with alcohol use, although there were more messages sent on both linking alcohol with relaxation.

- Evening programs more often associated alcohol with aggression than daytime programming did.

- Other associations, depicted equally on day and evening programming, connected alcohol use with the following: affective change of behavior, sexual enhancement, dependence, carelessness, and cognitive impairment.

- Since depictions show alcohol increases a person's social enhancement, the implication is that alcohol is desirable.

- The frequent association of alcohol with both relaxation and assertiveness sends a message that alcohol can be used as a tool or a cure-all for stress and/or other problems.

- Researchers believe the suggestion that alcohol can cure like an aspirin or that a drink can give someone courage or self-confidence sends a dangerous message.

- The messages about alcohol affecting change say basically that alcohol can be used to change a mental situation or mood.

Apart from actual programming on television, many messages are being sent about alcohol use in the commercials between the programs. In fact, at certain times of the week, there are many more associations depicted in the commercials than in the programs themselves. A classic example is Saturday and Sunday afternoon sports programming. Here, large segments of the games are sponsored by brewery companies who tout beer drinking as a way to gain friends and enhance male bonding. In short, the messages seem to indicate, if you're going to have fun you're going to have to drink beer. Further, they imply if you're going to be serious about sports, you will probably enjoy drinking.

The fact that these commercials are also so entertaining to watch and sometimes produce such a comedic effect does even more to lure viewers into their not-so-subtle messages about the benefits of drinking. Critics note that sending this message out to adults is one thing, that adults should be able to think for themselves about the merits and demerits of drinking. The problem is that much of the viewership of Saturday and Sunday sports programming consists of children and adolescents who don't have the same base of experiences to evaluate the drinking associations shown. Weekend sports commercials are thus a way of reaching the younger-age audience with dangerous messages about drinking. With all of the attention the federal government is paying to the impact of television on children, this seems to be an area that is vastly overlooked, possibly because there are so many profits generated from this type of sports advertising and the lobby is just too powerful. Television sports programming is also a fairly rare type of daytime programming because it draws good viewership from both adults and children, and it may not be easy finding advertisers that wish to target both demographics. In any event, not much is being done about restricting these messages about beer drinking.

THE MEDIA AND TOBACCO

One of the longest running controversies in the media has been the depiction, especially by way of advertising, of tobacco use. Advertising tobacco products on television and radio has long been banned by the federal government. Also, in 1985, the American Medical Association passed a resolution encouraging the government to install a *complete* ban on the advertising of tobacco products. This urging exacerbated an already intense debate between health professionals and consumer groups on one side and the tobacco and advertising industries on the other. Among the questions debated were (1) would such a ban be constitutional, given the broad freedom of speech powers granted the media in this country, and (2) would such a ban really lead to decreased use of tobacco products.

Reports in the media indicated that the advertising industry was united in opposing a complete ban on the advertising of tobacco. Still, as researchers John H. Crowley and James Pokrywczynski discovered, "most of the published opinions came from the leaders of advertising's major trade associations, people whose instincts are honed to oppose any kind of government intervention."[26]

To find out how advertising practitioners felt about the issue of banning tobacco advertising, Crowley and Pokrywczynski surveyed advertising professionals in Milwaukee and Minneapolis. The survey results found no clear support either for or against a total ban on tobacco advertising. However, the survey did find that smokers are "somewhat more resistant than non-smokers to the idea of a ban but that advertising specialists have not been especially swayed by trade publications' strong resistance to a ban."[27] The researchers concluded, "Most believed, contrary to the tobacco industry position, that advertising entices young people to smoke. These specialists report their views shaped as much by the general press as by the specialized trade press."[28]

Industry and government leaders have been more certain about the pros and cons of the proposed ban. A former president of the American Advertising Foundation, Howard Bell, said such a ban would "fail to meet the constitutional requirements that government must meet before banning truthful commercial speech."[29] Leonard Matthews, former president of the American Association of Advertising Agencies, has noted, "This ad ban is an attempt to control people's behavior by limiting their knowledge. It's censorship, pure and simple."[30] Matthews has also gone on record as opposing the belief that an advertising ban would diminish the amount of smoking in America.[31]

On the other side of the issue, people like former U.S. Surgeon General C. Everett Koop told congressional hearings, "Advertising constantly and deliberately recruits new smokers among youngsters and encourages established smokers to puff more."[32]

The print media, newspapers and magazines, derive a healthy share of advertising revenues from advertising products that are essentially unhealthy and which carry package labels so stating that fact. Yet some tobacco advertising appears by many critics to be targeted to youths and seems geared to the premise of increasing smoking in society. Despite tobacco industry denials of both these claims, the federal government under the Clinton administration took steps to limit the amount of advertising targeted to young users and would-be users. On August 23, 1996, President Bill Clinton unveiled a list of restrictions on tobacco advertising and sales to adolescents, and called cigarette smoking the most significant public health hazard facing Americans. Clinton authorized the Food and Drug Administration to curb the industry's access to youngsters through "advertising that hooks children on a product."[33]

The rules would restrict the distribution of cigarettes and smokeless tobacco based on their classification as devices that deliver the drug nicotine. The tobacco industry filed suit in 1995 in a federal court to block the plan, soon after the FDA first proposed regulating tobacco products. Health and Human Services Secretary Donna Shalala said she expected the tobacco and advertising industries to file additional lawsuits to seek to stop or modify the August 1996 regulations. Shalala and Clinton stressed that they were not interfering with the rights of smokers who are old enough to buy tobacco products.

The new regulations impressed the AMA. Lonnie Bristow, president of that organization, said, "What we saw today was every bit as important as when Jonas Salk stepped out and said he had found a safe [polio] vaccine."[34]

The Clinton rules included requiring young people to show proof of age before buying cigarettes; banning most vending machine sales; limiting tobacco company sponsorship of sporting events; eliminating cigarette logos on baseball caps, T-shirts, and other merchandise, and restricting nearly all tobacco advertisements, including billboards, to simple black-and-white text.

Among the key targets of the new regulations, especially the ones limiting and restricting advertising to minors, was the Joe Camel billboard, magazine, and newspaper advertising campaign. Many critics of the Camel campaign have argued that youths are the demographics that find it most appealing and are encouraged to develop the smoking habit by it. The Clinton administration hoped that by limiting all advertising to simple textual messages, this kind of provocative imagery would be eliminated. But the Clinton regulations didn't appear to be the final word on the subject, given the strong lobby the tobacco and media advertising industries have in Washington. Shalala said further lawsuits will be forthcoming.

Some media stories about the health hazards posed by smoking are more empirically based than others. In the final analysis, these are the ones consumers should be basing their opinions on. The problem is they don't always come from the popular press but intead from more staid magazines that are often free of the pressures of advertising. *Consumer Reports (CR)* is an excellent example. *CR*'s January 1995 issue carried an excellent article entitled, "Secondhand Smoke: Is It a Hazard?" Included in the detailed article was a table listing exactly what levels of probable human carcinogens are contained in sidestream smoke, or smoke which curls off the end of a smoldering cigarette and is ingested by others near the smoker. [35]

The table, which originated from the Occupational Safety and Health Administration, noted that sidestream smoke is the main component of secondhand smoke and is different in composition from the mainstream smoke that smokers inhale. In fact, sidestream smoke actually contains more of several carcinogens than does mainstream smoke. For instance, sidestream smoke contains from one to four times the component Polonium-210, from five to ten times the amount of Benzene, 30 times the concentration of Aniline, and up to 40 times the amount of N-nitrodiethylamine.[36] Based on empirical data such as this, *CR* refuted the tobacco merchants' claim that there is still a doubt as to whether secondhand smoke is an actual health hazard. The editors noted:

They [the tobacco industry] are using a little bit of scientific uncertainty and a lot of public relations to suggest there is still a serious debate about the health hazards of breathing smoke from other people's cigarettes. . . . [But] a number of studies make a consistent case that secondhand smoke, like firsthand smoke, causes lung cancer. . . . Other studies have found strong links between passive smoking and a host of other ills, such as asthma and bronchitis in children. Furthermore, evidence is mounting that secondhand smoke contributes to the development of heart disease.[37]

In using empirical data and describing some of the studies done by medical researchers and their results, the article got much closer to the truth of the issue than other opinion-based stories would have been able to do.

VIOLENCE, THE MEDIA, AND PUBLIC HEALTH

No other area of television's content and impact is more widely studied than violence in programming and its association with real-life acts of violence. For decades, critics of television, viewers, and even sponsors have worried about the amount of violence depicted on television entertainment programs. They have speculated about the possible effects of such depictions and have wondered how many criminals had used televised acts of violence as their blueprints.

So many different groups have been concerned about this that the government has gotten involved in several ways. The Federal Communications Commission has spoken out on the issue and encouraged the concept of "family hour" evening programming and asked networks to be especially mindful of the kind of violence depicted during the early prime-time hours when children are still up and watching. And recently, the Clinton administration signed into law a telecommunication act requiring that all television sets manufactured in the future contain the so-called "V-chip," whereby parents can block out questionable violent programming that their children could see.

The concept of the V-chip is controversial, especially within the television industry. Some critics say it could result in more violent programming on television, as producers abdicate their responsibility of controlling violence in shows since parents can block out whatever they want anyway. Others wonder how many parents will actually take the time to block the programming out, especially if they want to see it themselves. Proponents, however, hail the measure as a way of gaining at least some control over the prevalence of violence on television.

In September 1996, the AMA responded to the issue by distributing new guidelines to 60,000 physicians nationwide to help educate them and their patients about media violence. "Our children spend more time learning about life through media than in any other manner," said AMA Trustee John Nelson, M.D. "The link between media violence and real life violence has been proven by science time and again."[38]

Dr. Nelson illustrated his point with a personal example of a family friend who was viciously beaten, raped, forced to drink Drano, and then shot in the back of the head during a robbery attempt in 1974. Upon their arrest, he said, the killers coldly explained they had emulated what they had seen in the movie *Magnum Force*, which they watched a total of 22 times. "The reality of this story is as chilling today as it was the day it happened in 1974. But this is not an isolated incident," said Dr. Nelson. "Think of how advanced our media has become and how many lives it has influenced since then."[39]

AMA survey results released in 1996 indicate that 68 percent of parents want a stronger, more effective movie rating system, and 81 percent want a rating system for television shows and computer games, while 72 percent want one for music. David Walsh, Ph.D., president and founder of the National Institute on Media and the Family and contributing author of the AMA guidelines, has noted it is a tragedy that while the nation is wringing its hands about violence in young people, we are simultaneously entertaining them with it. According to AMA research, homicide rates doubled in each of the cities studied within the 10 to 15 years after the introduction of television.[40] The television industry responded to all this concern with a rating system in 1997.

The Physician Guide to Media Violence is designed to educate and empower physicians and in turn, their patients about the harmful effects of media violence, particularly on children. In addition, the guidelines provide physicians with a list of thirteen tips for parents to take home and use to help reduce their families' exposure to media violence.

The AMA is not the only medical group that has taken a strong stand against media violence as contributing to public health risks in the United States. A 1993 conference convened by the Annenberg Washington Program and the Center for Health Communication of the Harvard School of Public Health studied the issue of violence, public health, and the media.[41] At that conference, Harvey V. Fineberg, dean of the Harvard School of Public Health, noted that violence is a public health concern, as much as, or more than, a criminal problem. Violence calls for preventive as well as punitive action, he said, explaining that a public health approach to violence begins with a scientific assessment of epidemiological data to identify patterns and risk factors. He echoed Mark Rosenberg of the Centers for Disease Control and Prevention by citing the following example to show how different television's version of murder is from the real thing:

The public conception of homicide is that you walk into a convenience store late at night; there's a robbery going on, and you—unlucky you—are caught in the crossfire. In fact, the data show, most homicides are not related to any other felony. The assailant and victim—almost invariably male—usually know each other. Most often, alcohol is involved, and a firearm is present. What emerges, then, is a very different scenario: Two young men who know each other, sitting around drinking, talking. An argument starts about something. It escalates, it flares. Someone has a gun, pulls it out, and—boom—that's it.[42]

Harvard Sociology Professor Nathan Glazer has found little evidence to support the view that real-life, objective conditions shape public consciousness of events or social maladies. And University of Texas researcher Maxwell McCombs points out that we all rely on secondhand information to tell us what is important. The facts themselves, Glazer explains, become shaped by the need to compete with other claims. As a result, rhetoric, drama, and the art of gaining access to the media are central to our efforts to call attention to social problems from the very beginning. Shaping the facts to make them more compelling is a practice well known to advocates for particular social causes.[43]

As noted in chapter 1, Daniel Yankelovich, chairman of DYG, Inc., and WSY Consulting Group, Inc., believes there are seven stages in the public's journey from raw opinion to what he calls public judgment:[44]

1. Awareness.
2. A sense of urgency or a demand for action.
3. A search for solutions.
4. Reaction and resistance.
5. Wrestling with alternative choices.
6. Intellectual assent.
7. Full resolution—moral, emotional, and intellectual.

The Annenberg/Harvard conference concluded that the mass media often do an excellent job in the early stages of the process, by bringing issues to the public's attention and creating a sense of urgency about them. But then they often move on to the next issue waiting to be discussed, contributing little to the difficult process of working the problems through. Journalists, it was noted, traditionally present positions as adversarial—positions on issues like abortion or gun control, for example—that rarely correspond to the real views of most people. This style of presentation even retards progress, contributing to the gridlock that so often sets in when we try to grapple with these issues.

In contrast, if journalists saw their job as exploring the conflicting values surrounding an issue, then the media could become more useful as a forum for generating the actual process of public deliberation. Sometimes, entertainment programs in prime time, such as *NYPD Blue*, *Law and Order*, or *Hill Street Blues* will go this far. More often, however, the emphasis is on the action and the violence rather than the values giving rise to both.

Some public affairs programming also gets to this level of values discussion, however. Roundtable discussions of journalists and leaders from other walks of life are a good example. ABC *Nightline*'s occasional "Viewpoint" program is a good example of a television news organization taking an hour or more to deal with such issues as televised violence in America. Bill Moyers, with his in-depth public affairs programs on PBS like *The Public Mind* series is another excellent example. Sadly, however, much of this kind of programming is relegated to late-night hours or to PBS, which has limited viewership in competition with other popular network and cable channels.

As for entertainment programming, the challenge is clear: Producers who are concerned about the growing level of violence depicted in shows must find a way to present compelling programs that put violence in America into perspective and look at the issues and values surrounding the violent acts. This is not an easy task, given a viewing public conditioned to action/adventure films where the emphasis is, in fact, on the violence and its quick resolution by killing the bad guys. But that resolution lasts only until the next violent film comes along with its myriad acts of brutality, because the focus is on the violent acts and not on the issues giving rise to them.

According to Neil Hickey, senior editor of *TV Guide*, there is more televised violence than at any time in the medium's history flowing into American homes. Further, it's coming from many more sources than ever before: home video, pay-per-view, and cable, as well as from broadcast networks and stations. Hickey describes it this way:

The overwhelming weight of scientific opinion now holds that televised violence is indeed responsible for a percentage of the real violence in our society. What is new is that psychologists, child experts, and the medical community are just now beginning to treat televised violence as a serious public health issue—like smoking and drunk driving—about which the public needs to be educated for its own safety and well-being.[45]

To find out just how much violence is being televised, *TV Guide* commissioned a study of one day in the life of television. Thursday, April 2, 1992, was chosen as a typical, heavily viewed, non-sweeps night, and the results were an eye-opener. In the 180 hours of programming observed, there were:

• 1,846 individual acts of violence—purposeful, overt, deliberate behavior involving physical force against other individuals.

• 175 scenes in which violence resulted in one or more fatalities.

• 389 scenes depicting serious assaults.

• 362 scenes involving gunplay.

- 673 depictions of punching, pushing, slapping, dragging, and other physically hostile acts.
- 226 scenes of menacing threats with a weapon.

Researchers discovered that newer program forms, such as music videos and reality shows, are significantly increasing the amount of violence on television. Additionally, commercials for violent theatrical movies and TV series have become a major source of televised violence.

In the news arena, newscasts are parading strong and persistent displays of murder, muggings, and mayhem to draw in viewers and boost ratings.

In the fictional programming alone—which accounted for 95 percent of the total—researchers found an average of 185 scenes of violence per channel among the ten channels monitored. Well over a third of all the violence (751 scenes) involved some sort of life-threatening assault.

Not surprisingly to some observers, cartoons were the most violent, with 471 scenes. Promos for TV shows were next (265); then movies (221); toy commercials (188); music videos (123); commercials for theatrical movies (121); TV dramas (69); news (62); reality shows like *Top Cops* and *Hard Copy* (58); sitcoms (52), and soap operas (34).

Add to these programming hours the unmeasured number of hours spent watching videos on VCRs, and you get an idea of how much violence there is on just one day and night of television. The study's conclusion: Violence remains a pervasive, major feature of contemporary television programming, and it's coming from more sources and in greater volume than ever before.[46]

In his book *Hollywood vs. America*, film critic Michael Medved echoed the belief that Hollywood does indeed influence social behavior. He writes:

The most profound problem with the popular culture isn't its immediate impact on a few vulnerable and explosive individuals, but its long-term effect on all the rest of us. The deepest concerns about Hollywood go beyond the industry's role in provoking a handful of specific crimes and involve its contribution to a general climate of violence and self-indulgence.[47]

Medved adds that scientific and academic support for this conclusion increases every year, with official statements linking media messages and antisocial conduct from the American Academy of Pediatrics, the American Medical Association, the National Institute of Mental Health, the National Commission on the Causes and Prevention of Violence, the U.S. Public Health Service, the National Parent-Teacher Association, the U.S. Attorney General's Task Force on Family Violence, and the National Education Association.

Dr. Jennings Bryant of the University of Alabama has stated, "Some of the most durable and important effects of watching television come in the form of subtle, incremental, cumulative changes in the way we view the world."[48]

Dr. George Gerbner, former dean of the Annenberg School of Communications at the University of Pennsylvania, discovered that more than 90 percent of all programs offered during children's prime viewing hours were violent. For the Saturday morning time slot, this programming contained an average of more than 25 violent acts per hour.[49] A later study, done by the National Coalition on Television Violence, found that 72 percent of all children's programs contained more than ten acts of violence per hour.[50]

Dr. Thomas Radecki, research director of the National Coalition on Television Violence, points out that the destructive impact of the popular culture is not only a children's issue. He says there is overwhelming evidence that adults as well as children are affected by the glamorization and promotion of violence. TV-watching adults, he says, are more likely to purchase handguns, support military solutions to world problems, and overestimate the amount of violence in the real world.[51]

MOVIES AND HEALTH ISSUES

There is no shortage of commercial films that deal with medical, public health, and environmental issues. Just as movies about other issues (i.e., the theories posited and detailed in *JFK*), films about illnesses can cause us to jump to conclusions and believe some things are true before they have been proven to be so. The best of these films stick to the facts as they are known when the movie is produced; the worst will vacate or go beyond these facts in the interest of heightening dramatic elements. When films do this, they can produce a larger fear in the audience about certain health risks, and can produce false hope that cures are close at hand.

A look at just a few of the films that deal with medical and/or public health and environmental issues shows how popular and influential these movies can be:

- *Lorenzo's Oil*. A family suffers through a son's fight with a debilitating nerve disease.

- *Rain Man*. A man travels across country with his brother, an autistic savant, and comes to understand and love him for the first time.

- *Outbreak*. A killer virus is cut loose on the unsuspecting population of a placid community.

- *Awakenings*. A doctor searches for a cure for a peculiar form of sleeping sickness exhibited by a patient at an institution.

- *Charly*. A mentally retarded man responds positively to treatment, reaches the status of genius, and then correctly diagnoses his approaching relapse into retardation.

- *Phenomenon.* A 1996 version of a similar theme about the rise and fall of a warm-hearted genius.

- *Medicine Man.* An eccentric medical researcher and his young assistant find a cure for cancer in the South American rainforests only to lose it to a sweeping fire and the devastation wrought by a company wrecking a section of the jungle. This film has the distinction of trying to advance two risk themes at once: the hope of finding a cancer cure, and the need for saving the rainforests.

- *The China Syndrome.* A television reporter and cameraman assist a nuclear power plant engineer, on the verge of a breakdown, in saving California from a nuclear meltdown and in alerting the public to the dangers of nuclear power.

- *Ordinary People.* The lives of a mother, father, and surviving son are torn apart by the death of their older son and brother. A psychiatrist intervenes to rescue the father and his son, while the wife and mother move deeper into denial and out of reach of therapy.

- *The Prince of Tides.* Another film where a psychiatrist saves the day in helping an attempted suicide victim and her long-suffering brothers piece their lives back together.

- *The Three Faces of Eve.* A woman's multiple and often incompatible personalities surface during the course of several visits to her therapist, who helps her to overcome the multiplicity.

- *My Life.* A young father-to-be discovers that he has cancer and looks to several sources for cures before dealing with the finality of the disease.

- *Coma.* Doctors at a metropolitan hospital experiment with inducing comas in unsuspecting patients for private gain.

These and other films have made a lasting impression on the minds of many moviegoers and have either heightened their sense of insecurity about health risks, made them aware of risks they didn't know existed, or possibly even distorted the reality of these risks.

Some films, like the highly acclaimed *Lorenzo's Oil*, can go a long way toward creating a public understanding of a health risk. But even they often fall short of the mark of depicting a totally accurate view of the risk and possible cure. Medical writer Christine Gorman noted that *Lorenzo's Oil* did more than tout a possible cure for a rare and fatal hereditary disease; it also vilified the medical community for reacting so slowly to the possibility of a home-brewed cure.[52] That possible cure was a combination of vegetable oils developed by Augusto and Michaela Odone that may have improved the condition of their son Lorenzo, 13 at the time of the film, who suffered from a degenerative nerve illness called Adrenoleukodystrophy.

The movie depicted this oil—called Lorenzo's Oil—as being the answer the family was looking for, and it left that impression in the minds of the audience. Gorman notes, however, that a study from France concluded that the remedy is worthless, at least for the milder, adult form of the ailment.

Resarchers Dr. Patrick Aubourg and his staff from the St. Vincent de Paul Hospital in Paris reported in the *New England Journal of Medicine* in 1993 that they found no improvement in 24 patients who had taken Lorenzo's Oil for up to 48 months.[53] There appears to be universal agreement that the oil does decrease the level of toxic compounds in the blood that probably cause the disease. The problem, apparently, is the oil cannot reverse existing nerve damage that results in blindness and paralysis.

But even the results of the French study may not be universally accepted. Dr. Hugo Moser of the Kennedy Krieger Institute in Baltimore, Maryland, believes Lorenzo's Oil may delay the onset of the symptoms.[54] Thus, the question remains open about whether the oil is partially preventive. And the question regarding the movie is whether or not it proposed a single anecodotal case as being universal. In other words, because Lorenzo Odone was helped, if not cured, by the oil, does that mean other sufferers from the disease will be as well?

It is difficult for any commercial film to both entertain in high dramatic style and educate the public in an accurate manner about the dangers of and possible cures for health risks. Entertainment values and the often slow and multifaceted truth about a health risk are often at odds with each other, much like speed is often at odds with accuracy in a newsroom. The problem is further exacerbated when you have a film like *Lorenzo's Oil* which promotes itself as being a serious, no-nonsense look at a real life disease and features a well-known, highly credible star like Susan Sarandon. It is much the same situation as having Oliver Stone direct a well-edited film like *JFK* with its highly acclaimed star Kevin Costner. Stone had realistic films like *Platoon* to his credit, while Costner had just come off what seemed to be an objective look at Indians in the Old West in *Dances With Wolves*. Credibility reeks from films like these and attaches itself to the next project these professionals produce. It is not hard to understand, then, why many moviegoers left theaters believing in the broad conspiracy theories portrayed in *JFK* as fact, or in Lorenzo's Oil being a cure for a dreaded nerve illness.

On the other hand, with films like *Outbreak* or Stephen King's *The Stand*, there is a sense among moviegoers that these fall more squarely into the entertainment category and flow from a long line of science fiction thrillers featuring giant ants, mutant spiders, or killer bees. There is less danger of these films unduly panicking or subduing the public about health risks. Still, both films and television remain powerful forces in influencing all our perceptions and beliefs about issues such as health hazards.

THE INTERNET AND MEDICAL NEWS

Television and movies aren't the only visual electronic media where people can get news and impressions about various health risks. The burgeoning Internet is replete with resource guides, Web sites, chat groups, exchange opportunities among medical and dental professionals and research scientists, on-line journals, magazines and reports, home medical guides, and myriad other references. Anyone needing information about virtually any aspect of health or medicine will find it on the Internet. Never before has so much information been made available at one access point for the general public. In fact, the problem may be there is just too much of this information available. Some might find the sheer quantity of data overwhelming. But the Internet will offer a goldmine of information about health risks.

Journalists should also take advantage of the resources available on the Net. It can provide instant background and a solid context for any story on health issues.

It is always wise, however, to know something about the sponsors of the various Web sites, because a site funded by a pharmaceutical company, for example, may not be the most objective source about the risks associated with various drugs and medications.

A quick check of just one of the Internet guides, *Magellan*, found more than twenty sub-categories of medical resources under the overall topic of "Health & Medicine." Included in those sub-topics and the number of Web sites for each are public health (49); sexually transmitted diseases (32); women's health (68); family health (64); dentistry (19); addictions (22); mental health (85), and sports medicine (9).

The following are brief excerpts from the *Magellan* reviewers showing the kinds of information and discussion available from each of these categories, together with their Internet addresses:

Public Health

- *Agency for Toxic Substances and Disease Registry Home Page.* This agency identifies hazardous substances in the environment and their relation to adverse human health outcomes. Through education and outreach, the agency strives to prevent the causes from becoming effects. http://atsdr1.atsdr.cdc.gov:8080/

- *Federal Information Exchange (FEDIX)/The National Institute of Allergy and Infectious Diseases (NIAID).* FEDIX operates this page for those interested in information about NIAID. This site offers users a general overview of the institute and separate pages for information and programs. http://web.fie.com/web/fed/nih

- *Go Ask Alice.* This site is for people with any health, sexual, emotional, or nutritional question. This is an interactive question and answer line found at the Healthwise Web site created by the Health Education division of Columbia University Health Services. http://www.cc.Columbia.edu/cu/healthwise/alice.html

- *Health World Online Home Page.* In its infancy in 1996, Health World Online is already one of the most comprehensive health and wellness sites on the Web. This voluminous site offers in-depth sections on food, fitness, nutrition, health care, public health, and even free access to abstracts. http://www.healthy.net/

- *The Malaria Database.* The Malaria Database is a complex Web site providing important references to researchers. It is more pertinent to the microbiologist, parasitologist, geneticist, or medical professional than to the entomologist. http://www.wehi.edu.au/biology/malaria/who.html

- *American Heart Association (AHA).* The American Heart Association Web site includes details about AHA programs for youths, teachers, businesses, and health-care providers. http://www.amhrt.org

- *Global Health Network.* Designed to be a network for people working in public health around the world, this expanding and ambitious Web site aims to cover the collection, organization, monitoring, and disbursement of epidemiological data with the goal of reducing the incidence of diseases. http://info.pitt.edu/HOME/GHNet/GHNet.html

- *MedAccess.* MedAccess' mission is to be the premier provider of health and wellness information on the Internet, and it's well on its way. At this site are thousands of pages and records on general health and healthcare. http://www.medaccess.com/home2.html

Sexually Transmitted Diseases

- *AIDS Information via CHAT Database.* This is a conversational hypertext access technology that will answer plain-English questions about AIDS and related issues. telnet://debra.dgbt.doc.ca:3000/

- *AIDS Resource List.* This is an extensive index of AIDS and HIV-related sites. Links are provided to dozens of valuable resources such as the Red Ribbon Net, the Safer Sex Page, AIDS Virtual Library Page, the Art AIDS Link, several newsgroups, and much more. http://www.teleport.com/~celinec/aids.html

- *Risks of Oral Sex.* A site for anybody new to sexual activity. Although there's little here aesthetically, this portion of the Safer Sex site is still a good resource for anyone interested in safety. Included are statistics and other helpful data. http://www.cmpharm.ucsf.edu/~troyer/safesex/persp/perspectives.1.2.html

- *RedRibbonNet.* This is a source of information and research data on HIV and AIDS. Users will find Shopping at the Red Ribbon Mall, Live Chat in the Red Ribbon Coffee House, updates on the Latest Red Ribbon Events from around the country, and information on AIDS. http://worldclass.com/redribbon/

- *Disease/Pregnancy Prevention.* This site provides a somewhat humorous quiz on condom use and directions on how to use them most effectively. Users will also learn about latex squares (Dental Dams) and other disease/pregnancy prevention devices. gopher://gopher.uiuc.edu/11/UI/CSF/health/heainfo/sex/prevent

- *HIV Database.* This site provides technical information about how scientists collect, collate, analyze, and publish genetic sequences of the human immunodeficiency virus. Researchers will find information about gag proteins, global variations in the virus and so forth. http://hiv-web.1an1.gov

- *Herpes—The Evasive Intruder.* A useful on-line introduction to the herpes virus. Sections cover diagnostics, symptoms, transmission, treatment, diet, recurrences, self-help, and commercial products to treat herpes. http://inet-access.net/~herpes

Women's Health

- *Breast Cancer Answers.* This site has current and archived articles on the latest news about breast cancer prevention, screening, and treatment. You can also send an e-mail and get personal replies to your breast cancer questions. This site also contains a list of links to related sites. http://www.biostat.wisc.edu/bca/

- *Breastfeeding Information.* This page is an index of birth-related information. Links are provided to information on breastfeeding, nutrition tips for pregnancy, breastfeeding and feminism, non-standard lactation, and more. http://www.efn. org/~djz/birth/breastfeeding.html

- *Brigham & Women's Hospital.* This is the home page for the Brigham & Women's Hospital in Boston and contains the Brigham Hospital *Gopher*, as well as pages for Radiology, Thoracic Surgery, the Decision Systems Group, the Division of Pulmonary and Critical Care Medicine, and links to related services. http://bustoff.bwh.harvard.edu/

Family Health

- *Columbia/HCA Healthcare Corporation.* This excellent resource for health enthusiasts contains something for everyone, with surveys, fitness tests, health tips, recipes, several original articles, a physicians' corner and nursing stations, contests and games for kids, and a myriad of details. http://family.starwave.com/index.html

- *Family Planet.* Answers about questions ranging from potty training to finding quality childcare are found on this site. Also provided is information on choosing the best school for your child. http://family.starwave.com/index.html

- *Blue Cares.* Learn about the health care policies provided by Blue Cross and Blue Shield, and also find complete coverage of the latest news in health care as well as labeled diagrams, detailed pictures, and so forth. http://www.bluecares.com

- *Boots (the Chemists).* Helpful information on family health topics like pregnancy and homeopathy are presented here in a cleverly illustrated and clearly organized format. Boots' health library allows you to pull "books" off the shelves on vitamins, aromatherapy, and so forth. http://www.boots.co.uk/

Addictions

- *CVaNet—Substance Abuse Information.* The CVaNet–Substance Abuse site provides information on substances abused, a directory of facilities and other resources, a training calendar, and a question and answer area. Users will find Internet and community-based resources and numbers for hotlines. http://freenet.vcu.edu/health/vatc/vatc.html

- *Join Together.* This is a resource center dedicated to reducing the harms associated with the use of illicit drugs, excessive alcohol, and tobacco. Its Web site presents the results of surveys, has a 24-hour news update section, and provides community action guides and more. http://www.jointogether.org/

- *NicNet.* NicNet is The Arizona Nicotine and Tobacco Network Web site, with resources and local information regarding tobacco and smoking research. Users will find numerous links to on-line resources, grouped into categories such as treatment and prevention. http://www.medlib.arizona.edu/~pubhlth/tobac.html

- *Cocaine Anonymous.* Information and a self-test for addiction to cocaine are provided at this site. http://www.ca.org/

- *Habit Smart.* This is designed as a resource for people with destructive habits and addictions of all types, with documents and links to other addiction-related links on the Web. Users will find the document "Coping with Addiction," which addresses questions and issues related to addictive behaviors. http://www.cts.com/~habtsmrt/

Mental Health

- *Alt.support.grief.* This is an on-line support group for people who have lost a loved one. The primary topics are mutual support and assistance in how to cope with grief. news:alt.support.grief

- *CyberPsychologist.* The CyberPsychologist Web page provides examples of self-help psychology. Specific cognitive-behavioral methods help reduce stress and depression, overcome addictive habits, improve relationships, and enhance personal and career satisfaction. http://www.cyberpsych.com/cyberpsych

- *Mind Tools.* This is a resource of problem-solving shareware, thought techniques, applied psychology, and links to psychology-related topics designed to help users optimize the performance of their mind. http://www.mindtools.com

- *Pendulum.* This is a high-traffic mailing list which functions both as an on-line support group and center for dissemination of information for bipolar, or manic-depressive, people. Typical topics include making it through the day, and problems at home, work, and school. mailto:majordomo@ncar.ucar.edu

- *Psychiatry On Line.* Psychiatry On Line is a monthly international journal of psychiatry for mental health professionals. Articles at the Web site generally address current concerns in psychiatry, among which could be depression, dementia, organic brain disorders, and so forth. http://www.priory.com/journals/psych.htm

Sports Medicine

- *Slam Dunk Science.* This resource shows how scientists figure out how to help runners run quicker, how to make basketball shoes that support faster pivots, and how to analyze what athletes are doing to their bodies while they are competing. http://www.tufts.edu/~jlarsen/video.html

- *Dr. Pribut's Running Injuries Page.* This is a good resource for everyone who runs. Users will find all kinds of advice, strategies, and articles on common running injuries such as ankle sprains, knee problems, and so forth. http://www.clark.net/pub/pribut/spsport.html

- *The San Francisco Spine Center.* This site contains valuable information for sufferers of back pain or spinal injury. There is even a newsletter, "Back Talk," with advice on posture, exercise, the proper use of gym equipment, and so forth. http://www.spinenet.com/

- *Center for Arthroscopic Surgery.* This site advertises the Los Angeles-based center's services for people suffering from industrial or athletic knee injuries. Users will find information about this facility and how to sign up for treatment. http://mmink.cts.com/mmink/dossiers/cas.html

NOTES

1. Michael Pfau, Lawrence J. Mullen, and Kirsten Garrow, "The Influence of Television Viewing on Public Perceptions of Physicians," *Journal of Broadcasting and Electronic Media* 39(4) (Fall 1995), pp. 441–458.

2. Ibid.

3. Ibid.

4. Ibid.

5. Ibid.

6. Ralph Crawshaw et al., "Patient-Physician Covenant," *The Journal of the American Medical Association* 273(19) (May 17, 1995).

7. Nancy Signorielli, *Mass Media Images and Impact on Health* (Westport, Conn.: Greenwood Press, 1993), p. 49.

8. Ibid., p. 44.

9. Ibid., p. 45.

10. Ibid., p. 49.

11. Rita Rubin and Dr. Harrison L. Rogers, Jr., "Under the Microscope: The Relationship between Physicians and the News Media," a report published by the Freedom Forum First Amendment Center at Vanderbilt University, 1995, p. 38.

12. Ibid.

13. Ibid., p. 39.

14. Ibid., p. 40.

15. Janet A. Bridges, with Christine M. Price and Terri R. Breaux, "Health Belief Messages About Alcohol Consumption in Network Television Entertainment Programs: A Preliminary Report," presented to the Association for Education in Journalism and Mass Communication, Washington D.C., August 1995.

16. Ibid.

17. "TV Drinking Problem," *Dallas Morning News*, November 11, 1989, p. 3C.

18. Nancy Signorielli, "Drinking, Sex, and Violence on Television: The Cultural Indicators Perspective," *Journal of Drug Education* 17 (1987), pp. 245–260.

19. "Smoking Taboo, Drinking OK, Adolescents Say," *Chicago Sun-Times*, May 18, 1991, p. B2.

20. Dennis Lowry, "Alcohol Consumption Patterns and Consequences on Prime Time Network TV," *Journalism Quarterly* (Spring 1981), pp. 3–8.

21. George Gerbner, M. Morgan, and N. Signorielli, "Programming Health Portrayals: What Viewers See, Say, and Do," in D. Pearl, L. Bouthilet, and J. Lazar, eds., *Television and Behavior: Ten Years of Scientific Progress and Implications for the Eighties* 2 (Rockville, Md.: U.S. Department of Health and Human Services, NIMH, 1982), pp. 291–307.

22. Bridges et al., "Health Belief Messages About Alcohol Consumption in Network Television Entertainment Programs."

23. Ibid.

24. Ibid.

25. Ibid.

26. John H. Crowley and James Pokrywczynski, "Advertising Practitioners Look at a Ban on Tobacco Advertising," *Journalism Quarterly* 68(3) (Autumn 1991), pp. 329–337.

27. Ibid.

28. Ibid.

29. "Tobacco Ad Hearings Begin," *Editor & Publisher*, July 26, 1986, p. 16.

30. "Ad Ban Hearing," *The 4A's National Newsletter* (September 1987), p. 1.

31. "Free Speech and Advertising: Who Draws the Line?", transcript from the Institute for Democratic Communication, College of Communication, Boston University, 1987, pp. 15–16, as cited in John H. Crowley and James Pokrywczynski, "Advertising Practitioners Look at a Ban on Tobacco Advertising," *Journalism Quarterly* 68(3) (Fall 1991), p. 331.

32. "Surgeon General, Justice Department Disagree on Tobacco Ads," *Editor & Publisher*, August 16, 1986, p. 20.

33. "Clinton Unwraps FDA Rules Limiting Tobacco Ads, Sales," *The Commercial Appeal*, August 24, 1996, A1.

34. Ibid.

35. "Secondhand Smoke: Is It a Hazard?" *Consumer Reports* (January 1995), pp. 27–33.

36. Ibid.

37. Ibid.

38. "AMA Survey Shows 75 Percent of Parents Disgusted with Media Violence," news release of the American Medical Association, Chicago, Ill., September 9, 1996, p. 1.

39. Ibid.

40. Ibid.

41. Margaret Gerteis, *Violence, Public Health, and the Media*, report based on the conference "Mass Communication and Social Agenda-Setting," convened by the Annenberg Washington Program of Northwestern University and the Center for Health Communication of the Harvard School of Public Health, October 20–21, 1993.

42. Ibid, p. 7.

43. Ibid., p. 8.

44. Ibid., p. 10.

45. Neil Hickey, "How Much Violence on TV? A Lot, Says *TV Guide*," a report by the Center for Media and Public Affairs, Washington, D.C., 1993.

46. Ibid.

47. Michael Medved, "Researching the Truth About Hollywood's Impact," adapted from *Hollywood vs. America: Popular Culture and the War on Traditional Values* (New York: HarperCollins/Zondervan, 1992). Adapted for the Joseph & Edna Josephson Institute.

48. Ibid.

49. Ibid.

50. Ibid.

51. Ibid.

52. Christine Gorman, "Cold Water on Lorenzo's Oil," *Time*, September 20, 1993, p. 76.

53. Ibid.

54. Ibid.

8

Covering the Health Care Story

Millions of printed pages, countless hours of media debates and news reports, and innumerable workshops and panel discussions have been devoted to covering the many aspects of the U.S. health reform story. Still, the goal of this chapter is to set in broad context for reporters the general pattern of the health reforms and health reform proposals, together with the rationale for the seemingly endless debates on the reformation.

The legendary late speaker of the House, Tip O'Neil, once declared in his 1993 book that "all politics are local."[1] The same can be said of the current shifts in media coverage of the health care story from the national to state and local levels.[2] The health reform story is also undergoing transformation from a national political story to a business story.[3] These tendencies do not, however, negate the essence of demonstrating the interrelatedness of the state and local health reform initiatives to the national health policy developments.

Discussions in this chapter focus on the national- and state-level reforms, with specific emphasis on the latest state reform initiatives and the challenges posed. The most recently passed piecemeal health legislations at the national level, including Medical Savings Accounts (MSAs) for the Medicare population sub-group, are also discussed.

Media critics contend that one key limitation of health care reporting is the tendency for undue focus on politics at the expense of substance.[4] This, they claim, appears to derive from a lack of relevant technical expertise on the part of health care reporters. Consequently, the source materials in the chapter notes and references should be useful to reporters for improving their technical mastery of health care reform.

Journalists covering the health care story are likely to find the chapter materials useful for several reasons. Among them:

- The continuing concerns and public debates over health reform are, to a large degree, driven by the chronic federal deficits. Thus, reader interests are likely to continue into the foreseeable future. Consequently, health reform debates and reporting are most likley to continue dominating mainstream media. This is because political and economic issues, as well as a program for social change, typically underlie the push for health reforms.[5]

- This necessitates that reporters familiarize themselves with the historical context of the health reform debate, as well as obtain a more coherent understanding of an array of recently developed, frontier terminologies in use that characterize the new provider arrangements.[6] These are needed to understand and communicate the health care story more accurately and effectively to the larger public.

- The health care story lacks a clearly defined boundary. Being multi-dimensional, it encompasses aspects of consumer access, financing, insurance, health manpower, ethics, quality, cost, legislation, technology of care, provider delivery systems, and so on. These, then, are linked to an array of other issues, including provider practice of defensive medicine and malpractice insurance reforms. Studies have also shown that workers in companies furnishing retiree health insurance benefits plan to retire five to sixteen months sooner than workers in firms without the coverage.[7] The fear of losing health insurance coverage also decreases voluntary job mobility from 16 percent to 12 percent per year.[8]

WHY REFORM HEALTH CARE?

Health care reform goals include containing the high-growth cost factors, broadening access, and maintaining quality of care. The culprits of cost growth factors are many. First, as real incomes grow, the United States continues to spend a disproportionately large share of its national income on health care. Private and public health care costs become increasingly more burdensome as the elderly population grows more rapidly. Also fueling the burden is the discovery and use of high-tech medical diagnostics and treatments.[9] Further, life expectancy improves, and the real productivity of the country falls.[10] This set of complicated, intertwined factors has raised serious concerns in the minds of ordinary citizens, politicians, journalists, media critics, health policy experts, political scientists, economists, sociologists, and other interest groups.

In America, health spending represented 12 percent of the gross national product (GNP) or $666 billion, in 1995. Since the decade of the 1960s, growth in per capita real health care expenditures exceeded the growth in per capita real GNP by a factor of more than 2 to 1. During 1994, for example, the U.S. productivity was barely above 1 percent while the country spent slightly over 14 percent, or roughly $1 trillion of its GNP, on health care: the largest among OECD (Organization of Economic Cooperation and Development) countries. Health care costs in America remained high in 1994. However, according to the Medicare Office of National Health Statistics, health spending for the first time in more than 30 years grew at a slower rate of 6.4 percent. The 1994 health expenditures of $949.4 billion translate to $3,510 per person, and is distributed as follows:[11]

- 38.4 percent to hospital care.
- 18.9 percent to physician services.
- 8.2 percent to drugs and medical sundries.
- 8 percent to nursing home care.
- 5.8 percent to program administration.
- 20.6 percent to other spending and personal health care.

Absent any major, effective policy intervention in the United States to reverse or moderate the rapid growth trend, the health share of the GNP is projected to be 20 percent by the year 2030.

Health care cost containment initiatives have a rich history, with various policies being designed to restrain the growth of specific aspects of care. Policies aiming to restrict physician charges have been implemented. They include the 1992 physician payment reform for medical procedures and tests, capitation-based physician payments in managed care contracts, and other plans designed to tighten the control of individual practitioners.[12]

Managed care expanded substantially early in the 1980s, when health care cost growth doubled and employers who paid roughly 40 percent of all health care services sought to gain control of health insurance premiums. Hospital care cost containment efforts include the Diagnostic Related Groups, or DRGs. However, DRGs have now extended to outpatient care, to prevent the so-called Ballooning Effect.[13] Program administration costs are being reformed through the integration of more efficient information systems, network technology, and health care delivery systems.[14] Drug cost control reforms, particularly Medicaid program drug benefits, include the 1990 Public Law 101–508, requiring the U.S. drug manufacturers to grant the federal Medicaid outpatient drug program the deepest discounts granted to any other large purchasers of drugs, such as large hospitals and purchasing groups.[15]

The imperatives of health reforms are not limited to the United States, however. Cumulative growths in nominal per capita health spendings of selected OECD nations from 1970–1989 are as follows: 12.2 percent in Canada, 13.8 percent in France, 8.4 percent in Germany, 14.4 percent in the United Kingdom, and 11.7 percent in the United States.[16]

The growth rates in nominal health expenditures, or the percentage of GNP devoted to health care, can be compared across countries, and also show high increases in developed countries around the world.

Studies have shown that countries that are most successful in containing health care costs have centrally controlled health budgets.[17] Health care expenditure components also differ among the countries. For example, U.S. hospitals cost 40 percent more than Canadian ones. U.S. hospitals treat sicker patients, have higher bureaucratic overhead costs, and severely underutilize the capacities of decentralized high-tech equipment. However, even for similar indications, U.S. hospital care costs 22 percent more per patient.

Direct comparisons of international health expenditures can be problematic however, because the financing (e.g., fee-for-service versus capitation), delivery systems (e.g., private versus public and nonprofit providers), and health outcomes (e.g., infant mortality rate per thousand of child-bearing age women) of the medical care sector of these countries can differ appreciably.[18]

The lion's share of health care expenditures in total income is not "bad" in and of itself, except when framed in the context of the society's scarce resources. The critical concern is whether the high health care expenditures are justifiable, based on the health sector's relative productivity. This point is relevant because a dollar's worth of resources allocated to health care is no longer available for other competing uses. The foregone alternative uses (such as public higher education and interstate highway construction) to which the scarce social resources were not put are the real costs of health care to the society.

Renowned health care policy experts question whether the high health expenditures justify the benefits to society. For example, are physicians cost-justified, from the social viewpoint, to practice "defensive medicine" when its real worth is not outcome-justified?[19] One popular example is when physicians order extra diagnostic tests, such as a CAT scan, to confirm an already conclusive x-ray result. Society in this case could be spending excessively on health care relative to the real benefits received. Excessive spending of a limited income beyond social necessity simply means that some other uses remain unmet. Renowned health policy experts argue that a fully insured population spends roughly 40 to 50 percent more than a population with a large deductible, and their health status is not measurably improved by the additional services.[20]

RADICAL VERSUS PIECEMEAL HEALTH REFORM

President Clinton's proposal for a comprehensive health reform package failed to pass the Congress in 1994. However, health care in the United States is undergoing gradual, piecemeal reforms.[21] The objectives of these partial reform efforts remain familiar: they influence cost controls, access expansion, and maintaining quality of care. Therefore, print and broadcast media reporting of the health care story is continuing, despite the lack of a broad-based, universal, national reform.

Since January 1995, the new Republican-dominated Congress has taken the piecemeal approach to health reform. The marginalist framework contrasts sharply with the radical transformation ("fix the entire old system") originally proposed in the President's Health Security Plan.[22] That plan, which favored universal coverage, was designed around Enthoven's concept of managed competition.[23] Critics deemed the plan too radical for America in the sense that it obviates a focus on individual care.[24] Critics also contend that Clinton's plan was too bureaucracy-laden and would have granted unlimited access to a full range of medical treatments and services, including high-tech medicine, to everyone, regardless of their ability to pay.[25]

Health reforms are currently progressing piecemeal simultaneously at the national, state, and local levels.[26] The multi-directional movements toward managed care health reforms appear to be widening access to care. Specifically, those that were unable to afford medical coverage are increasingly being allowed access to some form of basic health care, largely through managed care programs.[27] This incentive-driven trend, largely occurring at the state levels in the form of Medicaid reform, is consistent with the earlier prediction of a health economist.[28]

Current implementations of the gradualist, piecemeal reforms have mechanisms in place for reviewing physicians' use of expensive tests, procedures, and fees, including high-tech treatments and expensive pharmaceuticals (e.g., bio-tech drugs). The gradualist approach is consistent with the economist's view in that it allows for an evaluation of the incremental benefits relative to the marginal (additional) costs of a changed, piecemeal policy.

The economist's ability to look back and compare the incremental benefits and costs of the implemented health policy is one way to judge the improvements in social welfare. In other words, all else equal, a socially beneficial resource reallocation occurs if the piecemeal policy benefits some individuals without making others worse off. The Republicans' marginalist approach seems to suggest that it is more cost-effective to focus on reforming specific aspects of the national health system one at a time, such as health care financing or complete reorganizing of indigent health care (e.g., Medicaid) or, most recently, that of the elderly (i.e., Medicare).

The recent GOP-led Congress is also popular for favoring health reform policies that do not significantly redistribute resources from the middle and upper classes to the poorer segments of the population. The Republicans argued that the president's failed universal health insurance would have increased the middle-class share of health costs, which is a form of redistribution. The current approach to U.S. health reform is, as noted earlier, gradualist and similar to that of the Republic of China or Taiwan.[29]

Current health reforms in the United States appear to be sporadic, however. This reflects the slow, but steady, undercurrent that drives the continuous process for reforming health. Despite an absence of a broad national reform, states are taking the lead in innovative designs of their own reformed systems.

STATE REFORMS AND THE MEDICAID PROBLEM

Despite the demise of Clinton's health reform plan, the reform issue is not dead and is proceeding more at the state level these days. It is worth noting, however, that the occurrence of state reforms does not necessarily nullify the need for reform efforts at the national level, and those are progressing as well, albeit more slowly.

State health reforms have the basic goals of containing the rapid growth of Medicaid spending, reducing the number of the uninsured and the working poor who are without coverage, and minimizing cost-shifting to the providers.[30]

The cost-shifting problem occurs because of the tightened Medicaid reimbursements, leading the providers to absorb a growing share of indigent health care costs. As a result of the failure of the Congress to pass a broad national health reform, the states, as major buyers of health care and partners in the joint federal/state Medicaid program, are faced with the congressional mandate to expand Medicaid services and rising Medicaid costs with fragile resources. The states are now spearheading most of the health reform efforts.

Some of the factors underlying the rapid growth of health care expenditures at the state level also include technological progress, and the moral hazards arising from the overuse and abuse of health care resources when patients don't pay full cost of care because they are insured.[31] Growths of the poor, elderly population, the uninsured and the mostly jobless poor who use the non-profit community hospitals for basic care also play increasingly vital roles in the rising cost of health care at the state level. States are now more active as the federal government attempts to balance its budgets by mandating increased roles for the states in the financing of indigent health care, incarceration, and public education.[32]

The U.S. Health Care Financing Administration (HCFA) is responsible for granting states Section 1115 waivers, thereby giving them permission to replace federal Medicaid with state-styled managed care arrangements. The states are increasingly experimenting with a variety of major health reforms, particularly in dealing with access to care and financing of the indigent (traditional Medicaid) and the uninsured. Insurance reforms include subsidizing insurance costs for small businesses and reforming state insurance laws to eliminate or reduce practices that exclude, limit, or deny affordable coverage (e.g., for pre-existing conditions of the "uninsurables"). The other reform initiatives include:

• Pilot testing of the medical individual retirement accounts, such as medical savings accounts, which include tax incentives for health coverage.

- requirements that employers participate in the cost of employee health programs or pay the government taxes to fund a similar coverage.

- capping malpractice awards to reduce physician needs to hedge against expensive malpractice suits by performing excessive tests.

- elimination of frauds.

- controlling administrative costs of health programs.

Related reforms at the state level include expanding and redefining the concept of Medicaid and setting up on a large scale the use of Medicaid managed care programs. Also, some states are submitting applications to HCFA for Section 1115 waivers to expand Medicaid coverage to include the uninsured.

In 1996, literature documented five primary approaches to reforming health care at the state level: insurance reform, state purchasing alliances, Section 1115 waivers, universal coverage law, and expanded coverage for children. All states except Pennsylvania, Massachusetts, and Hawaii have instituted insurance reform. Section 1115 waivers have been approved for eight states and were pending in seven others in 1996. Universal coverage laws were found in six states in that year, while two others instituted incremental coverage and three states were studying it. Fourteen states developed expanded coverage for children in 1996, while fifteen states had state purchasing alliances.

Some states, including Tennessee, sought Section 1115 health reform waivers from HCFA primarily to cover indigent care (Medicaid), and sometimes, the uninsured and uninsurable residents. In other states, such as Oregon, Hawaii, and Florida, the waiver is a first step, integral effort toward establishing a more comprehensive, universal coverage system and broader private sector participation.

The problem is that the capacity of states to generate funds to finance coverage is severely limited. Therefore, most state reforms are largely Medicaid-based. Of course, they sometimes include broader initiatives to cover uninsured health care, through means such as subsidizing the insurance costs of small businesses.[33]

Medicaid consumes about 20 percent of state government budgets. State health reforms focus largely on this segment of care receivers. On average, federal financial participation is 57 percent of the Medicaid dollar. Federal participation in the Medicaid funding has allowed states to become increasingly creative in writing off some of the accounts to the federal government. Federal budget shortfalls are now reducing the ability of states to subsidize indigent care. Arizona's implementation of Section 1115 waiver created a statewide Medicaid managed care program. Oregon's reform included a prioritized list of health services and an expanded use of its managed care for Medicaid enrollees. Oregon, unlike Tennessee, guarantees fair reimbursements to providers of care under its Medicaid managed care system.

TennCare is a comprehensive health care plan that covers roughly 2 million Medicaid and uninsured Tennesseeans. Tennessee's Medicaid program costs grew from $500 million in fiscal 1986–87 to roughly $3 billion in fiscal 1992–93.[34] During 1992–93, the federal share of Tennessee Medicaid was 67.5 percent.

TennCare aims to contain costs through managed care and managed competition. The state share of the Medicaid burden was growing too rapidly, and it applied for a Section 1115 waiver. The original proposal had the goal of saving the federal government $1.5 billion by fiscal 1999–2000. HCFA approved the TennCare program on November 18, 1994, with implementation on January 1, 1994. Under this program are twelve large, competitive networks of providers under the label of Managed Care Organizations (MCOs). The MCOs contract with physicians, hospitals, and other primary care practitioners and organizations, to provide indigent care. TennCare's budget for 1996 was $3.3 billion.

However, TennCare's largest MCO, Access Medplus, was found deficient in nine major areas. Access Medplus has 250,000 covered lives with a $400 million TennCare contract, and has served 25 percent of the 1.2 million indigent care recipients. It almost became financially insolvent and had to be rescued by Methodist Health Systems, securing the needed capital and setting up a for-profit management company, MCMC.[35]

Several experts feel Tennessee providers' experiences under Medicaid have worsened under TennCare. Provider reimbursements for care are significantly lower, compared with private payers. Therefore, funding and quality of care are major concerns of state health reforms. Publicized concerns of TennCare providers, particularly the physicians, included insufficient reimbursements. The Tennessee Medical Association, TMA, representing 6,700 of the state's 10,000 physicians, filed a lawsuit in 1993, a few days before TennCare was to replace Medicaid. That did not stop TennCare from going into effect, however. The suit was later dropped after the state's new governor, Don Sundquist, addressed most of TMA's major concerns, including a clause that would have subjected physicians to criminal penalties for refusal to treat TennCare patients.[36] As recently as March 1996, however, a survey of TennCare physicians revealed their concerns about TennCare's stringent rules guiding physician prescribing.[37]

Publicized concerns of the TennCare patients include an inability to receive timely medical attention, additional medical complications due to late care, reduced quality of care, and lack of coverage for specific medical conditions. The state is also experiencing a surge of indigents from its neighboring states who seek free care in Tennessee. The state's inability to effectively monitor and contain this infringement compounds TennCare's challenges.

On July 1, 1996, Tennessee launched a new initiative under TennCare, called TennCare Partners (TP). It is the state's Medicaid program for mental health and substance abuse. TP, developed over a two-year period, won federal approval in April, 1996, taking effect three months later.[38] TennCare Partners has goals similar to TennCare itself. They are to expand medical, mental health, and substance abuse treatments to Medicaid patients and the uninsured. Rather than deal directly with doctors, hospitals, and pharmacists, the state contracts with private companies to manage mental health services and pay-related expenses. The BHOs (Behavioral Health Organizations) contract for health providers to treat patients.

TennCare and TennCare Partners cover roughly 1.2 million Tennesseeans for $3.3 billion annually. Prior to formation of the partners program, Memphis Mental Health Institute provided alcohol and drug abuse programs. TennCare Partners is set up to provide similar coverage at a much reduced rate and with reduced mental health benefits. Only two BHOs operate under the Partners system. They are Tennessee Behavioral Health, Inc., and Premier Behavioral Systems of Tennessee. Tennessee Department of Mental Health and Mental Retardation oversees TennCare Partners. The BHOs will apportion a capitation of $21.84 monthly per patient to the providers of mental and substance abuse services. The launching of TP benefited from lessons of TennCare. Thus, interim assessments of the integrated mental health sub-system show positive prognosis.

REFORMING LOUISIANA MEDICAID

Roughly 40 percent of Louisiana's 4.32 million residents are on Medicaid or are uninsured altogether. The state, like several others, earlier applied for a Section 1115 waiver, pending in 1996. If approved, the initiatives other states are implementing could help Louisiana prepare for its challenges.

Currently in that state, however, indigent care is provided under a fee-for-service arrangement in state academic health centers. The federal government also recently restricted the amount that states can reimburse hospitals for treating Medicaid patients at a time when the dwindling federal budget is constraining the states' ability to absorb the additional costs of care. Therefore, indigent-care access is challenging to Louisiana, as it is to other states with large underinsured or uninsured populations.

Louisiana's indigent care crisis has moderated somewhat through reduced funding for indigent health care, particularly to the nursing homes, as well as by shifting more care to home health care. There are gradual reductions in services, as well as in health personnel staffing at state facilities. In the meantime, Governor Mike Foster has asked his Secretary of the Department of Health and Human Services, Bobby Lindahl, to halt the movement toward privatization of the state's Medicaid program. Meanwhile, that secretary had to approach the legislature to cut funds elsewhere.

One issue under debate in 1996 centered on charging indigent care recipients a $3–$5 co-payment. While this covers little in the way of costs, many feel it limits access to needed care. Studies have shown that the poor spend a larger share of their disposable incomes on cigarettes, liquor, and various forms of gambling. These are all potentially addictive, but they are also conscious spending decisions. Total spending on these items is likely to exceed the minimum annual co-payments for health care.

Individuals on Medicaid also tend to receive welfare checks. Some have suggested having the state deduct monthly from the welfare payments to the indigent an amount sufficient to cover the co-payments for their health care benefits.

Others have suggested taxing the behaviors that pose significant health hazards and risks to the indigent, as well as the institutions that support or provide these activities. Those tax funds could then be used to augment the public funds for the health care needs of the indigent and uninsured.

NATIONAL PIECEMEAL HEALTH REFORMS

The failure of the 104th Congress to enact some form of broad health care legislation has resulted in more sporadic enactments of piecemeal reforms at the national level. Such reforms are taking many forms. The 1995 Health Insurance Reform Act, approved unanimously by the Senate Labor and Human Resources Committee, is designed to cut the linkage of health insurance to employment. Dubbed the biggest health care measure passed in ten years, the Health Insurance Portability and Accountability Act (HIPPA) of 1996 was signed into law in September 1996, by President Bill Clinton to take effect July 1, 1997.[39]

HIPPA, a bipartisan initiative, forbids health insurance firms from dropping individuals or groups of individuals from coverage if they fall sick. The second major provision forbids insurance companies to refuse coverage of new workers with pre-employment medical illnesses. An exception is if the worker is without coverage for more than 63 days between jobs. Third, self-insured individuals can deduct from taxes 80 percent (as opposed to the old 30 percent) of their health insurance premium by the year 2006. HIPPA also allows the terminally ill to withdraw from life insurance plans without tax penalty.

Medical Savings Accounts, MSAs, have a set of built-in incentives for responsible consumption of medical services. HIPPA provides for a limited testing of MSAs as a way to hold down health care costs. Specifically, a four-year pilot program was authorized to create a maximum of 750,000 tax-free MSAs for employees in business with fewer than 50 workers. The MSAs operate like the IRA and, as such, are market-based.

The viability of MSAs as an incentive-based, piecemeal health care finance policy reform alternative to a broader reform plan has received scant media coverage. This despite its introduction in Congress after the 1994 demise of the Clinton plan, and also despite its recent inclusion in the HIPPA.

Oregon's health reform legislation exempts employees from state taxes on funds placed in employer-sponsored MSAs. Even without legislation, private-sector firms such as Golden Rule Insurance Company are enrolling large numbers of employees in voluntary MSAs. MSAs attempt to balance the conflicting goals of efficiency (i.e., patient benefits exceed costs of care) and equity (i.e., subsidizing low- more than high-income workers or treating equally individuals of different incomes).

The proposed MSA reform advocated by economists Mark Pauly and John Goodman will involve the use of tax credits for purchasing a mix of catastrophic coverage (to cover large medical bills above a given deductible) and MSAs (fixed-dollar or predetermined amounts set aside for routine health care services). This arrangement is capable of reducing the currently distorted efficiency incentives and also achieve equity. The current problems of "moral hazard" can therefore be reduced significantly by pricing medical care to reflect true costs and letting the consumer bear the full cost. Consumers, being frugal, could then decide among care providers offering similar quality services in the medical marketplace. Competition among providers, in turn, will encourage efficient production of care.

Portability of MSAs is an added advantage when workers relocate. Arizona's 1994 health care reform legislation grants tax exemption for employee contributions to employer-sponsored MSAs. Funds not expended in one year can be rolled over and added to future deposits. MSAs are also favored by insurance companies.

Singapore devised a three-prong MSA scheme for financing health care. The 1984 Medisave aspect, based on the concepts of free choice, self-reliance, and personal accountability, requires workers to save for medical care and pay providers directly for the services. Deposits to Medisave account for about 7 percent of personal incomes. Roughly 95 percent of workers participate. Medisave balances become part of the holder's estate upon death. Medishield, the risk-pooling insurance component begun in 1990 for catastrophic care, limits the moral hazard factor (e.g., it imposes lifetime spending limits). Finally, Medifund, a need-based endowment fund established in 1993, not yet used intensely, subsidizes hospital indigent care.

Some U.S. experts feel the Singapore experiment has expanded the access to health care. Public hospitals are more efficient and now compete with private-sector care, although, overall, per-capita health spending rose about 2 percent faster than before the MSA programs, mainly due to providers competing more fiercely to acquire and treat patients with the latest in innovative medical technologies and procedures.

Is the MSA likely to succeed in the United States, based on the Singapore experience? There is no simple answer, as a number of factors must be considered first. For example, Singapore is a city-state, a British-style health system preceded its reformed MSA design, and its cultural orientation, demographics, and government system differ from America's.

Some observers in the United States, like Dr. Joseph Newhouse of Harvard, attribute between 50–75 percent of the growth of the U.S. health costs to technological changes. New technologies simply refuse to completely displace old ones, some feel. Therefore, technology may not be an additional cost-driver, unlike in Singapore, if the MSA scheme is widely instituted in the United States.

Finally, America needs to recognize the cost implications of "provider-induced demand" (demand creation) and devise mechanisms to curtail it in a reformed MSA system. This is because medical care decisions are jointly made by patients and their physicians under the MSA scheme.

To conclude, whatever form they are taking, incremental reform efforts in the United States must resolve the ills of the wasteful health care system.

MEDICARE MEDICAL SAVINGS ACCOUNTS (MSAS)

Medicare is the only major U.S. health insurance plan that has not yet undergone a major overhaul since the mid-1980s. The GOP-sponsored Medicare Preservation Act of 1995, a part of the efforts to balance the federal budget over seven years, seeks to reduce the annual growth rate of Medicare from 10.5 to 6.4 percent. Congressional Republicans expected the $270 billion in projected savings to preserve the long-term solvency of the Medicare system beyond 2002, and also give elderly Americans the choice of private insurance now available to the younger population. The Congressional Budget Office, however, expected the GOP-proposed Medicare overhaul to increase the federal deficit by $3.5 billion in seven years.

One actively debated, free market effort for reforming Medicare is privatization through MSAs. This option permits Medicare enrollees to combine a private, high-deductible, catastrophic health insurance plan with a restricted, personal savings account funded by Medicare for defraying routine medical expenses such as office visits.

The GOP plan would give Medicare recipients $5,100 in 1996, with $3,000 used to purchase a $3,000-deductible private insurance policy from, say, Golden Rule or similar insurance companies. The balance of $2,100 would be deposited into a personal MSA to cover routine medical expenses and deductibles. Medical bills exceeding MSA deposits, but less than the catastrophic deductible, could be paid out of pocket or with personal funds that otherwise would have been used to purchase a private, medigap insurance policy. Medicare payments for MSAs will increase yearly under the GOP plan, not to exceed $6,700 per enrollee in 2002.

Medicare cost savings from implementing MSAs are expected to account for $220 billion of the $270 billion reduction in the GOP-sponsored Medicare cost containment bill, according to the National Center for Policy Analysis. State health reform plans such as Oregon's and Arizona's allow for tax-free contributions to MSAs. Several employers and private insurers currently offer MSAs along with the standard health insurance plans.

MSA advocates and several health-care policy experts promote the benefits of MSAs. These benefits include:

- a wider latitude for health care providers and users to make joint medical care decisions which are absent from managed care plans;
- financial incentives that lead to a more efficient production and use of medical care (this operates via lowered moral hazard effects);
- a provision that undisbursed funds at year's end can be withdrawn and taxed or rolled over to the next year.

The potential problems and unresolved aspects of the MSA provision in the Medicare bill are not adequately debated in the public press. Discussing them is important, as they are relevant in any meaningful accounting of the expected net social benefits of a reformed health system design. The troubling aspects of MSAs follow:

- *Cost-Shifting.* Seniors who become catastrophically ill after one year of an MSA coverage can switch back to the traditional fee-for-service care. This tends to insure MSA health insurance companies at the expense of fee-for-service health plans. Medicare patients gain financially, at least for the first year, by deferring early intervention and ignoring preventive care while hedging against large losses thereafter by switching health plans when they become seriously ill.
- *Adverse Selection.* The natural end result of the progressive cost-shifting is that Medicare program costs are likely to rise. Health insurance risks can no longer be pooled to minimize program costs if the healthy individuals are not also present in the actuarial pool. Democrats and the White House were concerned in 1996 that healthy elderly people would likely self-select themselves into the MSAs for personal financial gains and leave the more ill, financially burdensome elderly patients to the traditional Medicare and HMO health plans.
- *Post-Deductible Utilization.* Several studies of the current health insurance designs show that once the deductibles are met, there are no incentives for the insured individuals to minimize utilization of health services. The proposed MSA under Medicare has a $3,000 deductible for 1996. Once this is met, there is no reason to suppose that the MSA-insured elders will behave any differently from any other person under the standard fee-for-service model.
- *Physician-Induced Demand.* The very ill elderly patient may not be able to make a well-informed decision jointly with the physician. This opens up opportunity for providers to pursue their personal goals of income maintenance to achieve a target income stream. Inducement occurs when therapeutically unneeded care is

provided to insured patients. Evidence is mixed on this, however, as the true measure of the benefits of care is the health outcomes of the intervention.[40]

- *Miscellaneous Uncertainties.* The MSA concept, which appears to be theoretically appealing, has not been tested on a large-scale audience to gauge the extent to which the MSA incentives reduce health services utilization costs. How MSAs relate to existing health benefit programs such as managed care is unclear, also. Thus, administering MSAs could be problematic for health benefit plan managers. How MSAs will impact the total cost of employer-sponsored health plans is also debatable.

- *One Size May Not Fit All.* Similar to the other programs, such as IRAs and other savings accounts at banks, there are potentially many ways to design an MSA. Their complexities are also likely to increase with experience. The structure of an MSA can determine how many and which employees buy them. Studies have shown that, compared to the standard plan, a budget-neutral, high-deductible MSA design raises the out-of-pocket costs for workers needing significant amounts of health care. However, the alternative—also a high-deductible, comparative benefits MSA plan—increases costs to the employer.

The MSA approach to reforming Medicare appears to have attractive features. However, there are legitimate concerns. Therefore, there may be merit in allowing the private health insurance industry, working with the government and private employers, to experiment with varieties of MSA plans. This could be done over a sufficiently long time period of about two years, necessary to collect adequate data for evaluating the projected cost implications for Medicare. How implementation of MSAs alters the cost structure of other managed-care plans for the elderly should be evaluated.

Finally, findings of the Medicare MSA experiment can be useful as a guide for designing broad-based MSA plans for workers.

THE CHALLENGE OF REPORTING ON HEALTH CARE

Organizing a reformed health system is challenging. Consumer access to quality care, sufficient provider reimbursements, and reliable funding are required for successful implementation. These are, however, major challenges to contend with—especially in those states with large urban concentrations of low-income residents. Therefore, for Louisiana's initiatives to succeed during a period of rapidly evaporating federal supports, the state must create and implement a set of creative financing and legislative devices that guarantee reasonable access to needed health care that does not compromise quality.

Reporting on health reforms in the future is likely to pose increased challenges to the media, especially in light of the arguments for and against the concept of "public journalism." Public journalism is a vague term to many that connotes the news media's going beyond reporting of an issue to helping readers and viewers solve the problem. Jay Rosen, a journalism professor at New York University and an advocate of the idea, contends that the media were instrumental in the failure of President Clinton's failed health reform efforts. He argues that the media reported "too much of the process and minutia in politics," thereby reinforcing the standard public belief that the nation is incapable of effectively addressing its social problems. He maintains that public journalism would not cover up the story but "help the community come to public judgment." The role of public journalism, Rosen declares, is to (1) focus on the readers and viewers and not on, say, health care experts, and (2) help the public work through a problem by providing information and insuring that the public understands there are some choices to be made, that the choices involve tradeoffs, and that they have consequences.[41]

This second aspect of public journalism is consistent with the economists' view of the resource allocation problem in a world of finite resources. Critics of public journalism—such as former NBC News President Michael Gartner—contend that public journalism is dangerous in that it takes the journalist over the line of reporting and into the role of social worker. To some degree, future media reporting on health care is likely to be influenced, to some degree, by the outcome of this debate on public journalism.

Further challenges to the media include informing the public on the comparative effectiveness of the fee-for-service and the managed approach to providing care. This way, individual purchasers of the different health plans are likely to be informed sufficiently to judge whether they have made a value-maximizing decision in selecting from among alternative health plans.

NOTES

1. Tip O'Neil, with Gary Hymel, *All Politics Are Local and Other Rules of the Game* (New York: Random House, 1993).

2. Intergovernmental Health Policy Project, *Fifty State Profiles: Health Care Reform, 1995* (report prepared for the Henry J. Kaiser Family Foundation by the George Washington University, Washington, D.C.).

3. Julie Robner, "Covering Health Care: Are Reporters Missing the Beat?", a supplement to *Advances* (Princeton, N.J.: Communications Office, The Robert Wood Johnson Foundation, Issue 3, 1996).

4. Ibid.

5. Martin J. Feldstein, *The Politics of Health Legislation* (Melrose Park, Ill.: Health Administration Press, July 1996).

6. American Association of Retired Persons, *Reforming the Health Care System: State Profiles, 1995* (Washington, D.C.: AARP, 1996).

7. B. C. Madrian, "The Effect of Health Insurance on Reitrement," Brookings Papers on Economic Activity, 1994.

8. Employment-based Health Insurance and Job Mobility: Is There Evidence of Job Lock?", *Quarterly Journal of Economics* 109 (February 1994), pp. 27–54.

9. David M. Cutler and M. B. McClelland, "Determinants of Technology Change in Medical Practice," in David A. Wise, ed., *Advances in the Economics of Aging* (Chicago: University of Chicago Press, 1996).

10. Joseph B. Newhouse, "Medical Care Costs: How Much Welfare Losses?", *Journal of Economic Perspectives* 6 (Summer 1992), pp. 3–21.

11. American Pharmaceutical Association, *Special Report: Opportunities for the Community Pharmacist in Managed Care* (Washington, D.C., 1994).

12. American Association of Retired Persons, *Reforming the Health Care System.*

13. Albert A. Okunade, "Production Cost Structure of U.S. Hospital Pharmacies Time-Series, Cross-Sectional Bed Size Evidence," *Journal of Applied Econometrics* (August 1993), pp. 277–294.

14. Paul F. Larson, Marion Osterweis, and Elaine Rubin, eds., "Health Workforce Issues for the 21st Century," *Health Policy Manual IV*, The Association for Academic Health Centers, Washington, D.C., 1994.

15. Albert A. Okunade, "Effects of the 1990 Federal Medicaid Drug Rebates Policy on Dispensed RX Volumes," invited paper presented at the Annual Meeting of Southern Economic Association, New Orleans, La., November 1995.

16. George Schieber, Jean-Pierre Poullier, and Leslie M. Greenald, "A U.S. Health Expenditure Performance: An International Comparison and Data Update," *Health Care Financing Review* 13 (1992), pp. 1–15.

17. John Hutton, Michael Borowitz, Inga Olesky, and Bryan R. Luce, "The Pharmaceutical Industry and Health Reform: Lessons from Europe," *Health Affairs* 13 (Summer 1994), pp. 98–111.

18. Schieber et al., "A U.S. Health Expenditure Performance."

19. R. Labelle, G. Stoddart, and T. Rice, "A Re-examination of the Meaning and Importance of Supply-induced Demand," *Journal of Health Economics* 13, pp. 347–368.

20. Newhouse, "Medical Care Costs."

21. Albert A. Okunade, "Piecemeal Reform Offers Wider Health Care Choices," *The Commercial Appeal* (Memphis, Tenn.), September 17, 1995, p. B6.

22. The White House Domestic Policy Council, the President's Health Security Plan, the complete draft (New York: Times Books), 1993.

23. Dev S. Pathak and Alan Escovitz, eds., *Managed Competition and Pharmaceutical Care: A Challenge to the Profession* (New York: The Haworth Press, 1996).

24. David Brown, "Darwin's Presence Shadows Health Care Debate," *The Commercial Appeal* (Memphis, Tenn.), September 25, 1994, p. B5.

25. Les Seago, Jr., "Educated Guesses: Health Care Reform," *Update*, The University of Memphis, January 30, 1995, p. 2.

26. Robert H. Miller, Helene L. Lipton, Kathryn S. Duke, and Harold S. Luft, "The San Diego Health Care System: A Snapshot of Change," *Health Affairs* 15 (Spring 1996), pp. 224–229.

27. Frederic R. Curtiss, "Managed Care: The Second Generation," *American Journal of Hospital Pharmacy* 47 (September 1990), pp. 2047–2052.

28. Seago, "Educated Guesses."

29. John W. Peabody et al., "Health Systems Reforms in the Republic of China.

Formulating Policy in a Market-Based Health System," *JAMA* 273 (March 8, 1995), pp. 777–781.

30. Cyril F. Chang, "TennCare: Tennessee's Answer to Health Care Reform." *The Journal of Medical Practice Management* 9 (1995), pp. 259–262.

31. William G. Manning et al., "Health Insurance and the Demand for Medical Care: Evidence from a Randomized Experiment," *American Economic Review* 77 (June 1987), pp. 251–277.

32. Albert A. Okunade, "Do State-Level Public Health and Prison Expenditures Impact Higher Education Appropriations?", paper presented at the Annual Meetings of the Association for Research in Nonprofit Organizations and Voluntary Action, Cleveland, Ohio, November 1995.

33. Mary Powers, "No Real Calamaties in Mental Health Switch; Providers Adjust to TennCare Partners," *The Commercial Appeal* (Memphis, Tenn.), August 1996, pp. A1, A5.

34. Chang, "TennCare."

35. Johnson Cato, "Methodist Hopes Access Medplus Deal Doesn't Lead to Acquisition," *Memphis Health Care News*, March 22, 1996, p. 3.

36. Richard Locker, "Doctor Group Calls Off TennCare Lawsuit," *The Commercial Appeal* (Memphis, Tenn.), July 12, 1995, p. A3.

37. Patrick Graham, "Survey by TMA Finds Physicians Fearing Managed Care's Influence in Prescriptions," *Memphis Health Care News*, March 8, 1996, p. 17.

38. Powers, "No Real Calamities in Mental Health Switch."

39. "Some Health Reform," *The Commercial Appeal* (Memphis, Tenn.), September 4, 1996.

40. Labelle, Stoddart, and Rice, "A Re-examination of the Meaning and Importance of Supply-Induced Demand."

41. Robner, "Covering Health Care."

9

Ethical Issues in Risk Communication

In a sense, this entire book has incorporated an ethical analysis of how well reporters are performing their tasks in alerting the public to possible health and safety risks. In writing or talking about journalists describing the risk posed by copycat terrorists who may try to emulate the acts of the Oklahoma City bombers, reporters are talking about an ethical dilemma: alerting the public to a serious threat verses panicking them needlessly if the threat is actually a misguided prank. When reporters warn about the potential impact of global warming, there is an ethical dimension: Should you run the risk of panicking the public when even the experts can't agree on the seriousness of this threat or when it might occur? On the other hand, when journalists withhold information about potential health hazards which they might think will create a panic, you have an ethical dilemma as well: Is it better to inform the public, despite the possible panic it will cause, or keep them in the dark about what may be a real threat?

The following case study shows how tricky the waters of some ethical dilemmas can be for journalists.

VICTIMS AND THE PRESS: A CASE STUDY

Robert Logan of the University of Missouri developed this case study to show some of the many ethical questions facing reporters in dealing with risk communication stories.[1]

Alice Waters's seven-year-old daughter Julie has leukemia. Her illness was diagnosed in its early stages last year. Julie's physicians believe her condition can be successfully treated.

Alice Waters, 37, lives in a mobile home in an unicorporated area a few miles from Metroplex, a city of 1.5 million. Ms. Waters's street is the only residential section in the area. At the north end of the street—which has twelve mobile homes on each side facing one another—are four large service stations. They catch traffic off the interstate that runs a quarter-mile away to the west. At the south end of the street (about a quarter-mile away) are two large tanks that are a relatively small storage facility for Big Oil, Inc. Next to this—starting almost in her backyard—is the boundary of a successful, seven-hundred-acre grapefruit orchard, which borders on a municipal landfill. About a quarter-mile away are large well fields that are the principal source of drinking water for Metroplex.

Three years ago, a six-year-old boy in the household two doors down from Ms. Waters was diagnosed as having leukemia. He was not as lucky as Julie; his diagnosis was late in the progression of his disease, and he died last year. Then an infant girl became the second baby born with birth defects in the neighborhood within seven years. Both families moved before Ms. Waters came to the neighborhood two years ago.

Internal specialists Dr. Earnest and Dr. Sincere met Julie soon after she was admitted to the hospital in October 1990. They were instrumental in getting funding for Julie's care when her mother was unable to pay. They are members of Worried M.D.'s for Social Responsibility, a self-proclaimed liberal, national public-interest group that gets actively involved in national political issues.

The physicians told Ms. Waters that they were suspicious about the causes of Julie's illness. Two cancer and birth-defect incidents on the same street, the physicians said, were not a coincidence.

Last year, they began to collect water samples from the well near Ms. Waters's house. They sent the samples to a well-regarded testing lab in another city. Since then, they have tested the water at a professional lab every four months. Every test revealed traces of more than ten human-made and natural chemicals often associated with oil storage tanks, pesticides from grapefruit orchards, gas-station leaks, lead from auto emissions, and a large landfill.

But each chemical occurs consistently at six to fifteen parts per billion, which is considered safe for drinking water via standards set by the Environmental Protection Agency (EPA). At higher levels, these chemicals are associated with carcinogenic risks or increases in birth defects, but the levels found at Ms. Waters's well head are within safety thresholds set by the EPA. There is no evidence the chemicals are associated directly with the health problems found in Ms. Waters's neighborhood.

At a fund-raising party last night for mayoral candidate Sam Clean, Drs. Earnest and Sincere privately tell Clean what they have found. Clean is a well-known public figure, has a reputation as an environmentalist, owns a successful health-foods restaurant chain, is media wise, and looks good on

TV. He is a long shot to become mayor and needs fresh issues to draw attention to his candidacy.

Today at 11:00 A.M., news radio station KAOS begins running as the top story in its twenty-minute news rotation, "Clean Attacks City's Lack of Cleanup." In the story, Clean gives a soundbite attacking city officials for "ignoring cancer-causing agents in water in a neighborhood where children have died, which is next door to the city's water supply." He describes the neighborhood's medical problems and describes (without naming) Julie and Alice Waters. The news report explains that water from the neighborhood has several "toxic agents believed to cause cancer at higher levels" and points out that the city's water wells are within a quarter-mile of oil tanks, gas stations, a grapefruit orchard, a landfill, and septic tanks. County officials are said to be unavailable for comment. The report runs throughout the day at twenty-minute intervals.

By 2:30 P.M., calls to the switchboard have jammed the newsroom. The callers who get through are frightened about their drinking water. City Hall's switchboards are jammed. The callers sound upset and ask whether their water is safe to drink.

By 4:00 P.M., reporters from the local ABC affiliate are already knocking on doors in the trailer park and sending live reports from the scene. Neighbors tell them where Alice and Julie Waters live.

By 4:15 P.M., your managing editor gives you the story. You are an ambitious reporter for *Metroplex Today*, the only morning newspaper in Metroplex. Both of you realize this is clearly page 1 potential, but you have only a few hours before deadline for the next morning's edition. After a few phone calls, you discover that the mayor, the city council, and most city and county officials are out of town at a retreat and are unavailable for comment. The regional EPA office is not answering the phone.

A trusted spokesperson for Regional Hospital tells you that Sincere and Earnest are furious at Clean for releasing the story and have no comment. She fills you in with all of the above information. The same Regional Hospital spokesperson says Ms. Waters does not want to be interviewed. She suddenly realizes that her husband, whom she walked out on several years before, might see the story and return to town.

Sam Clean, of course, is more than happy to talk to you.

Among the questions facing reporters covering this story are the following:

- Is Clean a reliable enough source on whom KAOS radio could base its reports?
- Should KAOS have broadcast the story?
- Should you respect Ms. Waters's wishes and leave her and her daughter out of the story?
- Are Dr. Earnest and Dr. Sincere reliable sources?
- What do you tell the public about whether the water supply is safe?

Other questions include:

- Would you be working on the story at all if KAOS and the ABC station had ignored it?
- If Ms. Waters decides to do the TV interview later today, do you then include her comments in your story?
- If city and county officials remain unavailable, how do you handle their side of the story? Does that delay publication until you can get more information, or do you go with what is available despite the alarm-sounding element in the story?

And finally, you must deal with these questions about sounding that alarm in the community:

- Are there any unbiased sources you can contact about the risk assessment? Who?
- How do you handle the discrepancy between the information from the EPA and the skeptical scientists and environmentalists?
- What is the public's probable reaction to reporting this story? Should your newspaper take any precautions to prevent public panic, and if so, what should they be?
- How risky is the water compared to risks we take for granted, such as traveling by car? Can you think of a relevant comparison for your article comparing the relative risk of the water to a well-known risk?
- Is it the media's role to speak for a society that is averse to many risks? How might the media accomplish this function?

Often the resolution to these issues lies not on either extreme at all. Often it is not a matter of either disclosing or withholding the story, but rather finding some middle grounds, some way of telling the story where there is a balance created between keeping the public in the dark or panicking them. This middle ground was what Aristotle had in mind when he developed his concept of the Golden Mean.

SEARCHING FOR THE PASSAGE

In searching for the kind of ethical Northwest Passage that can guide them to proper ethical resolutions, many journalists have come to look to voices from the past who spent lifetimes studying the appropriate way to respond to tough questions. One of the most prominent of these voices was Aristotle, the fourth-century biologist and philosopher who still speaks across the generations to journalists today.

The Golden Mean

Artistotle, first and foremost, believed in the importance of education. He believed that morality was intertwined with a person's education; in general, the more a person knows, the better chance he or she has of becoming an ethical person. In searching for the passage to virtue, Aristotle developed his Golden Mean. It says moral virtue is the appropriate location between two extremes. The idea for this mean came to Aristotle from Confucianism's central belief in harmony and equilibrium. To Aristotle, the two extremes to generally be avoided are excess, on the one hand, and deficiency on the other. It represented a sharpening of Plato's idea of temperance, which was one of his four cardinal virtues. In moral virtue, excellence is regarded as a mean between excess and defect. Courage, for instance, is halfway between cowardice and temerity; modesty is a mean between shamelessness and bashfulness; righteous indignation stands between envy and spite, and so on.[2]

To Aristotle, the emphasis in ethics should be on a person's character rather than his behavior, because behavior is simply an outward manifestation of what is inside that person.

The Golden Mean wasn't intended by Aristotle to be the same for every person. It could easily vary depending upon a person's foremost loyalties and goals, as well as the situation itself. The important thing is for the person—in our case the journalist—to identify what the extremes are. In the case of the water contamination story cited above, the two extremes might be represented by (1) publishing an alarmist story that might not be totally supported by credible sources and facts and (2) ignoring the story altogether. The Golden Mean might be represented by giving the story the play it legitimately deserves, keeping in mind nothing has been proven yet about the level of danger involved, and noting that all sources have not been heard from yet about that risk level.

It should be noted that Aristotle was not encouraging people to strive for some average consensus or some timid action that would not alienate anyone. He was not necessarily promoting a bland compromise. That the mean can change for different individuals is indicated by his suggestion that, for a person prone to one extreme, he or she might lean more toward the other this time. Clifford Christians, Mark Fackler, and Kim Rotzoll explain:

The mean is not only the right quantity, but it occurs at the right time, toward the right people, for the right reason, and in the right manner. The distance (between extremes) depends on the nature of the agents as determined by the weight of the moral case before them. Consider the Greek love of aesthetic proportion in sculpture. The mean in throwing a javelin is four-fifths of the distance to the end; in hammering a nail nine-tenths from the end.[3]

Plato's Cave

Many students of philosophy will best remember Plato, Aristotle's pred-
ecessor, as laying down his four cardinal virtues of temperance, justice,
courage, and wisdom. To Plato, the virtuous person was one who evidenced these traits by his actions. But just as applicable to journalists is the
metaphor of the cave which Plato used to illustrate how the virtuous person
should behave with others.

Plato's cave is a metaphor for human existence. There are prisoners at
the bottom of the cave; they are forced to stare at a wall on which images
and shadows are depicted. The prisoners believe the images they see are
real. They play shadow games and award prizes to those with the keenest
eye. The images are, of course, not true representations of reality; they are
produced by puppeteers who stand on a ledge behind the prisoners and
parade their relics and objects for the prisoners to see on the wall. There
is a fire behind the puppeteers which projects these images onto the wall.
There is, at the apex of the cave, an exit to the outer world. This world
represents truth and attainment of that which is real and good.

To Plato, those chained to the wall are the unenlightened (Nietzsche calls
them the "herd"). To be liberated, they must be compelled to exit the cave
and move into the light of the outdoors. Over time, the prisoners will prefer
the real objects of the outside world to the blurred images of the cave, even
though they are harder to reach initially. He or she will enjoy the thrill of
knowledge of the higher things to the shadow games of the cave's bottom.
The ascent into the higher world away from the shadow world represents
the mind freeing itself from both the bondage of the things which pollute
the soul and the untruths of the cave.

Plato suggests that the cave represents how far our nature is enlightened
or unenlightened. The images on the wall can be likened to human education and the aculturalization process. And, indeed, the longer we stare
at the images on the wall and believe the charade of the puppeteer, the
more entrenched into intellectual darkness we become.

This is where journalism comes into play. We can certainly all agree that
newspaper reports, television news shows, and so forth are part of our
education. Their mediation between us and the events that affect us is apparent, especially those events to which we have no direct, personal access.
That the media have a large impact on our concept of reality is evident. In
terms of the cave allegory, there is no doubt that journalists play at least
some role, too, in our understanding and embracing of the images. So Plato
would caution the journalist to watch the imagery and to not sensationalize
or distort it. He would also ask the journalist to help readers or viewers
find their way in the outside world and connect their own personal worlds
to the greater world.

For the public health journalist, he would caution him or her to obtain as much knowledge as is humanly possible about the risk to be covered in the story before either unnecessarily alarming the public or sedating them when a real danger might actually exist.

The Importance of Duty

Out of the Age of Enlightenment came eighteenth-century philosopher Immanuel Kant, who taught the world to judge virtue on the basis of his *categorical imperative*. Kant believed this guideline could be used in any situation to determine which is the more virtuous way to act. Essentially the categorical imperative states that we should act in a way that we would like to see become a universal law for all future, similar situations. It is more of an absolutist perspective than, perhaps, Aristotle or Plato had in mind, but it is one also highly connected to the concept of *duty*.

Duty becomes a key factor for Kant, so much so that he believes it determines the moral worth of an act; that we must act from duty and not from inclination, and that we cannot act only in accordance with duty but, rather, for the sake of fulfilling our duty. In other words, to Kant, intention is everything. If we act in accordance with duty without meaning to, the action has no moral worth. We must, therefore, know our reasons for acting before we act.

Duty incorporates many aspects of human actions, and one of the most important is to act so that people are always an end, never only a means to an end. We must respect our moral duty, and this, in turn, will lead us to respect others. If this reasoning sounds familiar to traditional Judeo-Christian thought, it is. But Kant moves one step beyond and combines duty and respect into his famous categorical imperative.

Kant asks, "Can you also will that the maxim of your action become a universal law?" This question has become Kant's theme and key guideline. It has also become a strict moral code for his followers to ponder. Kant is an absolutist and unrelenting; there are no circumstances under which moral law will change, and everything is a universal.

To Kant, moral principles are truths in the same way mathematics are truths, and we are bound to them. We are thus bound to our duty to universal moral law and to our duty to others, even so far as to help them realize their duty and moral obligations.

This strict code gives journalists much to think about before the story goes into print or on the air. The intent of the story must be a good one, and the ethics used in getting it and presenting it must also be within the boundaries of that which could be a universal law. This is no easy task, and it certainly requires journalists to resist the temptation of hyping a story beyond the facts.

Mill and the Principle of Utility

Whereas Kant emphasized the intent of an act as the deciding moral determinant, John Stuart Mill—also a product of the Age of Enlightenment—tended to focus more on the consequences of an act. In his *Essay on Liberty*, Mill attempted to convert men and women to a peculiarly exclusive moral doctrine. He wished to moralize all social activity—religion and art, together with education and politics—and to mark each with its own emphatic imprint. He also wished to create a society that was morally homogenous and intellectually healthy because most of mankind, according to Mill, could succeed in reaching a level of education sufficient to allow them to be ethically and socially moral and to make rational and virtuous judgments as to which actions are right.

Mill argued that truth allows us to function well in our relation to others. However, in certain cases, the ends must be evaluated before the truth is sought, he would say. This is where his *principle of utility* fits in. One must keep in mind the consequences that may occur if one were to write the truth that could harm an individual's personal or social well-being.

Utilitarianism is a theory of ethics that says the rightness or wrongness of an act is determined by the amount of happiness its consequences produce for the greatest number of people. And that action is not necessarily dependent on the motive; an agent's bad motive may lead to others' happiness, thus rendering the act virtuous in the eyes of Mill.

Mill's doctrine would cause a journalist to moderate his or her absolutist position on publishing the truth to first ask what the possible consequences of airing that truth might be on the public.

In a sense, however, Kant and Mill are not often that far apart in their reasoning because—in thinking about what your motives are for publishing a story (i.e., will the story help or hurt the public)—the journalist is considering his or her intentions. They differ, however, with Mill stating that a bad motive can produce a good result and, thus, be ethical.

The Question of Relativism

A common thought among some people, when surveying these and several other determinants of moral action, is to say, "It doesn't really make any difference which course I take; ethics is all relative anyway."

Such a statement, however, suggests that all actions in a given situation are of equal moral value. That is simply not true. To see why, let's take a look at this idea of moral relativism in more depth. The first thing we find is that there are actually different kinds of relativism. Among them are the following:

1. *Conventional Relativism.* What is right or wrong is determined by the settled habits, traditions, and conventions of one's culture or society. This

honors these conventions and traditions, but it also permits intolerance toward dissenting minority views. Therefore, morality is conservative and possibly oppressive. Moral progress is thus very difficult. For a journalist who would simply follow the traditions and conventions of journalists who have gone before him or her in trying to decide how to solve an ethical issue involving risk communication, this could be troublesome. If the convention, for instance, is to always tell the truth in as much detail as you can, then the journalist would have no choice in considering the impact on a person with AIDS if the story about him appears in print.

To a conventional relativist, for example, women's suffrage and abolishing slavery were simple heresies and advocates were behaving immorally *until* the majority of the country sanctioned these changes with legislation.

Conventional relativism, therefore, provides little space for moral self-correction. Somehow the majority in society must first be swayed until morals undergo needed changes.

Finally with conventional relativism, individual judgment is subordinated to the group's judgment, which is generally seen as infallible.

2. *Individual Relativism*. This theory stresses the moral infallibiility of the individual. Therefore, if one thinks his or her action is moral, then it is. No one else may judge the rightness or wrongness of that individual's action, only the individual actor. But if each of us is right in our own ways, we can't have much to say to each other in moral matters.

Individual relativism may stress the virtue of *tolerance* for others' values, but if you believe intolerance is moral, for example, does that really make your opinion correct? Is this kind of relativism really a virtue of autonomy, or arrogance?

3. *Situational Relativism*. Morality is simply relative to the situation. It also means each situation is unique, so moral principles are useless, and generalizations are inappropriate. It leaves little room for discussion, and no general criteria for moral judgment are available.

Therefore, there is far more to analyzing the morality of actions than simply resorting to relativism as a way out. Situations, individual beliefs, and societal conventions must be analyzed alongside the moral principles—such as were discussed earlier—to find the best solution to the ethical puzzle.

Some Ethical Guidelines

Although journalists often resent the idea of mandatory codes of ethics for their work, they do welcome guidelines and principles that help them work their own way through the quagmire of dilemmas they confront. Fortunately, several journalists, educators, and philosophers have given a lot of thought to producing such guidelines. Two of them are discussed in this section.

The Society of Professional Journalists (SPJ) Ethics Handbook, *Doing Ethics in Journalism*, lays out a series of "Guiding Principles for the Journalist."[4] They are:

1. Seek truth and report it as fully as possible. Part of this principle is for journalists to inform themselves continuously so they can inform, engage, and educate the public. It also admonishes them to be honest, fair, and courageous in gathering, reporting, and interpreting information accurately; to provide a voice to the voiceless, and to hold the powerful accountable.

2. Act independently. Included in this principle are the warnings to guard the role a free press plays in an open society; seek out and disseminate competing perspectives; remain free of associations and activities that could compromise integrity; and recognize that good ethical decisions require individual responsibility enriched by collaborative efforts.

3. Minimize harm. Here, journalists are advised to be compassionate to those affected by their actions; treat sources, subjects, and colleagues as human beings deserving of respect and not just as means to an end; and recognize that gathering and reporting information might cause harm or discomfort, but balance those negatives by choosing alternatives that maximize the goal of truthtelling.

Many journalists have also received help from a series of criteria proposed by Ralph Potter of the Harvard Divinity School. Referred to as "Potter's Box," these criteria are:

1. Definition. Before any attempted resolution is considered, journalists must first be sure they have correctly defined the situation and explored all aspects and ramifications of it as is humanly possible within the time allowed. Included in this definition is the analysis of just what the ethical problem is. Sometimes when analyzed deeply, some situations really don't reveal as much of a dilemma as feared at first; other times they do.

2. Values. This criterion suggests that journalists analyze the ethical values involved in the situation. These values might be privacy versus the public's right to know; protection of a source versus adding credibility to an important story; misleading a source or going undercover to produce the truth, and so on. Often these values come in competing form and are the reason the dilemma exists in the first place. The journalist must start asking himself or herself which of these values seem paramount in the situation.

3. Principles. In this quadrant of the "box," the journalist should scroll back through the wisdom of the ages as produced from such sources as the Judeo-Christian tradition and the philosophers such as those discussed earlier in this chapter. What might these thinkers have to say across the years to the values inherent in the current dilemma? Journalists solving the puzzles might ask themselves, "How would Aristotle or Plato handle this situation? What about Kant and Mill?" Often colleagues in the newsroom who have confronted similar situations can also suggest valid principles that bear on the situation.

4. *Loyalties.* In this last quadrant (although the journalist might go around the box again to see if anything was overlooked), the journalist asks, "To whom or what do I consider my greatest allegiance owed in this situation?" To some extent, that probably depends on the answers to the questions obtained in the three previous boxes. Perhaps now the resolution is clear; perhaps there is only a stronger glimmer.

In any event, having taken the dilemma through such a system or set of criteria, the journalist can at least answer one question that could plague him or her in the future: "Why did I handle this story the way I did?" If he or she can believe they had a good reason for handling it that way, and if they tested it against the criteria mentioned above, at least they know they've done the best they can.

Sleep should come easier than if handling it more randomly.

The Role of Personal Involvement

The issue of a journalist becoming involved with his subjects and/or sources is always a controversial one in media circles. The fear is that such involvement will compromise the journalist's objectivity, which is held so sacred in newsrooms. However, the third general ethics principle discussed earlier admonishes journalists to minimize harm. That principle has led some journalists to wonder if they shouldn't become more involved with the people in their stories and those affected by them.

Writer Teresa Baggot has proposed what she calls a new kind of journalistic ethic—an *ethic of care*, an egalitarian ethic that pledges to consistently uphold human dignity and the community's well-being. According to Baggot, the ethic of care tries to "cause the least harm possible and sustain relationships among people. Journalists who follow it give voice to people whom society marginalizes and uncover the structures of injustice."[5]

The ethic of care was widely developed by Harvard social scientist Carol Gilligan who was somewhat dissatisfied with other theories of moral development. In particular, Gilligan sees women as having a different view of morality than men. She believes women's moral judgments are based mostly on the third criterion of cognitive development theory: they emphasize concern for others and their own image, and trust, loyalty, and respect.

To Gilligan, the ethic of care marks a different vortex of maturity. This ethic, with its concern for the other, for equity, and for the recognition of different points of view, marks points in the female individual's quest for attachment intimacy, and a sense of self.

In short, she believes the ethic of care is better than the ethic of justice. The reason is simple: if you care about someone else's well-being, you automatically care about them being treated justly.

As an example of the kind of ethic Baggot and Gilligan might deem appropriate, they would probably champion a reporter's scouring the streets of a major city, desperately seeking the seven-year-old daughter of a woman suffering from AIDS dementia. This is excactly what freelance writer Emily Adams did in Los Angeles in June 1992. About her experience, she wrote in a *Los Angeles Times* piece, "I couldn't image watching helplessly as a vibrant 25-year-old woman sank into forgetfulness and sometimes, bitter despair."[6]

It would also be the kind of ethic that might drive a reporter to become a spokesperson for the homeless, outcast children produced by a Third World country's civil war, choosing to devote her off-hours to obtaining funds to start an orphanage in that country for them.

Guided by the ethic of care, a journalist would interview sensitively and consider the effects of that interview should it be published. Baggot notes, "In the ethic of care, broad brush strokes are out."[7]

One story that caused journalists to discuss this basis of ethic was the media's revelation that former tennis star Arthur Ashe had AIDS. Many journalists argued that no useful social purpose was advanced by the revelation, and it only served to hurt Ashe and his family. Others, possibly those responsible for publishing the story, believed a social good was fulfilled and that it was worth the personal embarrassment to Ashe and his family. Still others say that kind of a decision is not the journalist's to make in the first place.

Baggot concludes her look at the ethic of care by noting:

Do journalists really need to apologize for acting human, or even, in some cases angelic? An ethic of care applauds their unorthodox professional approach and suggests it become convention. It also encourages journalists to approach their sources in a non-confrontational manner and to be on the lookout for stories that build up the community by supporting the good instead of always pointing out the bad.[8]

ETHICS CASES IN RISK COMMUNICATION

It is apparent, then, that stories involving elements of physical, mental, or emotional risk are fraught with ethical concerns. This section will examine a few stories to show how they were handled and see how well the cause of morality was served in them. The first story deals with the coverage of organ transplants; the second deals with the ethics of reporting environmental issues, and the third deals with a story on AIDS.

A Matter of Life and Death

That was the title given to an article by Deborah Baldwin on the media coverage of organ transplants. In it, she makes the observation, "Media coverage can play a large role in helping people pay for organ transplants, and sometimes in determining who gets them. To get that coverage, it helps to be a cute child."[9] The sobering fact is that some 34,000 Americans nationwide await organ transplants each year. New York City alone has some 200 such cases.[10] But, as in all cases with all kinds of stories, there must be something unique or heart-wrenching about a case in order for it to make it into print or on air.

The transplant that baseball great Mickey Mantle needed was a case in point. Here was a giant in sports who was an everyday household name. Was his transplant moved ahead of other lesser-knowns because of that? Probably. Then there was a case involving a 15-year-old New York boy, Simon Fischler, who needed a heart transplant and got one within days of coverage provided by *Newsday*. Did it help that he aspired to be a National Hockey League star and that his father, Stan Fischler, was a well-known professional hockey television commentator on Long Island? Probably. And there were the parents of a newborn in Detroit whose need for a heart transplant had been identified before birth who received media coverage— and the transplant—because the patient was an infant and the operation was so unusual.

In so many cases, news coverage leads to a quicker transplant as donors or their families see the stories and respond, even though there are other cases, just as needy, in line ahead of them. To correct this problem, Congress enacted legislation in 1984 creating the United Network for Organ Sharing, which maintains a central computer list of patients. The list, which was begun in 1987, intended to take some of the pressure off families searching for media coverage to help them get transplants.[11] Officially, transplant experts say there are several criteria for making the transplant list and securing a place in line. Among them are:

• the severity of the person's medical condition;
• length of wait;
• blood type;
• weight and other medical factors;
• proof of insurance coverage or the ability to pay for the operation.

Except for kidney transplants, there is no federal money available for organ transplants, so many families must try to convince their insurance companies that the risky operations should be covered. Those who can't must either come up with the money themselves or turn to fund-raising, in which the media become invaluable.

What about the pressure on medical reporters to respond to these requests for coverage? Anemona Hartocollis, the *Newsday* reporter who covered Simon Fischler, acknowledges that the coverage of people awaiting transplants isn't always fair: "I didn't really care how fair it was at that point. I only cared that he needed a transplant, and that moved me. It's not a pure process. I do stories on what appeals to me personally. I'm not sure that's wrong."[12]

Another reporter, Kristi Krueger, works in television news and has adopted the following guidelines:

I'm always looking for a peg. If a hospital calls, I'll say, "What's different? Is it a first? Is there a new piece of equipment or something else we can hook the folks in with?". . . . I hate to sound callous, and it does sound callous when you take so many calls.[13]

Some news media simply turn away requests for help from families awaiting transplants for loved ones, because the requests come too fast to keep up with and there is a general feeling of unease in responding to some and not others. One such paper, the *New York Times*, for instance, didn't cover the Fischler case. A science writer there says the *Times* only does stories that touch on ethical or scientific questions. Another paper, the *Washington Post*, doesn't carry regular items about organ or bone marrow recipients.[14]

Many media outlets, however, cannot afford to ignore the requests. Sometimes it depends on the size of the paper and the community it serves. In general, the pressures found in smaller communities make it impossible for newspapers and TV stations to ignore these requests. Brian Opanpa, reporter for the *Free Press* in Mankato, Minnesota, says, "We'll run a short item routinely (on fundraisers); bigger stories have to jump through the usual hoops."[15]

Stories on organ transplants are rife with ethical concerns. Is it right to feature one child needing a transplant and ignore another because the news value isn't as strong? How appealing does a child have to be, or how unusual must the procedure be, in order to rate such coverage? Organ transplant stories are a clear example of how the normal restraints of time, space, and news value come in conflict with the life-and-death needs of people awaiting transplants. You might actually help save the life of one patient with your coverage, but what about the others you deny coverage to who die while awaiting transplants?

Concludes Opanpa:

Ours sounds like a nice, pat policy. But what if two weeks later someone else calls, and you say we've already (done that story)? It's defensible journalistically, but how do you explain that to a family whose child is dying?[16]

Ethics and the Environment

Researchers William F. Griswold and Jill D. Swenson have studied the ethical dilemmas journalists face in one area of environmental coverage: waste disposal and treatment proposals in rural areas. In rural Georgia, for instance, disposing of other people's waste is a potential growth industry. Several communities have been asked to become the site of a hazardous chemical waste incinerator, sanitary landfill, or recycling plant. Almost all of these proposals come from corporations or governments in urban areas. Waste siting proposals are often marketed as economic development.[17] The reaction of the public to these siting proposals is almost always negative. In this climate, how should reporters handle these stories? Allan Mazur has noted, "When media coverage of controversy increases, public opposition . . . increases; when media coverage wanes, public opposition falls off."[18]

So, is it the job of the media to provide readers and viewers with information that can and will help them in mobilizing their opposition to these sitings? And should reporters support the "not in my backyard" sentiment of most of the audience? Also, should a journalist attempt to verify for himself or herself the benefits and/or risks of each proposal or rely instead on other experts—many of whom may have an ideological bias—to identify and classify these risks and benefits?

Some journalists ignore the thorny issue of risk assessment altogether and instead emphasize the human-interest stories. Is this a correct approach? Does the news media have an obligation to help find a way to dispose of its country's garbage once its landfill is full? The new rhetoric in media circles concerning *public journalism* suggests this is now the job of journalists: to go beyond reporting the problems the community faces and help citizens search for ways of solving the problem. But this is a controversial proposal among journalists, many of whom still believe it is only the journalist's job to point out the problems society faces and let other leaders look for solutions.

Elsewhere in this book, in the discussion of environmental journalism, it is noted that reporters covering the environment often take different approaches to their craft. Some believe in a strict objectivist stance; still others believe in advocacy journalism when discussing risks to the environment. Whichever approach one takes will affect the kind of ethic he or she brings to the story.

Sharon Friedman has studied enviornmental journalism and found much of it lacking. She writes that what is missing is the kind of data that

empowers readers and viewers, giving them information with which to make decisions. Control over environmental risks and hazards is a major factor for citizens, who are apt to accept a risk if they feel they have some degree of control over it.

But people seeing only facts without context in hazardous situations may decide
they are helpless to intervene or change a situation, and therefore do not participate
in the debate.[19]

Griswold and Swenson have identified three types of ethical orientations
common to American journalists that are related to environmental reporting[20]:

1. The marketing approach focuses on the commercial nature of the
media. Journalists using this approach try to give the audience what it
wants, seeing them as customers rather than students. Key loyalties of the
journalist are to the media company and its stockholders. Through a mix-
ture of the audience's awareness of its own needs and a free marketplace
ready to fulfill information needs, this perspective claims to serve the public
good. Implicit in this approach is having an audience which knows its own
needs and which asks for disturbing information from the press.

2. The community responsibility perspective is one more closely associated with smaller, more provincial media operating in smaller cities and
towns. Critics often view this perspective as boosterism and find problems
of objectivity associated with it. But those working in these communities
believe that they have a special responsibility to those they live with; that
they are a critical part of the community and are in a special position to
help the town look for solutions to its problems. The community perspective may be somewhat aligned with the ethic of care, discussed earlier.
Journalists may make their ethical decisions on the basis of how they will
affect and further the community's welfare rather than on the basis of strict
objectivity. In the instance of a potential waste disposal site being located
in or near town, these journalists may join with the community in adopting
an us-against-them orientation rather than report strictly on the facts of
how much risk or benefit is actually involved with the proposed project.

3. The professional orientation is more often associated with metro journalism. It emphasizes the traditional surveillance role of reporters and editors, and prescribes objectivity as an important idea for the journalist. The
reporter's ethical behaivior is based upon the degree to which he or she
conforms to a set of professionally agreed-upon principles of detachment
and verification of information. Fairness and balance are expected in the
presentation of all sides to the issue, and no advocacy stance is allowed.
But John Hulteng notes that this objective professional orientation requires
presenting the views of both sides in such a balanced and fair way that it
may be impossible for anyone but an expert to choose between them.[21]

What Griswold and Swenson suggest is an *environmental-development
ethic* that is based on the development news model created by a former
United Nations official. Basically this model urges journalists to adopt as
their ultimate goal the improvement of living conditions and quality of life

in their countries, but calls for them to take an independent stance from both government and big business so they can function as critic and evaluator of development projects. Further reviews of this model suggest the adequacy of development reporting can be assessed by testing it against the following questions:[22]

- Does the news emphasize development as process rather than events?
- Does the coverage present content critical of development projects, plans, policies, problems, or issues, as well as content supportive of it?
- Is there discussion of the relevance of development projects, plans, policies, problems, or issues on people?
- Is there information about development processes in other regions or countries?
- Do news reports compare the subject with original development goals and/or compare the subject with government claims for success?
- Does the news coverage make references to development needs of the people?

Griswold and Swenson believe this development news model is appropriate for environmental reporting because these issues are development in the broader sense of that term, which includes all processes of social change relevant to the well-being of society. They believe it would lead reporters toward helping citizens make more informed decisions on environmental questions, and is a more appropriate stance than following responsibilities toward media owners, community elites, or an abstract set of professional practices.

Yet the researchers warn that the model's focus on the community or the nation is likely to lead to trouble and may perpetuate disagreements among advanced and developing countries that lead to slow progress toward international pacts on environmental issues such as preserving the rainforests and protecting endangered species. So, instead, they suggest journalists take more of a global perspective on the ethical treatment of environmental stories. Nigel Dower has observed of this enlarged environmental perspective:

The scope of our moral relationships is in fact often viewed fairly narrowly in ordinary moral thought. That is, the scope is restricted to fellow human beings in our own society, to those living now, and to human beings as such. What the environmental perspective does is to invite us to see the scope of our moral relationships as greatly broadened to include fellow human beings throughout the world, to include future generations, and to include nonhuman life or the world of nature as a whole, rather than just fellow human beings.[23]

In relating this perspective to the problem of waste disposal siting in rural areas, Griswold and Swenson note each journalist would have been led to gathering enough information to make an independent judgment about the waste proposal presented to his or her community and, in making that judgment, to assess the human results of accepting or rejecting the proposal in other towns. And in the towns where newspapers did little or no reporting, the reporters would have been obligated to act; doing nothing, according to this perspective, is an immoral choice. In some communities, the journalists might have independently evaluated the benefits and risks of the proposal; decided that the plan for a bio-medical waste incinerator would solve local disposal needs, help the local economy, and involve minimal environmental risk; and reported so thoroughly. Or the newspaper might have acted in exactly the same way but, before agreeing to support the opposition campaign, would have reported on the proposal in a way to disseminate mobilizing information. In every case, it appears the probability of better informed public decision-making about important environmental issues would have been enhanced.[24]

"AIDS in the Heartland"

How to report on a dreaded disease that has social implications and is potentially embarrassing to its victims—that is just one issue facing journalists as they report on the spread of the AIDS virus across America and around the world. Jacqui Banaszynski of the *St. Paul Pioneer Press Dispatch* won a Pulitzer Prize for feature writing for her story called, "AIDS in the Heartland." As editor Deborah Howell noted about this series:

Many stories have been done on AIDS victims, but we have seen none that have approached the sensitivity, scope and impact of "AIDS in the Heartland." This series represents a major commitment . . . to foster an understanding of the human dimensions of AIDS. It was an assignment that required a particular combination of sensitivity, toughness, intelligence, tenacity and dedication to journalistic excellence. . . . "AIDS in the Heartland" cuts through the statistics. It chronicles the life and death of AIDS victim Dick Hanson, who is one of us—a native Minnesotan, a farmer, a political activist, someone's son and brother and uncle.[25]

The story, written by Banaszynski and photographed by Jean Pieri, tells the saga of Hanson and his partner, Bert Henningson, who also carries the AIDS virus. Hanson homesteaded his family's century-old farm south of Glenwood, Minnesota, and was also a high-profile liberal political activist in the area. The team of journalists spent many of Hanson's final days with him until his death on July 25, 1987, chronicling the challenges he and Henningson faced and how they learned to deal with them. An excerpt of series appears in the appendix of this book, but a short passage reads as follows:

"AIDS in the Heartland"
by Jacqui Banaszynski
St. Paul Pioneer Press Dispatch

Death is no stranger to the heartland. It is as natural as the seasons, as inevitable as farm machinery breaking down and farmers' bodies giving out after too many years of too much work.

But when death comes in the guise of AIDS, it is a disturbingly unfamiliar visitor, one better known in the gay districts and drug houses of the big cities, one that shows no respect for the usual order of life in the country.

The visitor has come to rural Glenwood, Minn.

Dick Hanson, a well-known liberal political activist who homesteads his family's century-old farm south of Glenwood, was diagnosed last summer with acquired immune deficiency syndrome. His partner of five years, Bert Henningson, carries the AIDS virus.

In the year that Hanson has been living—and dying—with AIDS, he has hosted some cruel companions: blinding headaches and failing vision, relentless nausea and deep fatigue, falling blood counts and worrisome coughs and sleepless, sweat-soaked nights.

He has watched as his strong body, toughened by 37 years on the farm, shrinks and stoops like that of an old man. He has weathered the family shame and community fear, the prejudice and whispered condemnations. He has read the reality in his partner's eyes, heard the death sentence from the doctors and seen the hopelessness confirmed by the statistics.

But the statsitics tell only half the story—the half about dying.

Statistics fail to tell much about the people they represent. About the people like Hanson—a farmer who has nourised life in the fields, a peace activist who has marched for a safer planet, an idealist and gay activist who has campaigned for social justice, and now an AIDS patient who refuses to abandon his own future, however long it lasts.

The statistics say nothing of the joys of a carefully tended vegetable garden and new kittens under the shed, of tender teasing and magic hugs, of flowers that bloom brighter and birds that sing sweeter and simple pleasures grown profound against the backdrop of a terminal illness. Of the powerful bond between two people who pledged for better or worse and meant it.

"Who is to judge the value of life, whether it's one day or one week or one year," Hanson said. "I find the quality of life more important than the length of life."

Much has been written about the death that comes from AIDS, but little has been said about the living. Hanson and Henningson want to change that. They have opened their homes and their hearts to tell the whole story—from beginning to end.

In analyzing the way Banaszynski and Pieri reported this story, media ethicists Jay Black, Bob Steele, and Ralph Barney concluded that the series showed the powerful connection between excellent journalism and ethical journalism.[26] They felt the reporter/photographer duo successfully navigated the treacherous waters of ethical questions that confronted them, including:

- informing the public;
- invasion of privacy;
- harm to family members;
- questions of taste about language and photos;
- potential manipulation of sources;
- confidentiality;
- promise-keeping;
- the two-way exploitative relationships between journalists and sources.

The ethicists concluded:

Banaszynski and her photographer Jean Pieri carried out their truthtelling responsibility with dedication and great skill. They also exhibited significant compassion and sensitivity in their reporting. Their paper was committed to publishing a powerful story about a painful issue. Excellence and ethics were tied together. . . . The journalists' careful and systematic process in making those [ethical] decisions serves as a model for other journalists.[27]

Specifically, they noted how well the journalists upheld the three principles of seeking and reporting the truth, acting independently, and minimizing harm. For instance, in seeking and telling the truth, Banaszynski did a great deal of research and preparatory interviewing before actually beginning the reporting on the primary sources. It took nearly a year to gain access to the people who would open their lives to news coverage. Once on the story, the journalists spent hundreds of hours over the course of a year reporting on Hanson and Henningson. Banaszynski was also open and honest with Hanson and Henningson about the type of story she was doing. She didn't want there to be questions of manipulation later.

In acting independently, Banaszynski realized she faced one of her greatest challenges. This was a story that affected her emotionally, and there was a great temptation to tell the story for Hanson and Henningson. In her own words, Banaszynski said:

The greatest challenge was to recongize my emotional involvement in the story— to use that emotion to breathe passion into my writing but to detach myself enough to remain focused on the truth. We discussed the ground rules. Everything I see goes in my notebook. I don't know how to not be a reporter. . . . I told them I would tell them about what I would write but I wouldn't show them my copy. (I told them that) when we talk and I don't use my notebook, it's not on the record, but I'll come back to you later to ask about it.[28]

Banaszynski further noted that it was important to collaborate with Pieri and her editors throughout the reporting and writing process to make sure everyone was agreed on the course the story would take.

Finally, in minimizing harm, the journalists realized they had to invade the privacy of the stricken couple, doing a story on an issue that could hold them up to public scorn, and still remain compassionate and respectful of them and their families. Here is where the real tradeoffs in reporting often occur as the reporter asks himself or herself about the ethics of deal-making among sources; leaving out certain details that would be enlightening to the public to preserve the privacy and dignity of the people involved in the story. Among the people Banaszynski agreed not to interview was Hanson's ex-wife because Hanson convinced Banaszynski she would be too vulnerable. Further, the editors of the *Pioneer Press Dispatch* also made a decision not to run a certain photo of Hanson and Henningson kissing because of the possible negative impact it would have on the readers and—by extension—on the paper and its ability to maximize its objectives with the series.[29]

All in all, "AIDS in the Heartland" emerges as a kind of textbook example of how an important, yet sensitive, story can be told well and still be told ethically.

Covering Sexual Abuse Stories

One of the difficult kinds of stories for journalists is that involving sexual abuse or rape. Journalists often discuss the merits and problems associated with keeping victims' identities confidential. Tradition and compassion usually dictate that confidentiality rule.[30] A major exception to that policy surfaced several years ago in the *Des Moines Register*, under the editorship of Geneva Overholser, now ombudsman at the *Washington Post*. The *Register* published a piece in which she wrote, "I understand why editors have made this choice [to withhold rape victims' names], but we're contributing to a reluctance to come forward."[31] A woman then came forward and asked the *Register* publish her name, and it did. The woman wanted to make the point that she was not to blame and that she rejected any stigma society might attach to the victim of a rape.[32]

Some other cases in which rape victims have been named include:

- The 1984 trial of four men charged with the gang rape of a woman in a New Bedford (Massachusetts) bar. The trial was televised, and several media outlets identified the victim.
- Several major outlets, including the *New York Times* and NBC *Nightly News* identified the plaintiff in the William Kennedy Smith rape case after her name had been revealed in tabloid newspapers in both the United States and England.

• The victim in the Mike Tyson rape case made her name public, and the media published and aired it.

   As researchers Tommy Thomason, Paul LaRocque, and Maggie Thomas point out, the dilemma of naming or not naming rape victims arises daily in America's newsrooms. The traditions of journalism—plus the experiential data—suggest strongly that names are extremely newsworthy and add credibility to stories. Add to that the fact that crime stories have strong readership, and editors are caught in a tough balancing act: judging the value of reporting names against the potential harm to the victim. And no victim is more vulnerable than the rape victim.[33] The researchers conclude, however:

Despite the publication of the names of rape victims in some high-profile cases and a belief by some that making victim names public will help remove the stigma from rape, newspapers remain reluctant to publish the names of sex crime victims. . . . Editors seem to be concerned that if more attention is not paid to victim privacy, laws will be passed to restrict public access to victim names. And victim advocates have been active in promotion of victim privacy.[34]

   In studying this thorny issue, ethicist Jay Black argues for journalists moving beyond their initial reaction of visceral or gut-level response: if it feels right, go for it; if it feels wrong, don't. He also argues for moving beyond deferring to laws or organizational policy statements or codes of ethics—or merely tradition. Ethics, he argues, demands philosophical thinking.[35] The problem is, journalists by and large don't do philosophical thinking. They operate on a fast-paced, deadline-oriented logic which is often at odds with thoughtful, reasoned decisions. He suggests that by following one of the reasoning models available—such as the Potter Box, for instance—journalists can make a more ethical decision. Within seconds, for example, a photojournalist can ask and answer the following questions posed by Salt Lake City photojournalist Garry Bryant:[36]

• Does the private moment of pain and suffering I find myself watching need to be seen? If so, does it tell the story or part of the story of this event?
• Are the people involved in such shambles over the moment that being photographed will send them into even greater trauma?
• Am I at a distance trying to be as unobtrusive as possible?
• Am I acting with compassion and sensitivity?

If the journalist simply addresses these questions, he or she will come a long way from strict reliance on gut instinct, journalistic tradition, or someone else's imposed code of ethics.

   When the victims are minors and are judged to be particularly vulnerable, the problem of naming them becomes most acute. Here, most editors do vote for confidentiality. One 1995 case, however, points up the challenges journalists confront even with this kind of story.

On July 12, 1995, the *Wabasha County Herald,* a 3,200-circulation weekly newspaper in southeastern Minnesota, ran a front-page story headlined, "Wabasha man sentenced for sexual abuse."[37] The story stated that the man was sentenced for six counts of criminal sexual conduct in a case involving his minor daughter. The story then named the man and described his assaults upon her from the time she was 8 until she was 16. His daughter told police her father had intercourse with her fifteen to twenty times, starting when she was about 11 or 12.

When the story appeared, the girl and her mother complained to the newspaper and then to the Minnesota News Council. Minnesota is the only state in the country having a council which hears complaints against media in its state. The paper's editor said he did not know how to report the story without identifying the victim, because her father was the defendant. He also noted the theory advanced by Overholser that the victims in assault cases should not feel shamed or in any way to blame.

In response, the news council sent him a paper it had previously distributed containing the advice of various state editors on how to handle such sensitive matters.

Despite an apology from the editor to the girl and her mother, they decided to pursue the matter before the news council. At the hearing, the council voted 11 to 2 that the newspaper had shown a lack of sensitivity in identifying the victim and urged the paper to consult people outside the newsroom, including sex-abuse therapists, for help in shaping a policy for covering such stories.[38]

Among the comments in the news council's paper were the following:

If the paper had consulted the girl's therapist first, it would have learned that she had still not come to terms with the attacks and was especially vulnerable to a public story about the crimes. She was powerless when it came to her father's attacks, and she was powerless when it came to the newspaper's publishing the story which identified her. At minimum, the editor should have notified her first that the story was about to be printed.

The *Herald*'s obvious primary loyalty was to the canon of journalism that, in effect, says "Print the news and be damned." The idea is that, to refrain from publishing all you know, you fail in your responsibility to the reader. Often this is a good precept to follow, but the news council found it lacking here. They raised the question: what duty does a journalist have to an innocent person? The SPJ Ethics Handbook guidelines cover this in its third principle of minimizing harm. Acknowledging the need of the media to tell the truth in all its uncomfortable details, council member Kate Stanley still voted to censure the *Herald.* Her reasoning:

This is a very special case. The girl's feelings and her future were more important than any public need to know. We need to minimize harm. It's a balancing act. She deserved special treatment. I don't know if she has an intrinsic right, but there's no huge benefit to be gained from disclosure.[39]

Bob Steele, an ethics specialist at the Poynter Institute believes that sometimes the media shouldn't report a story at all, if it means the details will cause a crime victim more harm. Instead, he suggests spending the paper's resources to cover the larger issues of familial sexual abuse and to help the community deal with it in that way. And Bob Franklin, reporter for the *Star Tribune* in Minneapolis, says his paper's policy is to avoid identifying victims except when you have a story newsworthy enough and a situation where you can't make any sense out of it without describing the relationship between abuser and victim.[40] To some, like Franklin, this is a clear policy. To others, there is a lot of room for interpretation as to when a story is newsworthy enough.

SOME ETHICAL GUIDELINES IN MEDICAL REPORTING

Journalists would do well to ask themselves the central question, "What responsibility does the media bear for societal attitudes about dangerous health problems such as cancer, heart disease, muscular dystrophy, and myriad others?" The answer to that question inevitably leads reporters into the arena of ethics in science and medical reporting.

Victor Cohn, former science editor for the *Washington Post*, tackled that question and came up with the following conclusions:[41]

1. Be Compassionate. Reporters should have compassion for their subjects. In looking at the 1974 story about first lady Betty Ford's breast surgery, Cohn recalled a letter he received which read in part: "While you might be doing some good at her expense by blazoning Mrs. Ford's operation, do you ever consider the harmful effects? I am referring to the statistics . . . that 38 percent of women with cancer cells in the nodes did not live five years after surgery. . . . Until I read your paper I had thought my chances were very good. . . . Thanks a lot!"

In reporting on statistics, point out that these are only averages, and that many people beat them. In response to the criticism that reporters often invade someone's privacy to report a medical story, realize it is true. In the case of public officials, however, that is often the unpleasant duty of reporters. In the case of lesser-known individuals, the decision is tougher. In all cases, however, report as humanely as possible.

2. Beware of Giving False Hope. Several years ago, a medical research team from Dartmouth administered a promising Alzheimer's drug to four elderly patients. The researchers then published a paper saying that, according to the patients' hopeful families, three of the patients showed marked improvement. When other journalists began asking questions, the researchers held a press conference. The results were many stories with headlines such as, "Alzheimer's Test Found Successful" and "First Breakthrough Against Alzheimer's." During the first two months following the stories, some 2,600 phone calls were logged at the medical center, many from desperate families.

The drug proved to be a failure. Cohn observes:

> I realized that we were too often being bamboozled by shaky "studies," by phony or unreliable claims and numbers, and by people who tell us this or that is true without presenting any credible evidence. A "scientist" or "environmentalist" or "public advocate" describes a study or makes a statement. It is striking. We report it. But should we? . . . We must learn to examine what we are told by some of the rules that make a piece of evidence worth examining. . . . it takes large numbers and careful studies to learn almost anything, and even a Dr. Famous can utter nonsense that no one else believes.[42]

3. Be Accurate. Accuracy should mean telling the viewer or reader the facts but not representing as such someone's non-facts—accurate reporting of science and health requires knowledge. Ask if the study was capable of securing the answers it originally sought to obtain. Ask if it could be interpreted to say something else. Ask if possible contaminating factors to the study were taken into account when the results were published.

Journalists should know that credible researchers must first form a hypothesis that they wish to test, and then try to disprove it by what is called the null hypothesis: to prove that there is no such truth. To support the hypothesis, the study must first reject the null hypothesis. Cohn suggests a parallel in law: the jury is instructed to begin hearing a case with the presumption of innocence and say to the prosecution, prove your case, provide the evidence to disprove innocence.[43] In like manner, reporters have a right to say to themselves about research studies, "I don't believe it. The researchers will have to convince me." It is in asking questions like those just suggested that a reporter becomes convinced of either the validity of the results or their invalidity.

Journalists, cautions Cohn, should also realize other things about science and medical research. Among his observations are the following:[44]

1. All science is almost always *uncertain*, or uncertain to a degree. Nature is complex, research is difficult, observation is inexact, all studies have flaws, so science is always an evolving story. It is thus important to tell all this to the public so people will understand why researchers say one thing today, and another tomorrow.

2. Scientists live with uncertainty by measuring *probability*. Do not trust a study if it is statistically insignificant. Also know that this may or may

not mean practical or clinical significance. Nor does it alone mean there is a cause and effect. Association is not causation without further evidence.

3. Statistically, *power* means the likelihood of finding something if it's there, say an increase in cancer in workers exposed to some substance. The greater the number of cases or subjects studied, the greater a conclusion's power and probable truth. So be wary of studies with only a small number of cases.

4. *Bias* in science means introducing spurious associations and reaching unreliable conclusions by failing to consider other influential factors or contaminating variables. Among them are failing to take account of age, gender, occupation, nationality, race, income, health, or behaviors like smoking. Watch for bias by asking, "Are there any other possible explanations?"

5. A common pitfall of science is that everything measured or studied varies from measurement to measurement. Every human experiment, repeated, has at least slightly (and sometimes markedly) different results. Ask, too, about any association's statistical strength—in other words, the odds. The greater the odds against an association's being a matter of chance, the greater its strength. If a pollutant seems to be causing a 10 percent increase above background, it may or may not be a meaningul association. If a risk is ten times *greater*—the relative risk in cigarette smokers versus non-smokers—the odds are strong that something is happening.

6. There is a *hierarchy of studies*—from the least to the generally most believable—starting with simple anecdotes and going on to more systematic observation or eyeballing, then proceeding to true experiments, comparing one population or sample with another under controlled or known conditions.

7. Many epidemiologic and medical studies are *retrospective*, looking back in time at old records or statistics or memories. This is often necessary, but also often unreliable. Far better is the *prospective* study that follows a selected population for a long period, sometimes years.

Asking these and other questions regarding the methodology used may prevent a false hope from being published or aired, and increase the chances that the story will emerge in accurate form.

NOTES

1. Phillip Patterson and Lee Wilkins, *Media Ethics: Issues and Cases*, 2nd ed. (Dubuque, Iowa: William C. Brown, 1994), pp. 149–151.

2. Clifford G. Christians, Mark Fackler, and Kim B. Rotzoll, *Media Ethics: Cases and Moral Reasoning*, 4th ed. (White Plains, N.Y.: Longman, 1995), pp. 12–13.

3. Ibid.

4. Jay Black, Bob Steele, and Ralph Barney, *Doing Ethics in Journalism* (Greencastle, Ind.: Sigma Delta Chi Foundation and the Society of Professional Journalists, 1993), p. 11.

5. Teresa Baggot, "Personal Involvement: Journalists, Compassion and the Common Good," *Quill* (November/December 1992), pp. 26–27.

6. Ibid.

7. Ibid.

8. Ibid.

9. Deborah Baldwin, "A Matter of Life and Death," *American Journalism Review* (June 1994), p. 42.

10. Ibid.

11. Ibid.

12. Ibid., p. 45.

13. Ibid., p. 43.

14. Ibid., p. 45.

15. Ibid., p. 44.

16. Ibid.

17. William F. Griswold and Jill D. Swenson, "Not in Whose Backyard? The Ethics of Reporting Environmental Issues," *Mass Comm Review* 20 (1 and 2) (1993), p. 63.

18. Ibid.

19. Sharon Friedman, "Two Decades of the Environmental Beat," *Gannett Center Journal* (Summer 1990), pp. 13–23.

20. Griswold and Swenson, "Not in Whose Backyard?", pp. 69–70.

21. Ibid., p. 71.

22. Ibid.

23. Nigel Dower, ed., "What is Environmental Ethics?", *Ethics and Environmental Responsibility* (Brookfield, Vt.: Avebury Press, 1989), pp. 11–37.

24. Griswold and Swenson, "Not in Whose Backyard?", p. 73.

25. Deborah Howell, ed., *St. Paul Pioneer Press Dispatch*, letter to the Pulitzer Prize Board, 1987, as contained in the book *1988 Pulitzer Prize Winners*, Knight-Ridder, Inc., 1989.

26. Black, Steele, and Barney, *Doing Ethics in Journalism*, p. 29.

27. Ibid., p. 30.

28. Ibid., p. 34.

29. Ibid., p. 36.

30. "Doing the 'Right' Thing: No One Said it Would Be Easy," *Newsworthy* (Fall 1995), p. 6.

31. Ibid.

32. Ibid., p. 4.

33. Tommy Thomason, Paul LaRocque, and Maggie Thomas, "Editors Still Reluctant to Name Rape Victims," *Newspaper Research Journal* 16(3) (Summer 1995), p. 42.

34. Thomason et al., "Editors Still Reluctant to Name Rape Victims," p. 50.

35. Jay Black, "Rethinking the Naming of Sex Crime Victims," *Newspaper Research Journal* 16(3) (Summer 1995), pp. 102–107.

36. Ibid.

37. "Doing the 'Right' Thing."

38. Ibid., p. 5.

39. Ibid., p. 7.

40. Ibid.

41. Victor Cohn, "Corrective Surgery," *Quill* (November/December 1992), pp. 17–18.

42. Ibid.

43. Victor Cohn, "Probable Fact and Probable Junk," *FACS NewsBackgrounder* (Los Angeles: Foundation for American Communications, 1994), p. 1.

44. Ibid., pp. 2–4.

Appendix: In-Depth Reporting Examples

The following stories illustrate some of the range of risks reported on by journalists today at three daily newspapers. They also show some of the reporting and writing techniques used in producing these stories, which alert readers to dangers existing in their world.

The first story, "AIDS in the Heartland," is part of a series by Jacqui Banaszynski and was published by the *St. Paul Pioneer Press Dispatch*. It received a 1987 Pulitzer Prize and is discussed extensively in Chapter 9. A brief excerpt from the series' concluding chapter follows it. This series was one of the first that put a human face on the AIDS story.

The second story is also part of a series, "Science vs. Stigma: Understanding Mental Illness." It deals with another facet of medical news: diseases of the mind. The story featured here, by Sue Goetinck and Tom Siegfried of the *Dallas Morning News*, shows how the mentally ill and their families must fight both the disease as well as stereotypes about it. It is a gripping story that focuses on the human aspect of mental illness, but it also includes an amazing amount of detail and insight into mental illness.

The third story, "Quacks Prey on Immigrants," is a story by Molly Gordy of the New York *Daily News*. It is part of a larger series entitled "Medical Menace," which focuses on the problem of medical mistreatment of New York City's Chinese immigrant population. Exhaustive reporting went into this series, which concerns the prescription for disaster when organized crime mixes with medicine.

"AIDS in the Heartland"

by Jacqui Banaszynski
St. Paul Pioneer Press Dispatch

(Chapter 1 of 3. Reprinted from the *St. Paul Pioneer Press Dispatch*, June 21, 1987)

The tiny snapshot is fuzzy and stained with ink. Two men in white T-shirts and corduroys stand at the edge of a barnyard, their muscled arms around each other's shoulders, a puzzled bull watching them from a field. The picture is overexposed, but the effect is pleasing, as if that summer day in 1982 was washed with a bit too much sun.

A summer later, the same men—one bearded and one not, one tall and one short—pose on the farmhouse porch in a mock American Gothic. Their pitchforks are mean looking and caked with manure. But their attempted severity fails; dimples betray their humor.

They are pictured together often through the years, draped with ribbons and buttons at political rallies, playing with their golden retriever, Nels, and, most frequently, working in their lavish vegetable garden.

The pictures drop off abruptly after 1985. One of the few shows the taller man picking petunias from his mother's grave. He is startlingly thin by now; as a friend said, "like Gandhi after a long fast." His sun-bleached hair has turned dark, his bronze skin pallid. His body seems slack, as if it's caving in on itself.

The stark evidence of Dick Hanson's deterioration mars the otherwise rich memories captured in the photo album. But Hanson said only this:

"When you lose your body, you become so much closer to your spirit.

It gives you more emphasis of what the spirit is, that we are more important than withering skin and bone."

Hanson sat with his partner, Bert Henningson, in the small room at Minneapolis' Red Door Clinic on April 8, 1986, waiting for the results of Hanson's AIDS screening test.

He wouldn't think about how tired he had been lately. He had spent his life hefting hay bales with ease, but now was having trouble hauling potato sacks at the Glenwood factory where he worked part time. He had lost 10 pounds, had chronic diarrhea and slept all afternoon. The dishes stayed dirty in the sink, the dinner uncooked, until Henningson got home from teaching at the University of Minnesota-Morris.

It must be stress. His parents had been forced off the farm and now he and his brothers faced foreclosure. Two favorite uncles were ill. He and Henningson were bickering a lot, about the housework and farm chores and Hanson's dark mood.

He had put off having the AIDS test for months, and Henningson hadn't pushed too hard. Neither was eager to know. Now, as the nurse entered the room with his test results, Hanson convinced himself the news would be good. It had been four years since he had indulged in casual weekend sex at the gay bathhouse in Minneapolis, since he and Henningson committed to each other. Sex outside their relationship had been limited and "safe," with no exchange of semen or blood. He had taken care of himself, eating homegrown food and working outdoors, and his farmer's body always had responded with energy and strength. Until now.

"I put my positive thinking mind on and thought I'd be negative," Hanson said. "Until I saw the red circle."

The reality hit him like a physical punch. As he slumped forward in shock, Henningson—typically pragmatic—asked the nurse to prepare another needle. He, too, must be tested.

Then Henningson gathered Hanson in his arms and said, "I will never leave you, Dick."

Hanson is one of 210 Minnesotans and 36,000 Americans who have been diagnosed with AIDS since the disease was identified in 1981. More than half of those patients already have died, and doctors say it is only a matter of time for the rest. The statistics show that 80 to 90 percent of AIDS sufferers die within two years of diagnosis; the average time of survival is 14 months after the first bout of pneumocystis—a form of pneumonia that brought Hanson to the brink of death last August and again in December.

"For a long time, I was just one of those statistics," Hanson said. "I was a very depressing person to be around. I wanted to get away from me."

He lost 20 more pounds in the two weeks after receiving his test results. One of his uncles died and, on the morning of the funeral, Hanson's mother died unexpectedly. Genevieve Hanson was 75 years old, a gentle but sturdy woman who was especially close to Dick, the third of her six children. He handled the arrangements, picking gospel hymns for the service and naming eight of her women friends as honorary pallbearers—a first in the history of their tiny country church.

But Hanson never made it to his mother's funeral. The day she was buried, he collapsed of exhaustion and fever. That night, Henningson drove him to Glenwood for the first of three hospitalizations—42 days worth— in 1986.

"Dick was real morbid last summer," Henningson said. "He led people to believe it was curtains, and was being very vague and dramatic. We all said to be hopeful, but it was as if something had gripped his psyche and was pulling him steadily downward week after week."

Hanson had given up, but Henningson refused to. He worked frantically to rekindle that spark of hope—and life. He read Hanson news articles about promising new AIDS drugs and stories of terminal cancer patients defying the odds. He brought home tapes about the power of positive thinking and fed Hanson healthy food. He talked to him steadily of politics and all the work that remained to be done.

He forced himself, and sometimes Hanson, to work in the garden, making it bigger than ever. They planted 58 varieties of vegetables in an organic high-yield plot and christened it the Hope Garden.

But Hanson returned to the hospital in August, dangerously ill with the dreaded pneumonia. His weight had dropped to 112 from his usual 160. He looked and walked like an old-man version of himself.

"I had an out-of-body type experience there, and even thought I had died for a time," he said. "It was completely quiet and very calm and I thought, 'This is really nice.' I expected some contact with the next world. Then I had this conversation with God that it wasn't my time yet, and he sent me back."

Hanson was home in time to harvest the garden, and to freeze and can its bounty. He had regained some of his former spunk, and was taking an interest again in the world around him.

"I'd be sitting next to him on the couch, holding his hand, and once in a while he'd get that little smile on his face and nod like there was something to hold on to," Henningson said. "And a small beam of life would emerge."

A month later, Hanson's spirits received another boost when he was honored at a massive fund-raising dinner. Its sponsors included DFL notables—among them Gov. Rudy Perpich, Lt. Gov. Marlene Johnson, St. Paul Mayor George Latimer, Minneapolis Mayor Don Fraser and Congressmen Bruce Vento and Martin Sabo—and radical political activists Hanson had worked with over the years, farmers who had stood with him to fight farm foreclosures and the West Central power line, women who remembered his support during the early years of the women's movement, members of the gay and lesbian community and other AIDS sufferers.

What started as a farewell pary, a eulogy of sorts, turned into a celebration of Hanson's life. Folk singer Larry Long played songs on an Indiana medicine man's healing flute. Friends gathered in a faith circle to will their strength to Hanson. Dozens of people lined up to embrace Hanson and Henningson. For most, it was the first time they had touched an AIDS patient.

"People are coming through on this thing and people are decent," Hanson said. "We find people in all walks of life who are with us on this struggle. . . . It's that kind of thing that makes it all worth it."

So when the pneumonia came back in December, this time with more force, Hanson was ready to fight.

"The doctor didn't give him any odds," Henningson said. Hanson was put on a respirator, funeral arrangements were discussed, estranged relatives were called to his bedside.

"He wrote me a note," Henningson said. " 'When can I get out of here?' He and I had never lied to each other, and I wasn't about to start. I said, 'You might be getting out of here in two or three days, but it might be God you're going to see. But there is a slim chance, so if you'll just fight . . .' ".

People from Hanson's AIDS support group stayed at the hospital round the clock, in shifts, talking to him and holding his hand as he drifted in and out of a coma. Friends brought Christmas to the stark hospital room: cards papered the walls, and a giant photograph of Hanson's Christmas tree, the one left back at the farmhouse, was hung.

The rest was up to Hanson.

"I put myself in God's healing cocoon of love and had my miracle," he said. "I call it my Christmas miracle."

He was released from intensive care on Christmas Eve day and since has devoted his life to carrying a seldom-heard message of hope to other AIDS patients, to give them—and himself—a reason to live as science races to find a cure.

"I'd like to think that God has a special purpose for my life," he said. His smile under the thinning beard is sheepish; faith is personal, and easily misunderstood.

"I don't want to come across like Oral Roberts, but . . . I believe that God can grant miracles. He has in the past and does now and will in the future. And maybe I can be one of those miracles, the one who proves the experts wrong."

Hanson has spent his life on the frontline of underdog causes—always liberal, often revolutionary and sometimes unpopular.

"Somewhere along the line Dick was exposed to social issues and taught that we can make a difference," said Mary Stackpool, a neighbor and fellow political activist. "That's what Dick has been all about—showing that one person can make a difference."

Hanson put it in terms less grand: "You kind of have to be an eternal optimist to be a farmer. There's something that grows more each year than what you put into the farm. . . . I've always been involved in trying to change things for the better."

He was born into the national prosperity of 1950 and grew up through the social turmoil of the 1960s. A fifth-grade teacher sparked his enthusiasm in John F. Kennedy's presidential campaign. He was 13 when his father joined the radical National Farmers Organization, took the family to picket at the Land O'Lakes plant in nearby Alexandria and participated in a notorious milk-dumping action.

He later led rural campaigns for Eugene McCarthy, George McGovern, Mark Dayton and his current hero, Jesse Jackson. He led protests against the Vietnam War, and was a conscientous objector. He organized rival factions to try to stop construction of the high-voltage power line that snakes through western Minnesota.

He was an early member of the farm activist group Groundswell, fighting to stop a neighbor's foreclosure one day, his own family's the next. The 473-acre Hanson farm has been whittled to 40 by bankruptcy; Hanson and Henningson are struggling to salvage the farmhouse and some surrounding wetlands.

He has been arrested five times, staged a fast to draw attention to the power line protest and stood at the podium of the 1980 DFL district convention to announce—for the first time publicly—that he was gay. That same year, he was elected one of the first openly gay members of the Democratic National Committee and, in 1984, made an unsuccessful bid for the party's nomination for Congress from the Second District. In 1983, he and Henningson were photographed in their fields for a Newsweek magazine story about gays responding to the AIDS crisis; neither knew at the time they carried the virus.

"He just throws himself into a cause and will spare nothing," Stackpool said. "He will expose himself totally to bring out the desired good."

Now the cause is AIDS. The struggle is more personal, the threat more direct. But for Hanson, it has become yet another opportunity to make a difference.

"He's handling this just as he would anything else—with strength and lots of courage and hope," said Amy Lee, another longtime friend and fellow activist. "And with that pioneering spirit. If there's anything he can do, any way he can help other victims, any time he can speak—he'll go for it."

Hanson has become one of the state's most visible AIDS patients. He and Henningson are frequently interviewed for news stories, were the subject of a recent four-part series on KCMT-TV in Alexandria and speak at AIDS education seminars in churches and schools throughout the state. Last month, Hanson addressed the state Senate's special informational meeting on AIDS.

"I want to take the mask off the statistics and say we are human beings and we have feelings," he said. "I want to say there is life after AIDS."

Rather than retreat to the anonymity of the big city, as many AIDS sufferers do, Hanson has maintained a high political profile in Pope County. He is chairman of the DFL Party in Senate District 15. He and Henningson continue to do business with area merchants and worship weekly at the country church of Hanson's childhood, Barsness Lutheran.

"I've always been a very public person and I've had no regrets," Hanson said. "One thing my dad always emphasized was the principle that honesty was the most important thing in life."

Hanson and Henningson use their story to personalize the AIDS epidemic and to debunk some of the stereotypes and myths about AIDS and its victims. They are farmers who have milked cows, slopped hogs and baled hay like everyone else. Their politics and sexual orientation may disturb some. But their voices and values are more familiar, and perhaps better understood, than those of some of their urban counterparts.

"It makes people aware that it can happen here," said Sharon Larson, director of nursing at Glacial Ridge Hospital in Glenwood.

That honesty has carried a price. A conservative Baptist minister from Glenwood criticized their lifestyle at a community forum and again in a column in the Pope County Tribune. Some of Hanson's relatives were upset by the Alexandria television show and demanded he keep his troubling news to himself. There have been rumblings in his church from people concerned about taking communion with him, and a minor disturbance erupted in a Glenwood school when his niece was teased about him.

But his connections also carry clout.

"It brings it a little closer home to the guys in the Capitol who control the purse strings," a fellow AIDS patient said.

When they speak, Hanson and Henningson touch on a variety of topics: the need for national health insurance to guarantee equitable care, the cruelty of policies that force AIDS patients into poverty before they are eligible for medical assistance, the need for flex-time jobs so AIDS sufferers can continue to be productive, the imperative of safe sex.

They also stress the personal aspects of the disease: the need for patients to be touched rather than shunned, the importance of support from family and friends and, most dear to Hanson, the healing powers of hope.

"I know there are some who die because they give up," he said. "They have no hope, no reason to have faith. Everything they're faced with is so desperate and dismal. . . . I believe the biggest obstacle for us who have AIDS or AIDS-related complex is fighting the fear and anxiety we have over the whole thing. Every positive thing, every bit of hope is something to hold on to."

Next month, Hanson and Henningson will celebrate five years together, perhaps with a gathering of friends and an exchange of rings. They exchanged vows privately that first summer while sitting in their car under the prairie night.

"We asked the blessing of the spirit above," Hanson said. "It was a pretty final thing."

At first blush, they seem an unlikely couple.

"Bert the scholar and Dick the activist. . . . In some ways they're just worlds apart," Stackpool said. "But politics brought them together, and now they take delight in those differences and in their special traits. They've figured out things many married couples never come close to figuring out."

Henningson is bookish and intense, a Ph.D. in international trade, a professor and essayist. He is a doer and organizer. He charts the monthly household budget on his Apple computer, itemizing everything from mortgage payments to medicine to cat food. He sets a hearty dinner table, which is cleared and washed as soon as the last bit of food is gone. He buries himself in his work during the week, becomes reclusive when he retreats to the farm on weekends and has worked hard over the years to control an explosive temper.

Hanson is more social, an easygoing, non-stop talker with a starburst of interests. He spent 12 years detouring through social activism before finally earning a bachelor's degree in political science at the university's Morris campus. He has a political junkie's memory for names, dates and events, thrills in company and is quick to offer refreshments, having inherited his mother's belief in friendship through food.

But they also have much in common.

Henningson, 40, grew up on a farm near Graceville, in neighboring Big Stone County. His life paralleled Hanson's in many respects: the radical farm movement, anti-war protests, involvement in liberal political campaigns.

Both suppressed their homosexuality until they were almost 30. Hanson kept so active with politics and the farm that he didn't have time for a social life. After acknowledging his homosexuality, his sexual life involved weekend excursions to the Twin Cities for anonymous encounters at the gay bathhouse.

"I had to taste all the fruit in the orchard," he said. "I had some real special relationships, but if they suggested it just be us I felt trapped, like they were closing in on me."

Henningson threw himself into graduate school, tried marriage and took on a demanding career in Washington, D.C., as an aide to former U.S. Rep. Richard Nolan. He divorced and returned to Minnesota, where he enrolled in a human sexuality program at the University of Minnesota. He had three homosexual involvements before meeting Hanson at a political convention.

"There were some major forces working in the universe that were compelling us together," Henningson said. "I don't know that we even had much to say about it. I've always believed in serendipity, but I also feel you have to give serendipity a little help. So I didn't sit back and wait for Dick to call—I called him."

Any doubts Hanson had about their relationship were squelched by his mother. She visited the farmhouse one Sunday morning with freshly baked caramel rolls, which she served Hanson and Henningson in bed. Henningson was accepted as part of the family, moved to the farm and eventually assumed financial responsibility for the family's farm operations.

"It was so good to work together, to sweat together, to farrow those sows and help the sows have those little piglets," Henningson said. "We literally worked dawn to dusk."

That hard but somewhat idyllic life has been altered drastically by AIDS. Hanson does what he can, when he can, perhaps baking cookies or doing the laundry. But the burden of earning an income, running the house and caring for Hanson has fallen heavily on Henningson's shoulders.

Hanson's medical bills—totaling more than $50,000 so far—are covered by welfare. Henningson's temporary job at the state Department of Agriculture, where he writes farm policy proposals, pays their personal bills, helps pay their apartment rent in the Twin Cities so Hanson can be near medical care during the week and allows them to keep the farmhouse.

"Dick's optimism is fine," Henningson said. "But you have to help optimism along now and then with a little spade work. I ended up doing all of the work with no help. What could have happened is that I could have grown resentful and blamed the victim.

"But I tried to put myself in his shoes—having pneumonia twice—and with all my anger and short temper, could I live with that? Could I even get through that? I'd probably have the strength to go to a field and dig a hole and when the time came crawl in and bury myself. But I don't know if I'd have the strength to do what he did."

So their commitment to each other remains absolute, perhaps strengthened by facing a crisis together.

"When you know that somebody's going to stand by you, and when they prove that they will, when they go through what Bert's gone through this past year in putting up with me . . . you just know it's very, very special what you have," Hanson said.

Each week, Hanson checks in at the AIDS clinic at Hennepin County Medical Center. He and Henningson make the three-hour drive to Minneapolis every Monday and spend their week in the Twin Cities. Henningson has work through June at the Agriculture Department. Hanson's full-time job is AIDS.

He has his blood tested to determine his white blood cell count—his body's natural defense system. It often is below 1,000; a healthy person's count would be closer to 5,000.

He has a physical exam, chats with two or three doctors, gives encouragement to fellow patients and collects hugs from the nursing staff. He is a favorite with the social workers, who tease him about his lack of interest in the women who flock to his examination room each week for a visit.

He does weekly inhalation therapy, breathing an antibiotic into his lungs to ward off the dreaded pneumonia. Then he buses to St. Paul for a long, healing massage from one of several local massage therapists who donate time to AIDS patients.

Thursday mornings find him at the University of Minnesota Hospital and Clinic for eye treatments. Doctors inject medicine directly into his eyeball to thwart a virus that is attacking his vision. Sometimes the needle punctures a blood vessel, leaving Hanson with bright red patches in his eyes.

On Thursday nights, he and Henningson attend an AIDS support group meeting, where as many as 30 patients, relatives and friends gather to share comfort and information.

For eight months, Hanson has taken AZT, or azidothymidine, an experimental drug believed to prolong life for AIDS sufferers. He takes other drugs to counter the nausea caused by AZT's high toxicity, and is watched closely for bone marrow suppression. He uses various underground treatments, all with his doctor's knowledge. He rubs solvent on his skin to try to stimulate a response from his immune system, and spreads a home-brewed cholesterol agent on his toast, hoping it will help render the virus inert.

He watches his diet to prevent diarrhea and takes various prescription drugs for depression and anxiety.

His spare time, what there is of it, is devoured by long waits for the bus or slow walks to his various appointments. He naps often to keep his energy level up and spends evenings watching the Twins on TV. Reading has become painful for him, straining his eyes and making him dizzy.

"It comes back and back and back many times," he said. "Is this my total life? Has the illness become such an all-encompassing thing that my life will never be judged by anything but this brand of AIDS?"

Weekends are spent on the farm, where Hanson often can be found kneeling in his flower beds. The impatiens, moss roses and Sweet Williams are planted especially thick this summer; Hanson was eager to see their cheerful pinks and reds cover the crumbling stone foundation of the old farmhouse. He insists on having fresh flowers in the house every day, even dandelions and thistles. Once, after pranksters broke the peony bushes in the church cemetery, Hanson gathered up the broken blossoms and took them home, placing them around the house in shallow bowls of water.

Or he can be found singing in the empty silo, practicing hymns for Sunday's church service. His voice is sweet and natural, with a good range. It is inherited, he says, from his mother, who sang to him when he was in the womb and tuned in opera on the radio in the farm kitchen when he was a youngster. He has sung for his brothers' weddings but is better, he says, at funerals.

On hot summer nights, he and Henningson sleep in twin beds in a screened porch upstairs. The room is kept cool by towering shade trees and constant breezes blowing off the marsh that winds in front of the house. From there, the men note the comings and goings of their neighbors: egrets and blue herons, Canada geese that feed on what Henningson called Green Scum Pond, a doe and her buff-colored fawn. There is an owl in the nearby woods, a peregrine falcon nesting in the farmhouse eaves and an unseen loon that sings to them at dusk.

If the weekend is slow, the weather is mild and his energy is high, Hanson can be found in a dinghy somewhere on Lake Minnewaska, the sparkling centerpiece of Pope County. He's a skilled fisherman, and remembers weekends when he would haul home a catch of 200 pan fish for one of his mother's famous fries.

"I find that going out in the garden is a good way to get away from things, or going fishing, or just visiting with people and talking," he said. "I don't want my whole life to be branded by AIDS."

Hanson awakes in the Minneapolis apartment on a recent morning to the sound of his mother's voice.

"It wasn't part of any dream," he said. "Just her voice, crystal clear, calling."

He has been running a fever for several days, and suffering headaches. His white blood cell count has dropped precipitously. His chatter, usually cheerful, is tinged with fear.

"I got pretty emotional about it," he said. "But Bert held me and said, 'Don't be afraid. Don't fight it.' And I remember a year ago when I was so sick, and she was reaching to me, and I was so scared I was almost pushing her away. And Bert said not to fight it, to let her comfort me even if she's reaching to me on a level we don't understand."

"There are days I think I'm just going to get out of this, put this whole thing behind me and get a job and go on with my life again. Then I have a rough day like this and I have to look at things much more realistically."

Hanson seldom talks of death. When his health is stable there seems little point. He has beaten the odds before and will, he says, again.

"Intermittently, there has been some denial," said his physician, Dr. Margaret Simpson, director of the sexually transmitted disease clinic at Hennepin County Medical Center. "That's not too surprising. When you're feeling good, it's easy to think this isn't true.

"But he's deteriorating again, and it's worrisome. I don't make predictions, but I think now in terms of weeks and months rather than months and years."

Hanson senses that urgency. But he remains a fighter. His attitude, he says, is not one of delusion but of defiance.

"I think I'll know when the time is right and it's coming," he said. "Should it be, I'm ready to meet my maker. But I'm not ready to give up and say there's nothing that will turn around so I can live."

A week later, Hanson is in the hospital. The headaches are worse, and doctors do a painful spinal tap to determine if the AIDS virus has entered his brain. His white blood cell count is dangerously low, but a transfusion is too risky.

It is the first hospitalization in six months, and only an overnight stay for tests, but it evokes painful memories of the past and fears for the future.

Henningson telephones Hanson's sister.

"I told Mary it may be only three or four months and we have to respond to him accordingly," he said. "Not treat him as someone who's going to die, but accord him the time and attention you want. We can't just say, 'See you next week.' It's not a matter of dealing with certitude anymore, but a great deal of uncertainty about where it's going to lead."

Hanson is quiet this evening and seems distracted. The Twins game plays silently on the hospital room TV, but relief pitcher Jeff Reardon is losing and Hanson pays only passing interest. He gets up once during the evening to vomit and occasionally presses his hand to his temple. But he never mentions the nausea, the throbbing headache or the pain from the spinal tap.

Henningson sits next to him on the bed and thumbs through their photo album, recalling lighter times.

Suddenly, Hanson waves his hand vaguely, at the room, at his life. "I'll miss all this," he confided. "I'll just miss all these wonderful people."

Then he and Henningson discuss—gently—the logistics of his death. Should he be placed in a nursing home if he becomes invalid? Should life-sustaining measures be used if he falls into a coma again? Should he donate his body to research?

The morbid conversation is held in matter-of-fact tones and seems to soothe Hanson. It is Henningson's way of pulling out the emotions, the soft rage and futility that Hanson otherwise would keep tucked inside.

"Talking about things like that helps you understand your mortality, and that it may not be much longer," Henningson said. "And that helps relieve your fears. Dick's fears are not so much for himself as for me. Will I live out here all by myself? Will I find someone else? I say don't worry about that, it's out of your control."

But Henningson, too, is shaken. He sits at the window next to Hanson's hospital bed, and holds his hand. Finally, he abandons the diversionary talk and cries. He is worried about losing the farm, about the political hassles involved in getting housing assistance, about getting a job after his contract with the state expires, about not having enough time left with Hanson.

And he can't help but worry about the AIDS virus in his body and his own health prospects. Although he guards his health carefully and is optimistic about medical progress on the AIDS front, he fears that the stress of caring for Hanson is taking its toll. He watches Hanson, and wonders if he is watching his own future.

Then he comforts himself with a wish.

"I want to be cremated and have my ashes thrown in Big Stone Lake. And from there I would flow to the Minnesota River, down to the Mississippi River, all the way to the Gulf. And I'll hit the Gulf Stream and travel the world.

"And I told Dick if he'd like to be cremated, they could put him in Lake Minnewaska, and he would flow to the Chippewa River and then into the Minnesota and the Mississippi and to the Gulf and around the world. And at some point we would merge and we'd be together forever."

He stops, perhaps embarrassed.

"You can't control what happens to people after they're dead," he said. "But even if it doesn't happen, it's a lovely, consoling thought."

"AIDS in the Heartland: The Final Chapter" (excerpted)

by Jacqui Banaszynski
St. Paul Pioneer Press Dispatch

(Reprinted from the *St. Paul Pioneer Press Dispatch*, August 9, 1987)

Dick Hanson died Saturday, July 25, at 5:30 A.M. Farmer's time, when the night holds tight to a last few moments of quiet before surrendering to the bustle of the day.

Back home in rural Glenwood, Minn., folks were finishing morning barn chores before heading out to the fields for the early wheat harvest. Members of the Pope County DFL Party were setting up giant barbecue grills in Barsness Park, preparing for the Waterama celebration at Lake Minnewaska.

In the 37 years Hanson lived on his family's farm south of Glenwood, he had seldom missed the harvest or the lakeside celebration. As the long-time chairman of the county DFL, it always had been his job to run the hotdog booth.

But today he was in a hospital bed in downtown Minneapolis with the blinds of the orange-walled room drawn against the rising sun. Doctors said a seizure the day before left him unaware of his surroundings, beyond pain and—finally—beyond struggling.

Yet those closest to him swore he could hear them, and knew what was happening, and knew it was time.

"Three times during the course of the night he brought his hands together and his lips would move, and you knew he was praying. I can't help but think he was shutting himself down," said Roy Schmidt, a Minnesota AIDS

Project official and longtime friend who stayed with Hanson that last night.

Hanson died holding the hands of the two people most dear to him—his sister, Mary Hanson-Jenning, and his partner of five years, Bert Henningson.

"Amazing Grace" was playing softly on a tape machine in the corner of the room. It was Hanson's favorite hymn, the one he had sung over his mother's grave barely a year ago.

This is the final chapter of Hanson's story. After having lived a year longer than most AIDS victims, he grew weary of fighting for his life and was willing—if not eager—for it to end. After his death, he was cremated and returned to his childhood church for a memorial service that was vintage Hanson—traditionally religious but politically radical and, inevitably, controversial.

Henningson is left behind on the farm with a legacy of love—and death. For now he, too, is sick, suffering early symptoms of acquired immune deficiency syndrome. No sooner will he finish grieving for Hanson than he must begin grieving for himself.

"Science vs. Stigma: Understanding Mental Illness"

(A two-section series reprinted from the *Dallas Morning News*, April 28–29, 1996: The following is the first of several stories in the series)

"Mentally Ill Fight Disease and Stereotypes"
by Sue Goetinck and Tom Siegfried,
staff writers of the *Dallas Morning News*

People express their prejudices carefully these days. Sexism and racism are supposedly taboo. Jokes about physical handicaps are condemned as tasteless. Nobody shuns cancer patients anymore.

But people with mental illness are still fair game.

They are satirized on *Seinfeld*, stereotyped in serial movies such as *Psycho* and *Halloween*, and ridiculed in George Carlin's comedy routines.

When John du Pont was arrested on murder charges, TV comedians exploited his mental illness for a few laughs. When rock star Kurt Cobain, who suffered from depression, committed suicide, *60 Minutes* commentator Andy Rooney derided him for not having a good enough reason.

George Will, a Pulitzer Prize-winning syndicated columnist, lampooned the Americans With Disabilities Act for protecting people with mental disorders. U.S. House Speaker Newt Gingrich, in his book on renewing America, lumped the mentally ill in with dangerous criminals.

"I'm so used to cruel and insensitive comments about mental illness that it doesn't surprise me," said Dr. Kay Redfield Jamison, a psychiatrist at Johns Hopkins University in Baltimore. "It's easy to make fun of."

But it's apparently not so easy to understand. Mockery, discrimination and stigma persist despite scientific research showing mental illnesses to be as real and as serious as any other sickness. Like cancer, diabetes and heart disease, mental illness can be chronic, debilitating or fatal. Even so, most health insurance plans don't offer equal coverage for mental disorders.

Compelling scientific evidence shows that mental illness is based in biology. Hallucinations in people with schizophrenia are allayed by medicines. Lithium tablets tame the terrifying emotional ups and downs afflicting victims of manic depression. Brain scans show abnormal biochemistry in people who are depressed.

"Mental illnesses are brain diseases," said Steven Hyman, director of the National Institute of Mental Health. "Based on biomedical research, there is absolutely no justification for separating out mental disorders from other serious brain disorders. They are brain diseases just as a stroke or a brain tumor is a brain disease."

Yet when it comes to mental illness, society has not caught up to science.

"The world's history has been one of fear and misunderstanding and superstition around mental illnesses," said Michael Faenza, president of the National Mental Health Association. "There's still a lot of misunderstanding. About half the folks out there think that mental illnesses are problems that have to do with character and self-discipline."

In one poll for the National Depressive and Manic Depressive Association, nearly 2 out of 3 respondents didn't know that mental illnesses have physiological causes. One respondent in 4 thought people brought depression on themselves. Many people think depression is no more than the blues, instead of a serious clinical disorder.

Despite the mountains of research, these and other misconceptions about mental illness are slow to die, mental health professionals say. And, they say, those misconceptions contribute to neglect of a major public health problem.

As many as 1 in 4 Americans will suffer a serious mental disorder at some point in their life; in any single year, mental illness of some sort afflicts more than 5 million Americans. The annual cost of treatment, based on 1990 figures, exceeds $67 billion—more than 11 percent of the nation's total health care bill.

Adding the costs of social services, disability payments, lost productivity and premature death pushes the annual cost of mental illness to more than $150 billion, according to NIMH.

The human costs are not recorded only in dollars, but also in deaths. Between 15 and 20 percent of people with major depression commit suicide, and victims of other mental disorders are at a high risk for suicide as well.

"Most suicide attempts are tied to mental illness—95 percent," said John Rusk, a psychiatrist at the University of Texas Southwestern Medical Center at Dallas.

Suicide often carries stigma similar to that of mental illness itself. Such stigma stems from a bias in society against the belief that mental illnesses are really manifestations of physical problems, said Dr. Kenneth Altshuler, chairman of the psychiatry department at UT Southwestern.

Because people can do so much with their minds, he said, some think they should be able to do everything.

"To me that's the real reason that mental illness has the stigma it does," Dr. Altshuler said. "We have a tremendous investment in the power of our minds. Wherever you go in the country or the world, you see people who have these ideas—that I can control it with my mind."

But people with mental illness say willpower simply doesn't work.

"People think for some reason you have control over it," said Rebecca Parks, a 42-year-old Dallas resident with schizophrenia. "You do not. Without the medication you do not."

Ms. Parks, who works at a bookstore, said she first became ill with schizophrenia when she was 23. With treatment, she hasn't had a psychotic episode for six years, she said.

But at first, she said, she blamed herself.

"I felt like such a failure and so weird that I was doing crazy things. Why couldn't I just stop?" she said. "Back when I first got sick, even the doctors didn't know what caused schizophrenia. I had a doctor tell me that it was my way to get what I wanted from my family. Nobody really thought it was biological back then."

Even now, in the face of scientific evidence and advances in medicine, the blame persists.

Dianne Shirley, a sales manager who lives in Dallas, said many of her co-workers don't believe that her son, who has been diagnosed with schizophrenia, has a medical condition. Because he also has drug abuse problems, people write off his mental illness and blame it on the drugs, she said.

But Mrs. Shirley said she thinks her son turned to drugs in an attempt to self-medicate his illness.

"There's not a person in the world who would say, 'I want to be mentally ill,'" she said.

Even among psychiatrists, old biases linger. In her book, *An Unquiet Mind*, Johns Hopkins' Dr. Jamison describes a colleague's reaction when she told him that she had manic depression.

Her colleague said he was "deeply disappointed" that she wasn't strong enough to resist a suicide attempt, Dr. Jamison writes.

And even though most of her colleagues are psychiatrists, it wasn't easy to reveal her illness, Dr. Jamison said in an interview. In fact, she doesn't necessarily recommend it.

"Most people aren't in that position (having psychiatrists as colleagues)," she said. "And it's terribly personal."

Scientists don't necessarily understand mental illness either, said Kenneth Kendler, a psychiatrist at the Medical College of Virginia in Richmond.

"It drives me nuts to sit on human subjects committees where people are approving very invasive treatments or research on cancer and you come to somebody wanting to do research on schizophrenia and you can get statements like, 'Well, that's just an emotional problem,' " he said.

People's reactions to mental illnesses may be inappropriate because such illnesses, especially the most severe, are hard to fathom, said Dr. Joel Feiner, training and clinical director of Mental Health Connections, a collaboration between the Dallas County Mental Health and Mental Retardation Center and UT Southwestern's psychiatry department.

"These are people who are pointing out to us those very things that we're very afraid of in ourselves," Dr. Feiner said. "And that is losing control and going to extremes and being banished. It's confounding. And when we can't understand something about ourselves, and about human nature, I think we have different ways to deal with it," he said. "We jump in and embrace it and make a career out of it like I do, or you investigate it like other people do, or you avoid it and laugh at it and demean it and make believe it's very different than you."

Or you fight.

In February, the National Alliance for the Mentally Ill (NAMI) launched a five-year campaign to fight the stigma of mental illness. The group plans to use public service announcements, rallies and local publicity to inform the public about mental illnesses, said NAMI spokeswoman Farrell Fitch.

Besides fighting stigma, NAMI wants to put mental illnesses on equal footing with other diseases in health benefit plans.

"Most people don't know, until they have to know, that these disorders aren't covered equally," Ms. Fitch said.

Most insurance plans have much more restrictive limits on care for mental illnesses than for diseases like cancer. Typical mental health insurance coverage might be limited to 20 visits with a counselor or psychologist and $50,000 over a person's lifetime.

Other medical coverage might have a lifetime limit of $1 million.

NAMI's employees have a lifetime limit of $25,000, said Ron Honberg, director of legal affairs for NAMI.

"We tried very hard to find a better policy," he said.

The inequities in mental health coverage have a long history, said UT Southwestern's Dr. Altshuler. Originally, he said, mental illnesses were simply excluded.

"Back in the '40s and '50s, there was no mode of really successful treatment and there was no way to measure the cost in advance. In those days everybody got psychotherapy, which was an open-ended, long-enduring thing," he said.

But now mental illnesses are largely treatable, so the limits on health insurance for them are pure discrimination, mental health advocates said at a schizophrenia symposium in Washington last month.

"It's simply false to distinguish schizophrenia from other physical illnesses on this basis," said Laura Lee Hall, director of research and policy at NAMI. "It's simply unfair to help one individual because her or his heart or stomach got sick but to shun another because their brain was the part of the body that got sick."

People with serious mental illnesses can exhaust their benefits with just a few stays in the hosptial, Dr. Hall said. If they try to turn to the public health care system, she said, they can be rejected if their income is too high.

Health insurance companies acknowledge the disparity in coverage for mental and physical illnesses.

"We have in this country a bifurcated system," said Don White, spokesman for Group Health Association of America, a trade association representing health maintenance organizations and other network health plans.

Mr. White said that because costs for mental health coverage have been difficult to control, employers often don't demand equivalent coverage for mental illnesses.

"The employer decides what kind of a package they're going to provide," he said.

And employers say they don't have a way of measuring whether someone is better off with more benefits.

"If an employer had a $50,000 cap versus a $100,000 cap, they don't have any insurance that their employee would be any better off," said John Kajander, executive director of the Texas Business Group on Health, a Houston organization representing employers who purchase health benefits for their employees.

Historically, Mr. Kajander said, employees have taken the maximum benefits allowed, he said. Employers were concerned that the system was being abused.

Psychiatrists, however, argue that the illnesses are simply not treatable under the caps of many health plans.

"There's no question that these illnesses—the more severe ones—are not treatable under a cap, any more than cancer is treatable under a cap, or heart attacks are," said UT Southwestern's Dr. Rush.

In an effort to control costs better, many employers are turning to separate managed care companies for mental health coverage, Mr. White said.

But psychiatrists say the managed care philosophy doesn't address the special needs of people with mental illnesses.

Because severe mental illnesses are for the most part chronic, patients often need lifelong care. In addition to getting prescriptions refilled, people with mental illnesses may require counseling or other forms of therapy.

And many patients don't even get the minimum benefits their policy promises, Dr. Altshuler said.

"If you have the benefit of 20 sessions, the likelihood is that you'll get four or five," he said. "The guiding force is to provide the minimum absolutely necessary."

"We used to try to get people well," he said. "Now they try to get you over the crisis."

The battle for parity in health insurance coverage is being fought in Congress, too. An amendment to the Kennedy-Kassebaum health care reform bill, approved by the Senate last week, would require equivalent coverage for mental illnesses. But that provision is likely to be removed in conference committee, when the House and Senate reconcile their versions of the health care bill.

Although discrimination against people with mental illnesses is still common, the news isn't all bad, researchers say.

The success of drugs such as Prozac and lithium has helped destigmatize psychiatric diseases. Personal testimonies by celebrities such as actress Patty Duke and journalist Mike Wallace have helped mental illness begin to creep out of the closet.

Awareness that historical figures such as Abraham Lincoln and former major league centerfielder Jimmy Piersall suffered from mental illnesses shows that people with the diseases can lead productive lives.

Still, mental health professionals say, most people remain ignorant until mental illness hits close to home.

"You know when people change? When they have a family member who is mentally ill," Dr. Kendler said. "Then they understand."

"Medical Menace"

(The first of a three-part series reprinted from the New York *Daily News*, July 18, 1996)

"Quacks Prey on Immigrants"
by Molly Gordy, *Daily News* staff writer

A thriving subculture of medical charlatans is preying on New York's Chinese immigrant community—and inflicting serious harm on a growing number of victims.

Posing as doctors and pharmacists, these hucksters have deprived patients of the use of their limbs and sight and plunged one into a coma.

They have caused brain damage, disfigurement and paralysis. They have subjected women to botched, nearly fatal abortions.

They perform amateur surgery, administer prescription drugs and give injections of unknown substances. They sell their patients toxic potions banned by the U.S. Food and Drug Administration.

And they advise even seriously ill people not to seek care from licensed physicians. The troubled areas are Chinatown, Sunset Park, Brooklyn, and Flushing, Queens—neighborhoods where the newly arrived are entering a new culture, often with limited English and scant familiarity with American medicine.

Coming from a system of herbal, holistic healing that bears no resemblance to ours, their victims are ill-equipped to differentiate between qualified Western medical treatment and malpractice.

The problem is compounded by the growing presence of illegal immigrants who are likely to seek out the cheapest health purveyor because they have no savings or insurance. They're also the least likely to complain to authorities if something goes wrong.

Unlicensed doctors are a problem in every immigrant community. But among most other nationalities, the main offenders are physicians who were authorized to practice in their homeland but haven't passed licensing tests here.

What's happening in the Chinese community is far more serious because of the volume of people posing as doctors with no conventional medical training at all.

During the past six months, aided by Chinese researchers wearing concealed tape recorders, the *Daily News* entered the world of these shadow doctors.

The impostors were startlingly easy to find. They conceal themselves behind nothing but language, reaching 500,000 readers by advertising in the city's four largest Chinese-language newspapers.

Their ads appear next to those of legitimate physicians, giving them a deceptive credibility. They eschew the initials, "M.D." in favor of the title "Dr." and usually include phrases like "20 years experience combining Chinese and Western medicine" or "Sai Jee," the Chinese-language term for Western-trained.

Many offer cancer cures, painless surgery and breast implants with "guaranteed no side effects."

"The newspapers take the advertisers' word for their credentials," said Dr. Marcus Loo, a board-certified urologist who's president of the 600-member Chinese-American Medical Society. "They never ask to see a diploma. You can claim anything you want."

The *News* checked the names of 45 such advertisers against the rolls of physicians licensed to practice in New York. Not one was a medical doctor.

News researchers, fluent in Cantonese and Mandarin, then visited 10 purported doctors to confirm that they were practicing medicine without a license—a felony. The researchers, all in good health, were equipped with hidden tape recorders.

Each of the 10 offered illegal, if not dangerous, medical services, sometimes under astonishing conditions.

To visit them and to discover, through legitimate physicians, the stories of patients who have been grievously harmed, is to come face-to-face with an unrecognized public health menace.

AN OFFER OF SURGERY

The young man climbed the stairs to the second floor of the tenement at 34 E. Broadway. There, he asked for Ke-Xie Ni, who advertises as a specialist in "dermatology, orthopedics, syphilis and relief of painful symptoms."

His ad also asserts "rich experience combining Chinese and Western medicine," using "Chinese medicinal herbs and acupuncture."

"I have two growths on my abdomen that I'd like you to check," the young man told Ni, referring to two harmless nubs of cartilage previously examined at Mount Sinai Medical Center.

Ni put on a stained lab coat, ordered the young man onto a filthy examining table, told him to pull his pants down to his knees. Then, inexplicably, Ni examined his penis.

"You can get a bad infection there," he said. "You need to be circumcised."

When the patient refused, Ni quizzed him about his sex life and told him he risked venereal disease and cancer if he refused the operation. Still, the patient insisted that Ni confine his examination to the two growths. Ni pressed them with his fingers and pronounced that they also must be removed.

Again, he offered to do the surgery immediately.

Shaking with fear, the patient paid Ni's $30 fee and made haste to leave.

"As I headed to the door, Dr. Ni followed me with a book of pictures of men with their penises in stages of decay," he said afterward. "He told me this is what would happen if I wasn't circumcised."

Ni is neither a licensed physician nor acupuncturist, state records show.

When a *News* reporter and photographer approached him for comment, they found the floor caked with dirt, holes in the linoleum and foot-high piles of old newspapers covering the examining table.

Initially, Ni was cordial.

"I am an herbalist. I only give out herbs," he said, although not a single jar or package was in evidence in his office.

But when Ni was asked about surgery, he suddenly grew hostile, making a telephone call in Chinese and locking his door to prevent the reporter and photographer from leaving.

As the photographer rushed to open the door, Ni tackled him from behind and began hitting him with the photographer's cameras. Racing out, the reporter summoned police from a pay telephone.

Because Ni's address is in the heart of Fuk Ching gang territory, 14 officers responded. Ni was taken into custody.

A SPINE DESTROYED

With five children and nine grandchildren to care for and a retired husband underfoot, the 64-year-old woman never seemed to get caught up on the housework in her Jackson Heights, Queens, home.

She was scrubbing the bathroom last June when a sharp pain seized her in the back. She ignored it. It returned during her vacuuming and reappeared over the dinner dishes. She willed it away.

By November, her misery was constant.

"I thought it was sciatica," said the woman, who asked to be identified only as Mrs. Wong. "Or at my age, maybe arthritis."

She consulted the Chinese papers to find a doctor. "We chose the most impressive one," she said. "It said he's been a medical school professor in China. There were all kinds of professional titles."

Her choice diagnosed an inflammation of the spine that he said he could eliminate by acupuncture in her hip. After four months of treatment, the pain was so bad Wong could no longer straighten up. Soon she could barely walk. Finally, Wong consulted Dr. George Liu, a licensed internist at NYU Medical Center and New York Downtown Hospital.

"I did an X-ray, looked at it and thought, 'Oh, my God!' " Liu recalled. "She had tuberculosis of the spine. If she'd been taking TB medicine during the time she'd been with the acupuncturist, we could have saved the bone. Instead, her spine was destroyed."

Wong is now too disabled to move without a walker. Yet she and her husband refused to name her acupuncturist, much less file a complaint. Liu said they're reluctant to offend someone in a respected position in Chinese culture.

"Of course, we regret that the ads aren't more truthful," said Wong's husband. "Someone should do something about that."

RX FOR DISASTER

The woman who visited the old man known as Royal Doctor Auyong in a tiny room at 254 Canal St. was lured by ads promising to cure diabetes, "95 percent guaranteed."

Although a licensed internist had certified that her blood sugar was normal, the silver-haired herbalist took her pulse and promptly "confirmed" that she had diabetes "very, very bad."

Then he showed her an acupuncture chart of the human body on the opposite wall.

"See, your problem is here," he said, pointing to the spleen—not the pancreas, which controls blood-sugar levels.

"You must eat only natural foods, like fruits and vegetables," Auyong advised. "Here in Chinatown, we see many people who live to be 120 years old because we only eat natural foods. Americans all die by age 70 because they eat chemicals."

"Don't fruits contain a lot of sugar?" the patient asked.

"Yes, but not the kind that harms you, because it's all natural," Auyong replied.

For $40, Auyong gave her three bottles of white powders.

"It's natural medicine, very good for you," he said.

"Yes, but what kind?"

"Very good medicine. You will see. You take this for three months, you have blood test, your diabetes will be almost gone," he said.

The patient told Auyong she was injecting insulin to control her blood sugar levels several times a day. She asked how this would interact with his medicines.

"You must stop taking insulin immediately," Auyong instructed. "Insulin is a chemical. Very bad for you. Like poison. Eat and drink only natural things, and you will get well."

That advice was "unethical and dangerous," said Dr. Robert Schiller, who practices conventional and herbal medicine at Beth Israel Medical Center.

"To stop taking insulin without medical supervision could put the patient into insulin shock or a coma," he said.

Auyong is not a licensed physician, state records show.

When a reporter visited seeking comment, he appeared surprised when told that it is illegal to advertise treatment of a specific disease and to promise a cure.

"No, no, this is natural medicine from Japan, 4,000 years old," he said. "Japanese people are very smart, do everything well. American medicine is only 200 years old."

A FACE DISFIGURED

She wanted to look beautiful and, in America, beholders of beauty seemed to prefer women with round eyes. So the middle-aged woman from northern China decided to follow the example of friends and have part of her eyelid folds removed by cosmetic surgery.

The standard procedure calls for making a fine, clear incision with expensive scalpels. It is normally done in a sterile operating room equipped with a coagulator to seal off excessive bleeding, special lights, a reclining chair and the anti-hemorrhage drug epinephrine, licensed surgeons say.

The woman, who speaks no English, turned instead to a Chinese man who presented himself as a surgeon. He performed the operation on his kitchen table. The results were disastrous.

Her eyelid started gushing blood. Lacking equipment or drugs to staunch the flow, the purported surgeon pressed a cloth to her eye for five hours before finally giving up and driving her to Elmhurst Hospital Center.

There, she discovered, he wasn't a licensed doctor, when the staff wouldn't let him accompany her into the emergency room.

"He must have nicked some eye muscles because she had one eye looking straight at me and the other permanently rotated down so it couldn't see," said Dr. Raymond Fong, the ophthamologist called into the case.

"There was also a disfiguring scar. I referred her to a cosmetic surgeon for the scar, but there was nothing I could do for her. She had lost the use of one eye."

Dr. Lily Chen, a plastic surgeon, said she's seen many people with infected eyelids who'd had surgery done in beauty salons.

"When they went to get the stitches taken out, the person who'd done it had disappeared," Chen said.

None have filed complaints, she said, possibly out of a widespread belief in Chinatown that some of the salons have gang connections.

A FINGER AMPUTATED

Renyu Lin works 60 hours a week as a mechanic in a SoHo garage, thick, black grease coating his hands, his face, his overalls and his long, wavy hair. It's easy to see how a tiny unattended cut on his index finger deteriorated into dry gangrene.

When Lin consulted Dr. Danny Fong, a licensed plastic surgeon, in January, the nail had rotted off the finger and his skin was blackened like coal to the first joint.

Fong asked him to apply a prescription ointment for two weeks to let the tissues underneath heal "because sometimes the dead part will separate by itself, and you don't have to do surgery."

Lin was reluctant. "I went to one pharmacy, they didn't have it," he recalled. "I don't have time to shop around."

So Lin went instead to an herbalist who, practicing unlicensed surgery, cut the fingertip off with scissors, leaving exposed bone.

An infection resulted, and Fong had to perform emergency surgery, amputating the finger down to the knuckle.

Lin refused to file a complaint against the herbalist, a fellow immigrant from China's Toisan province.

"He's a family friend. He was doing me a favor," the mechanic said. "He even called my house to see if I was all right."

ILLEGAL PRESCRIPTIONS

Li-Ye Cheng of 103 Mott St. advertises himself as a doctor of Eastern and Western medicine. A certificate on his wall also proclaims that he is president of the Chinese-American Acupuncture Society. But state records show that Cheng is neither a licensed acupuncturist nor a physician.

Complaining of back pain, a patient recently requested painkillers. Cheng gave him Indomethacin, an anti-inflammatory drug available by prescription only, and offered to send him for an X-ray at the radiology clinic at 8 Chatham Square.

"Doesn't that require a prescription?" the patient asked. "It's okay, they know me there," Cheng replied. "I can just make a phone call."

Reached for comment, Cheng said, "I just do massage, not acupuncture or medicine. "I don't have time to talk now. Goodbye."

Two other Chinese unlicensed physicians who advertise as acupuncturists also gave the patient prescription drugs, a medical laboratory has confirmed.

G. Y. Lo of Elmhurst, Queens, dispensed Indomethacin, a laboratory confirmed.

Zhi Hu Zhang of Manhattan dispensed prescription-only-strength 400-milligram pills of the painkiller ibuprofen and 200-milligram capsules of the anti-inflammatory drug Feldene. He also tried to give a patient an injection of an undisclosed substance "to fight infection."

State records show that Lo is neither a licensed acupuncturist nor a doctor. Zhang is licensed as an acupuncturist but not a physician. He does not have the right to dispense or prescribe drugs.

Called for comment, Lo claimed the patient brought the drugs with him. Zhang said: "These medicines are used very often in China."

Selected Bibliography

Baggot, Teresa. "Personal Involvement: Journalists, Compassion, and the Common Good." *Quill* (November/December 1992).

Baldwin, Deborah. "A Matter of Life and Death." *American Journalism Review* (June 1994).

Black, Jay, Bob Steele, and Ralph Barney. *Doing Ethics in Journalism*. Greencastle, Ind.: Sigma Delta Chi Foundation and the Society of Professional Journalists, 1993.

Bogart, Leo. "The American Media System and Its Commercial Culture." Occasional Paper No. 8. New York: The Gannett Foundation Media Center, March 1991.

Bridges, Janet A., with Christine M. Price and Terri R. Breaux. "Health Belief Messages About Alcohol Consumption in Network Television Entertainment Programs: A Preliminary Report." Paper presented to the Association for Education in Journalism and Mass Communication, Washington, D.C., August 1995.

Burkett, Warren. *News Reporting: Science, Medicine, and High Technology*. Ames: Iowa State University Press, 1986.

Carmody, Kevin. "It's a Jungle Out There." *Columbia Journalism Review*, May 19, 1995.

Chase, Alston. "Do Environmental Journalists Really Exist?" *Detroit News*, August 31, 1995.

Christians, Clifford G., Mark Fackler, and Kim B. Rotzoll. *Media Ethics: Cases and Moral Reasoning*, 4th ed. White Plains, N.Y.: Longman, 1995.

"Clinton Unwraps FDA Rules Limiting Tobacco Ads, Sales." *The Commercial Appeal* (Memphis, Tenn.), August 24, 1996.

Cohn, Victor. "Corrective Surgery." *Quill* (November/December 1992).

Cohn, Victor. "Probable Fact and Probable Junk." *FACS NewsBackgrounder*. Los Angeles: Foundation for American Communications, n.d.

Critchfield, Richard. "The Village Voice of Richard Critchfield." *Washington Journalism Review* (October 1985).

Crowley, John H., and James Pokrywczynski. "Advertising Practitioners Look at a Ban on Tobacco Advertising." *Journalism Quarterly* 68(3) (Autumn 1991).

Davis, Joel J. "The Effects of Message Framing on Response to Environmental Communications." *Journalism and Mass Communication Quarterly* 72(2) (Summer 1995).

Dorocher, Debra D. "Radiation Redux." *American Journalism Review* (March 1994).

Dower, Nigel, ed. *What Is Environmental Ethics? Ethics and Environmental Responsibility.* Brookfield, Vt.: Avebury, 1989.

Friedman, Sharon. "Two Decades of the Environmental Beat." *Gannett Center Journal* (Summer 1990).

Gandy, Oscar H., Jr. *Beyond Agenda-Setting: Information Subsidies and Public Policy.* Norwood, N.J.: Ablex, 1982.

Gerbner, George, M. Morgan, and N. Signorielli. "Programming Health Portrayals: What Viewers See, Say, and Do." In D. Pearl, L. Bouthilet, and J. Lazar, eds., *Television and Behavior: Ten Years of Scientific Progress and Implications for the Eighties* 2. Rockville, Md.: U.S. Department of Health and Human Services, NIMH, 1982.

Gerteis, Margaret. "Violence, Public Health, and the Media." Report based on the conference "Mass Communication and Social Agenda-Setting," the Annenberg Washington Program and Harvard School of Public Health, Washington, D.C., October 20–21, 1993.

Greenberg, Michael R., David B. Sachsman, Peter M. Sandman, and Kandice L. Salomone. "Risk, Drama and Geography in Coverage of Environmental Risk by Network TV." *Journalism Quarterly* 66(2) (Summer 1989).

Greenfield, Jeff. "America Rallies Round the TV Set." *TV Guide*, February 16–20, 1991.

Griffin, Robert J., and Sharon Dunwoody. "Impacts of Information Subsidies and Community Structure on Local Press Coverage of Environmental Contamination." *Journalism and Mass Communication Quarterly* 72(2) (Summer 1995).

Griswold, William F., and Jill D. Swenson. "Not in Whose Backyard? The Ethics of Reporting Environmental Issues." *Mass Comm Review* 20 (1 and 2) (1993).

Hayakawa, S. I. *Language in Thought and Action*, 4th ed. New York: Harcourt, Brace, Jovanovich, 1978.

Herbers, John. "Judgmental Reporting." *Nieman Reports* (Winter 1994).

Hickey, Neil. "How Much Violence on TV? A Lot, Says TV Guide." A report by the Center for Media and Public Affairs, Washington, D.C., 1993.

Hohenberg, John. *The Professional Journalist*, 4th ed. New York: Holt, Rinehart, Winston, 1978.

Hu, Yu-Wei. "Reconsidering the Theoretical Linkage between Risk Communication and Relative Personal Invulnerability: A Path Analysis." Paper presented at the Association of Educators in Journalism and Mass Communication annual convention, Washington, D.C., August 10, 1995.

In Their Name: Oklahoma City. The Official Commemorative Volume. New York: Random House, 1995.

Kaiser Family Foundation. *Covering the Epidemic: AIDS in the News Media, 1985–1996.* Designed by the Foundation and Princeton Survey Research Associates, and conducted by the Associates. Supplement to the July/August 1996 issue of *Columbia Journalism Review.*

Kenney, Charles. "Trashing Garbage." *Boston Globe,* November 30, 1993.

Killenberg, George M. *Public Affairs Reporting.* New York: St. Martin's Press, 1992.

Lichter, S. Robert, and Daniel R. Amundson. *Executive Summary of Food for Thought: Reporting on Diet, Nutrition and Food Safety.* Washington, D.C.; Center for Media and Public Affairs, February 1996.

McGill, Larry, and Andras Szanto et al. *Headlines and Sound Bites: Is That the Way It Is?* Research Report by the Freedom Forum Media Studies Center, New York, N.Y., August 1995.

McKibben, Bill. "Uncovered: The Changing Natural World." *Nieman Reports* (Winter 1992).

Medved, Michael. *Hollywood vs. America: Popular Culture and the War on Traditional Values.* New York: HarperCollins/Zondervan, 1992.

Minow, Newton N. *How Vast the Wasteland Now?* Speech at the Gannett Foundation Media Center, New York, N.Y., May 9, 1991.

Monks, Vicki. "See No Evil." *American Journalism Review* (June 1993).

Morrongiello, Christine, and Barbara Straus Reed. "The Accuracy of Breast Cancer Reports in Consumer Magazines." *Research Report No. 95–45,* School of Communication Information & Library Studies, Rutgers University, Princeton, N.J.

Patterson, Phillip, and Lee Wilkins. *Media Ethics: Issues and Cases,* 2nd ed. Dubuque, Iowa: William C. Brown, 1994.

Pearson, Bob. "AFP Mobilizes to Cover Quake." *News Photographer* (June 1994).

Pfau, Michael, Lawrence J. Mullen, and Kirsten Garrow. "The Influence of Television Viewing on Public Perceptions of Physicians." *Journal of Broadcasting and Electronic Media* 39(4) (Fall 1995).

Rivers, William. *Finding Facts.* Englewood Cliffs, N.J.: Prentice-Hall, 1975.

Rosenblatt, Roger. "Journalism and the Larger Truth." *Time,* July 2, 1984.

Rubin, Rita, and Harrison L. Rogers, Jr. "Under the Microscope: The Relationship between Physicians and the News Media." A report published by the Freedom Forum First Amendment center at Vanderbilt University, 1995.

Sandman, Peter M., and Mary Paden. "At Three Mile Island." *Columbia Journalism Review* (July/August 1979).

Schulte, Henry H., and Marcel P. Dufresne. *Getting the Story.* New York: Macmillan, 1994.

"Secondhand Smoke: Is It a Hazard?" *Consumer Reports* (January 1995).

Signorielli, Nancy. "Drinking, Sex, and Violence on Television: The Cultural Indicators Perspective." *Journal of Drug Education* 17 (1987).

Signorielli, Nancy. *Mass Media Images and Impact on Health.* Westport, Conn.: Greenwood Press, 1993.

Stein, M. L. "Covering Another California Disaster." *Editor & Publisher,* January 19, 1994.

Ullmann, John, and Steve Honeyman, eds. *The Reporter's Handbook*. New York: St. Martin's Press, 1983.

Walsh-Childers, Kim. "A Death in the Family—A Case Study of Newspaper Influence on Health Policy Development." *Journalism Quarterly* 71(4) (Winter 1994).

Walton, Deborah J. *A Study of Components and Variables Comprising Corporate Crisis Communication Plans*. Unpublished Master's Thesis, University of Memphis, 1993.

Westley, Bruce H., and Hugh M. Culbertson, eds. *Research Methods in Mass Communication*. Englewood Cliffs, N.J.: Prentice-Hall, 1981.

Williams, Frederick. *Reasoning with Statistics*. New York: Holt, Rinehart and Winston, 1968.

Index

About the Authors

JIM WILLIS is a former newspaper reporter and editor who now holds the Hardin Chair of Excellence in Managerial Journalism at the University of Memphis. Willis received his B.A. in Journalism at the University of Oklahoma and, following a dozen years with newspapers such as The *Daily Oklahoman* and *Dallas Morning News*, received a Ph.D. at the University of Missouri School of Journalism. He has been in college teaching since, and has taught at Northeastern University, the University of Missouri, and Ball State University, and was chair of the Department of Communication at Boston College before accepting his current endowed chair at Memphis. In 1995, Willis took a leave of absence from Boston College to return to his native Oklahoma City and cover the aftermath of the Murrah Federal Building bombing for the *Edmond Evening Sun*. He is the author of several books on journalism and the mass media including *The Age of Multimedia and Turbonews* (Praeger, 1994).

ALBERT OKUNADE is an authority in health care economics. He is Professor of Economics in the Fogelman College of Business and Economics at the University of Memphis. Okunade earned his Ph.D. in Economics from the University of Arkansas and has a broad primary research interest in health care and pharmaceutical care economics, and public health policies. He has published more than 40 journal articles, received grants, and presented more than 35 papers at professional association conferences. He has also written several guest columns for local and regional newspapers.

ISBN 0-275-95296-7

9 780275 952969

90000>

EAN

HARDCOVER BAR CODE

5274